Jim

From
David
X-mas 1982

GRAPES

A Vintage View of Hockey

DON CHERRY

with Stan Fischler

STEVE BABINEAU

Prentice-Hall Canada Inc., Scarborough, Ontario

*To Rose and Blue and all the honest
hockey players who played for me.*

Canadian Cataloguing in Publication Data

Cherry, Don, 1934-
    Grapes : a vintage view of hockey

ISBN 0-13-363499-X

1. Cherry, Don, 1934-   2. Hockey players—United
States—Biography.   I. Fischler, Stan, 1932-
II. Title.

GV848.5.C53A35   796.96'2'0924   C82-094867-5

*Every reasonable effort has been made to find copyright holders.
The publishers would be pleased to have any errors or omissions brought
to their attention.*

Prentice-Hall, Inc., Englewood Cliffs, New Jersey
Prentice-Hall International, Inc., London
Prentice-Hall of Australia, Pty., Ltd., Sydney
Prentice-Hall of India Pvt., Ltd., New Delhi
Prentice-Hall of Japan Inc., Tokyo
Prentice-Hall of Southeast Asia (PTE.) Ltd. Singapore
Editora Prentice-Hall de Brasil Ltda., Rio de Janeiro

ISBN 0-13-363499-X

Design: Gail Ferreira
Production Editor: Heather Scott McClune
Artwork: Jo-Ann Jordan and Victoria Birta

1 2 3 4 5 6 THB 87 86 85 84 83 82
Typesetting by Linotext Inc.
Printed and bound in Canada by T. H. Best Printing Company Ltd.

CONTENTS

ACKNOWLEDGMENTS

No championship hockey club could succeed without foot-soldiers who are willing to go into the corners and indulge in heavy checking. Likewise, this work could not have been completed without the grand efforts of a number of literary diggers led by the tenacious Michael Berger who industriously worked with Don's tapes and transcriptions. Michael's management of the flow of information was invaluable and the authors are more than appreciative of his help and diligence.

Many others assisted in the transcription of tapes, the typing of manuscript, and the other duties relevant to the book's production. To them we deliver a deep bow and a large round of applause—Richard Friedman, Paul Fichtenbaum, Phil Davis, Phil Czochanski, Sara Kass, Sharon Kopitnikoff, Debbie Klein, Joel Sherman, Andrew D'Angelo, Don Frumkin, Arthur Bulin, David Hom, Ralph Russo, Steve Ginsberg, George Hall, and Lori Weissman.

It would be an understatement to add that the book would not have come to fruition without the encouragement of Gerry Patterson and Janice Whitford, the latter of whom has been a beacon of literary guidance from the inception of the project. Fifteen years and fifty-five books have passed through this typewriter, and never have I enjoyed working with an editor more than Heather McClune. I have been equally delighted with the work of Gail Ferreira who created the book's terrific design.

Stan Fischler

GRAPES

A Vintage View of Hockey

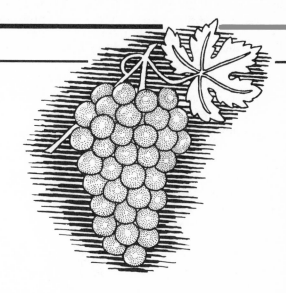

CHAPTER ONE

Close But No Cigar

I died on May 10, 1979; at 11:10 p.m. to be exact.

Two shots killed me. The first, which left me critically wounded, was fired by Guy Lafleur. The one that wiped me out came from the stick of Yvon Lambert.

Had I survived these attacks I have no doubt that I would still be coach of the Boston Bruins today and, quite likely, governor of Massachusetts. But, as my mother always said when she extracted my left *and* right hands from the cookie jar; you can't have everything.

For a time, I did have everything. Early in May, 1979, I was reasonably healthy, only twenty pounds overweight—which is good for me—and I had my family. There was my lovely wife Rose, who had stuck with me through all the battles, (my friends say there's a special place in Heaven for Rose for putting up with me) my beautiful daughter Cindy, my wonderful son Timothy, and most important, my friend and companion Blue—we never call her a dog—who is the Stan Jonathan of Dogdom.

And, of course, there was my job. I was coach of the Boston Bruins. Why, even when I think of it today I find the mere mention of it hard to believe. Me, Donald Stewart Cherry, coach of the Boston Bruins. For my money, there was only one role in history that could surpass running the Bruins and that would be being Lord Nelson commanding the fleet at Trafalgar. He was killed in that action too.

1

I loved coaching the Bruins more than Gretzky and Bossy love scoring goals. Ever since I was a kid growing up in Kingston, Ontario, I dreamed of being a general or admiral directing the troops. Kingston is one of Canada's most beautiful cities, with its preserved historic buildings and lovely waterfront. Also, hockey got started there, so it's not surprising that it's where I decided to enlist.

My luck, the troops I had on the Bruins were special. Very special. The writers liked to call them the Lunchpail Athletic Club. They put in a good day's work and never bitched about it. Anyone who has the good fortune to coach a team like that should count his blessings.

I counted and counted. Not only did I have a team I loved, but there was a constituency to boot. Boston fans are one of a kind. They are blue collar types who come to Boston Garden and give you what-for if you don't give them their money's worth.

There was one guy who always sat in the upper balcony. He had a piercing voice that reminded me of someone pounding on an organ with his elbows. If I was doing badly, he'd yell down, "Hey Cherry, you remind me of a town in Massachusetts. Marblehead!" I think the first time anybody was called Marblehead here was when King Clancy was refereeing. It's one of the classics that's hollered at every coach.

The most famous catcall ever heard in Boston concerned Harry Sinden. The Bruins were having a tough time when Harry was coaching in his first year, and one night a guy hollered, "Sinden! There's a bus leaving for Oklahoma at six a.m. Be under it!" Another time, when Bobby Orr had just joined the club and was skating rings around everybody, the guy hollered, "Sinden! Bench that kid. He makes the rest of the stiffs look bad!"

The trouble with these guys was that they would wait until the whole building was quiet and then start yelling. One night during my first year, when it was very quiet, a guy yelled, "Wake up the coach." I had a running conversation with him. I turned around and hollered, "Have another beer." This got some mild applause from the crowd. In the next period he kept it up, so I yelled, "Aren't you drunk yet?" The crowd gave me a standing ovation for that one.

One day, Terry O'Reilly got into a fight with Dave Schultz, and hurt his hand on Schultz's head. I didn't play Terry for the next game because he couldn't hold a stick, but I dressed him so Schultz wouldn't think he had kept Terry from playing. I forgot how much the Boston fans wanted to see Terry play and they kept giving it to me to play him. Finally I couldn't stand it any longer so at a stoppage of play, I waited until it was nice and quiet, then yelled as loud as I could, "Terry's hurt, but I don't want Schultz to know it." Do you know what reply I got? "Play him anyway, he gets enough dough!"

My first year, one guy was really giving it to Esposito and Cashman. He had Phil in tears of rage one night, and I heard Cash say, "Enjoy the game, you bastard. It's the last game you'll ever see in Boston Garden." I kept my eye on the guy, and after the period he was approached by two guys who looked like Dave Semenko. I never saw or heard from the guy again.

Another time in my first year, we won 3-2 and were booed. I asked one of the writers why the crowd was booing us and he told me that we hadn't covered the spread!

The crowd disliked Don McKenny and Ken Hodge and used to call them "Mary" because they weren't tough enough. But they loved, absolutely adored, Terry O'Reilly. It was said that if O'Reilly shot the puck into his own net, the crowd would boo the goaltender for not stopping the shot.

Tom Fitzgerald once wrote a glowing piece about Terry and someone said to him: "The only reason you people in Boston like O'Reilly is because his name is O'Reilly." Tom answered, "That's not true; we'd like him just as much if his name was Sullivan."

Then there was the media. If there was ever a better bunch of guys around, neither Blue nor I had heard of them. I'll tell you what great guys they were. Many times I would say something in a fit of anger that could really bury me. The sports writers would decide not to print any comments that could hurt me. It must have been the first time in history that writers helped and protected a coach. No wonder I loved them.

I should have been the happiest guy in the world as my Bruins prepared for the seventh game of the Stanley Cup semi-final round against the Canadiens. The series was tied at three games apiece. The writers had picked us to be out in four or five games so already we were away ahead of them. The Canadiens were worried. "Habs on the Ropes," the papers said.

Well, it was true. But Don Cherry was also on the ropes. I had to win this game, and everyone from Boston to Moose Jaw knew why. My manager, boss, and former buddy, Harry Sinden, was after my ass. Harry wanted my skin and the one way he could get me was if we were knocked off by the Canadiens.

Why Sinden wanted me out of my Bruins job is a good question, one I will deal with very shortly. For the moment, suffice it to say that there was a severe personality clash. We had grown farther apart than the Hatfields and the McCoys, and I can guarantee I liked Harry a lot more than he liked me.

All my players were aware of the friction between us. To be unaware they would have to have been spending their days and nights in some distant cave. They were aware, and in a sense, amused by the Cherry-Sinden feud, and they would have fun with it since they never believed I would be fired as long as we kept winning, and we kept winning.

Once, Bobby Schmautz and Gregg Sheppard were marching around in their underwear, singing "Onward Sinden Soldiers." Harry walked into the locker room to hang up his coat and saw the whole scene. Needless to say, Shep was soon gone and Schmautzie followed a little later.

I remember clearly the morning of the seventh game. We were preparing for our morning skate, to loosen up for the game. Somewhere, the team had found a picture of Harry and Tom Johnson, his assistant, and while I was sitting there, putting on my underwear, I saw them putting up this picture and laughing. I knew something was up, but at that point I didn't give a damn. But I thought I should keep the peace for a little while longer, so I went up to see what my little boys had done to piss Harry off today.

Under the picture was written, among other things, "Willard and Ben." For people who haven't seen the movie *Willard*, Willard was a guy who owned a rat named Ben, who was his best friend. I tore down the picture and threw it in the garbage can. But some of the players rescued it and put it back up, when who should come into the dressing room but Tom Johnson. Tom saw the picture, and immediately reported to his boss Harry what *I* had done. "Oh well," I thought, "I'm gone no matter what happens, and besides, it was right on the money."

I remember the players doing something similar during the Pittsburgh series, which we won three games to none. Cheevers was unbelievable in that series. On the morning of the first game, Harry called us all off the ice during our morning skate, and for the first time in five years, really interfered with our game plan. All of a sudden we are going to go over the Pittsburgh lineup, their individual lines and all, the morning of the game. We'd been in the playoffs before and had never done anything like this and all of a sudden, we were doing it for the Penguins.

So, when we all got off the ice, Harry had Pittsburgh's lineup on the blackboard and was telling us how wonderful they were, and how we had to be ready, and sacrifice, and all the bullshit that coaches go through before a game.

Halfway through the speech Harry made such a bad mistake that even I was embarrassed for him. He said "Pittsburgh has a great new winger named Hamilton, who's having a great year. He's scoring a lot of goals and we'll definitely have to watch him." How could Harry make such a blunder? The kid had just come up from the minors and had scored two lucky goals in one game. The players were killing themselves.

Harry left after his performance, and I got up and said, "We're the Boston Bruins; we don't worry about any other team, they worry about us. If we're executing the way we should, they won't win a game. But remember, keep your eye on Hamilton."

I left the locker room and, when I returned, there was Harry, reading the blackboard, only this time the players had written all over the Pittsburgh lineup: "So What? They Suck! Hamilton Who?" And, "Three Straight Games, No Problem!"

I just sighed. (Another nail in the coffin.)

I went back to the Manoir Le Moyne Hotel, where we were staying, and no sooner had I closed the door behind me than the phone started ringing. It was John Zeigler, President of the NHL. He said "Don, I have an article from the *Boston Herald* written by D. Leo Monahan, and it quotes you as saying that the NHL brass does not want a Boston-New York final, they want a Montreal-New York final because they want the big apple and a colourful Canadian team, so watch us get stiffed if it goes seven games."

Ziegler said, "Now I don't mind you calling us stupid among other things, but this article implies we are dishonest. I don't want to put a muzzle on you and your colourful remarks, which are usually good for the league, but we will not mention this again. Is that understood?"

Next thing I knew, I was getting ready for the game at The Forum. I put on my traditional Boston Bruin robe. I walked around, going from player to player, trying to get them relaxed but it was as if they had been in the trenches for too long and were suffering from shell shock.

I walked into the small room where the players fixed their sticks. Bobby Schmautz, my tough little right wing, and Terry O'Reilly, my big right wing were standing there arguing. Schmautz had a hacksaw in his hands and O'Reilly was carrying a blowtorch. Both were working on their sticks. Both wanted to use the vise that holds the sticks while they are being shaved and bent.

I have never in my life experienced anything to compare with the feeling of violence in that room. I honestly thought they were going to go at each other with their weapons, and these guys were, and are, the best of friends. This is just an indication of the fever pitch they were working themselves into for the game.

Take the whole business of deciding which goalie to start. I had used Gerry Cheevers in our quarter-final series against the Penguins and he was terrific. Mind you, I'm talking about an athlete who was 36 years old at the time stopping shots going more than a hundred miles an hour. Now, I didn't want to play him in every game against the Penguins. My other goalie was Gilles Gilbert, a French Canadian and a real stylist. Although he was younger than Gerry, he didn't have Gerry's heart. I had hoped to start Gilbert in Game Three of the Pittsburgh series, but he got so nervous he came down with a case of hives and I had to throw Cheevers into the breach.

I actually didn't have a chance to use Gilbert until the Montreal series. Everyone thought I was nuts to use Gillie because he hadn't played against the Penguins but they didn't figure on the psychological element that is so important in this game. I knew that Gilbert was coming up to the option year of his contract and I knew that if he expected to get a good new contract he would have to excel against the Canadiens.

But, just to be certain, I huddled with Blue. A reporter in Boston once asked me, "How do you pick your goalies?" As a joke I replied,

"Blue picks them for me. We go for walks and she picks which goalie is going to be hot." This really ticked Harry off. So whenever anyone asked me after that, I would say, "Blue says Cheevers is ready," or "Blue says Gillie is going to be hot tonight."

People wonder why coaches have dogs, and I have noticed that athletes often take their dogs for long walks. The reason is that the dog doesn't care whether you win or lose, he just wants to be with you. The joy a dog expresses in solitary walks with you seems to raise your spirits. No dumb questions, no criticisms, a dog just wants to be with you and love you. How could you not feel better?

I could hardly wait, after a game, to get home and take a moonlight walk with Blue. And I really did talk to her. If we had played badly, I'd say, "Well, Blue, we really blew it tonight," or "We really stunk the joint out tonight," or if we played well, "We were smoking tonight." She didn't care, she was always too busy chasing something in the bushes.

One time, the dog-walking idea backfired on me. I thought it would be a good idea to take a walk with Blue in the State Park that bordered our property in Boston. The place had stone fences and deserted mills that were two hundred years old. It was a very warm day and I decided to stop by a beautiful stream. I fell asleep and when I awoke, still a little sleepy, I decided to take a short cut through the woods.

Blue and I wandered for four hours, and she kept looking up at me as if to say, "You jerk." We went through woods and swamps and I got worried when it started to get dark. Finally, I heard tires on a distant highway, so we headed there. I found a piece of rope at a deserted farmhouse to put around Blue and we started along the highway. Two guys drove by and hollered, "Hey, there's Blue." Imagine, they recognized Blue and not me. They picked us up and I found out later that we had walked fifteen miles.

Anyway, Blue was the one who tipped me about playing Gilbert, and Gillie just came up great. We were down to the seventh game and I knew that he would play better than ever in front of the French-speaking crowd. French-Canadian hockey players have a special pride in their culture. Playing in The Montreal Forum is to them what a pilgrimage to Mecca is to a Moslem.

Of course it meant a lot to the English-speaking players as well. I looked at Brad Park and I could have cried. Here he was, 30 years old, should have been in the prime of his hockey life and yet, judging by his wan face, you would have figured he was playing the last game of his life. His knees had had all the cartilages taken out but they never took his heart out.

Park realized that this might be the last time he would get so close to sipping Stanley Cup champagne. He knew in his heart that if we could just get past the Canadiens we would destroy the New York Rangers in the finals.

Timothy and me in Boston Garden, 1975-76.

Rose, Blue, and me.

Cartoon by Bob Alexander that appeared in the Eagle-Tribune, April 29, 1979.

"What I'm thinking," said Park, "is that I have an opportunity here. How many other times will I have that opportunity?"

The Canadiens had won the Stanley Cup more times than anybody, but we sensed that they were tight. "We forced them into a situation where they're in big trouble," said Park. "Now they have to see if they can play loose. It's a first for them in this series. Now they're the team that has to win."

To beat Montreal, we had to get the puck past the big guy, Ken Dryden, who guarded their net. He was the scholar of the National Hockey League. He had a law degree and a great pair of legs; no other goalie could make that statement. He also had a clearer view of the game than most of the players. His professorial approach didn't fool me. Deep down, Dryden was as intense a competitor as anyone else on the ice; maybe more so—especially in the seventh game. Canadiens have never been the same since he left.

"We will gamble more," said Dryden. "We will take more punishment, knowing that there is nothing to save for another game to be played."

Fine. The rhetoric was superb, as it usually is before a seventh game. The question remained: How would it be translated on the ice? Well, it was a hell of a game. My guys were loose and the Canadiens, for some reason that to this day I still can't fathom, couldn't get themselves untracked.

The trick was to stop Guy Lafleur. Sounds easy. About as easy as bottling the Atlantic Ocean. I gave the job of shadowing Lafleur to Don Marcotte. For my money there wasn't a better example of a working guy than Marcotte. (I think it's a joke that he never won the Frank Selke award given to the best defensive forward.) Don's job was to hawk Lafleur on every turn and he was doing it well. I also knew that Scotty Bowman, my counterpart behind the Canadiens' bench, was trying to double- and triple-shift Lafleur to get him away from Marcotte. My answer to that was that if Lafleur could play 60 minutes, Marcotte could play 60 minutes.

"You follow him to the toilet if you have to," I told Donny, "but don't let him out of your sight."

For two periods he followed my orders to a T. Once the two of them collided and were simultaneously cut on the face. They just stood there glaring at each other, like a pair of medieval knights who had nothing but the utmost respect for each other.

After two periods, we led 3-1. Geez, but we could have had at least two more in the second period. Terry O'Reilly and Peter McNab had Dryden beaten but they couldn't put the biscuit behind him.

The trick for a coach between periods of a game like that one is to try to keep everything loose, especially when you have a team of guys who are up for every game. Keep everything loose and in perspective.

Treat it like any other game. What I did was to remind them of their jobs.

To Marcotte I said, "Watch Lafleur, keep with him." To Cashman I said, "Cash, stand in front, don't let him see anything." (This meant I wanted him to screen Dryden on shots from the point.) To Park, "Make sure your shots are on net." To Doak, "Don't run." (This meant that he shouldn't run *at* the Canadiens.) To everybody I said, "Don't get caught." and "Remember now, shoot low." We had found out during the season that if you put a low, soft, screen shot on net, Dryden would miss it.

I told Bobby Schmautz to "waste one." This meant—and very few people in the league have the balls to do this—shoot the puck around Dryden's head. That way, he would be straightened up and unprepared for a low shot.

So, this is the sort of thing a coach says between periods, and it's a funny thing. The players never answer back. They don't even say yes or anything else. They only nod, but they are ready.

We went out prepared for the third period, but Damn! The Canadiens got one at 6:10 and before nine minutes had gone by we were tied up at 3-3.

Then we got a break. Guy Lapointe, one of the best of Montreal's defensemen, hurt his knee and it was the Canadiens' turn to sag. With four minutes left in regulation time my nifty little right wing, Rick Middleton, got the puck behind the Montreal net. He came out front and stuffed it past Dryden to put us ahead, 4-3. There were exactly 3 minutes and 59 seconds separating us from the biggest victory of our lives.

Could we do it? Everybody had his assignment, but I could tell that they were tight. Too tight. I would have liked to call a three day time-out and review all assignments, remind the players that the best defense is a good offense, and return Donny Marcotte to the fray, reasonably well-rested. Under the circumstances, I felt as helpless as a guy trying to catch the gold ring on a merry-go-round while sitting on an inside horse. The game had somehow gotten out of my grasp. It was up and down, fast, faster, fastest. Next thing I knew, Lafleur was going off the ice for the Canadiens and Marcotte had come back to our bench, while the play was still on. I walked over to Donny and gave him a pat on the back. He looked up at me, exhausted, and then looked back onto the ice. Marcotte turned white. I heard him moan, "Oh, no!" Those deathless words will remain with me into my fourth reincarnation.

I looked out onto the field of battle and got that sinking sensation. I didn't have to count the players, I knew. *We had too many men on the ice.* My heart actually hurt then, and remembering now makes it hurt again.

I needed a large—about 40 foot long—invisible hook to instantly haul in my wandering minstrel. (Who will never be mentioned, we made a silent pact never to reveal his name.) If the referee and linesmen wore blindfolds for about a minute I might be able to get somebody's attention and get him the hell back to the bench before we were slapped with a two-minute penalty.

No such luck. Linesman John D'Amico, a hell of a nice guy, noticed that we had six skaters instead of the legal five. I could tell that in his heart of hearts he *didn't* want to blow the whistle on us and that even *he* was hoping that a Bruin would have the good sense to get back to the bench. I could see in his eyes that he was saying to himself, "Don, I hate to do this to you but I have to!"

D'Amico's arm went up and the sound of his whistle cut right through to my bone marrow.

The time of the penalty was 17:26. How did it happen? Why did it happen? I have asked myself these questions so many times!

For starters let me say for now and for an eternity that *I* accept full responsibility for the blunder of blunders. When a team gets caught with too many men on the ice at that stage in a hockey game, it has to be the coach's fault. I deserved to be court-martialed.

The confusion was rooted in the fact that Marcotte had stayed on left wing through three shifts. The other guy was nervous and got carried away. When he finally came back to the bench after D'Amico whistled the penalty he had tears in his eyes. So did my son, Timothy, who had been watching the game at bench level. I imagine I would have been crying, too, but, at that point, I suspect that all my bodily functions had gone on strike. At that moment I took a look at the Canadiens' bench. They looked like a pride of lions about to jump a wildebeest. There was only one thing to do. I called a time-out.

Were we ever in a mess. My trainer, Frosty Forristall, had tears in his eyes and two Bruins fans sitting next to our bench were bawling like babies. I wanted to cry myself but I couldn't. (That would come later.) I told the guys that we had to stop Lafleur, to stay between him and the net as much as possible.

Okay. The time-out was over. There was a face-off and the puck was in motion. I couldn't believe what a terrific job we were doing of killing the penalty. A minute had gone by and we still had the lead. Now it was 70 seconds elapsed and we were *still* ahead.

But the Canadiens mounted a counterattack. Jacques Lemaire, one of the most underrated players on that Montreal team, took a pass near our blue line. Lafleur was moving down the right side like the Japanese Bullet Train. Lemaire dropped the pass over to Lafleur. I figured he was going to try to move in on Gilbert, try a few dekes and get into a really good scoring position.

He was way over to the right, far, far out, sort of where I wanted him. A shot from there would be desperate, but he drew his stick back. He *was* desperate. For a split second I almost felt reassured. Then, his stick swung around the big arc and the blade made contact with the puck.

I can't tell you precisely how fast that puck travelled but anything faster than that shot had to break the sound barrier. Almost in the same moment Lafleur slapped the rubber, it bulged the twine in the left side of the net behind Gillie. There went the lead. *Boom!* Just like that.

We left the ice tied, 4-4, at the end of regulation time. The way my players plodded into the dressing room you would have thought that they had just finished a trek across the Sahara Desert—in uniform. I have seen teams in my eleven year coaching career that were down, but none as thoroughly subterranean as this one.

I knew that getting them to even a reasonable state of battle readiness for the overtime would be the chore of my life.

Before going into the room I had to get my frustrations out. It does no good for the players to see the coach upset, or for the coach to take his frustrations out on the players. So I left them alone for a while. Then I took a deep breath and walked into the room.

It was like a morgue. No jokes this time. I said to them, "Look, when we were down two games to none in this series going back to Boston, if I could have said to you, 'Would you be happy to go into the overtime of the seventh game?' what would you have said?" And they all yelled, "YES!"

I didn't know if I believed it, but they did and that's most important. They were banging at the doors to get going. There never was, nor ever will be, a better bunch of guys. I love them.

And, before you knew it, the buzzer was sounding for the start of sudden-death overtime.

To my surprise, we came out with more drive than I thought we had in us. Marcotte took a pass from O'Reilly when Dryden had one knee down on the ice. Marcotte shot it for the upper corner and started to raise his stick in celebration, as if the puck was going in. But Dryden, who was so damn big, got his shoulder in front of the puck—more by accident than by skill—and my heart was still in my mouth. The rebound came out to O'Reilly and, with an open net waiting to greet his shot, the puck bounced over his stick.

Back and forth the play whirred at a dizzying pace. The clock ticked past the nine minute mark and there was still no tie-breaker. My guys—particularly the older ones—were struggling. Park, Schmautz and Cashman had blood running into their underwear but they kept on going.

At last, Lafleur was off the ice and it seemed as if we might have a respite, but Bowman had some excellent infantrymen. One of them was a kid named Mario Tremblay who had gone into orbit along the right boards. Another was Yvon Lambert, who always looked as if he had two left feet until he put the puck behind your goalie.

Al Sims was alone on defense, with Park coming back, and I could see the fear in Al's eyes as Lambert sped to the goal crease while Tremblay, tantalizingly, waited for the precise moment to deliver the pass. Lambert eluded Park, accepted the puck at the lip of the net and pushed it past Gilbert before the goalie could slide across the crease.

The pain I felt when the red light flashed behind our goal cannot be measured in traditional human terms. To say that a piledriver applied to my stomach would not have created a deeper hurt would simply be minimizing the ache.

A lot of people—and I know that they don't have sadistic tendencies but it feels like they do—ask, "What were your feelings at that exact moment?" I tell you on Blue's head, it was sorrow for my players, especially those who had been given shots of novocaine before the game. The goal doesn't flash in my mind, but somebody's underwear, with blood mixed with the sweat, does.

I felt disgusted with myself for letting it happen. Sometimes when you have too many men on the ice it's the player's fault. But not this time. I hadn't spelled out the assignments plainly enough.

Strangely, I didn't even think of my job until a reporter asked me, "Do you think this will cost you your job?" I said, "My friend, after this loss, I don't really care one way or the other." But I knew I was gone. I had known I was gone as far back as Christmas. There was a slight chance of me staying if we had won the Cup, but at that moment I really couldn't have cared less.

I tried to punish myself by keeping the reporters out of the locker room for fifteen minutes, so they could bombard me with questions and really give it to me. They tried to be kind, but every question was like a knife through my heart.

We flew home on a charter right after the game. I sat with the players, as usual. No sense in changing now. I sat there sipping a beer, and I said to myself, "Well, what now? Do I become a company man? Do I change my principles even though I know they're right?" No sir. I decided then and there, to hell with it, I was gone.

When we landed at the airport the guys were going to the 3B's, their favourite bar. I was feeling so run-down and sick with the flu that I couldn't go. As I think back now, I should have gone, no matter how sick I was. It would have been our last time together.

I could not duck the blame in the disaster. I was captain of the ship, the ship went down, so I was at fault. The temptation was to start feeling sorry for myself but I felt more grief for my players like Park, Ratelle, and Cash—the old warriors—who might never get this close to winning the Stanley Cup again.

And then there was my goalie, Gilbert. We had had our differences before the Canadiens series, but I couldn't quarrel with his effort this time. He faced 52 shots in the last game and was called out onto the ice after the winning goal. He had been chosen star of the game. When Gillie skated out onto the ice to take his bow, his lips were pursed and he had a far-away look in his eyes. If he had been wearing a steel helmet and a tunic I would have guessed that he was a shell-shocked soldier who had just survived a trench bombardment in World War I.

Survival was very much on my mind at this point in time. I knew that Harry Sinden was after my hide and I didn't have to be told that Lambert's goal killed me. Now there was a matter of reincarnation.

I could have been reborn as a yes man. But that would have meant a 180-degree change. If I had to kiss someone's ass to keep my job, I couldn't live with myself—and I couldn't coach either.

Sure, I might fool some people, but I could never fool the players. One thing my guys have always known is that they could count on me to go to bat for them. That's why they were willing to produce for me. You could say I'm crazy but I wouldn't change that for anything in the world.

The question before the house, as well as all of Boston and parts of Canada, was how Harry would dispose of me and no less importantly, how I would dispose of him.

I drove home; Rose was there. She said that it wasn't my fault but I knew better. Blue wanted to go for a walk. "Sorry Blue, no walk this time. Even you couldn't make me feel better." I went to bed, to dream of blood and sweat . . . Sorry guys.

CHAPTER TWO

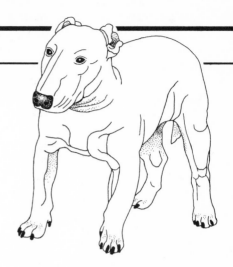

I'm Not Wild About Harry

There were Frick and Frack, Hope and Crosby, and, finally, Cherry and Sinden. Anything closer than us would have had to be welded together. He was my boss and I was his employee but our relationship had a brotherly quality about it that had all the elements of permanence. (For the first couple of years at least.)

I had heard of Harry long before I met the man. In Canadian hockey circles he was something of a mini-legend. Like me, he had come up through the ranks. At one point he worked as a boilermaker for General Motors and played hockey as a sideline. He was a defenseman and a hell of a good one, at that. On the smallish side, he was reminiscent of Brad Park in size and style. He could really move the puck well but he wasn't rough. (When you think about that it's fascinating because Harry later became the architect of one of the toughest teams of all time, The Big Bad Bruins of the late 1960s and early 1970s.)

Before Harry turned pro he played for a team from Whitby, Ontario, called the Dunlops. It was a senior division club, sponsored by the Dunlop tire people and it was solid enough to be asked to represent Canada in the 1958 World Championships in Oslo, Norway.

Although they were considered a ragtag team, the Dunlops won the whole shebang and Harry, like the other guys on the club, became an instant Canadian hero.

15

He turned pro in 1960 with Hull-Ottawa of the Eastern Pro League and the following season he was a regular with Kingston in the Eastern League. In 1962-63 he was like the Bobby Orr of the league. He had 10 goals and 56 assists for 66 points, won the leading defenseman award and was the league's most valuable player.

You would figure that the Boston Bruins, who were holding a mortgage on the bottom of the NHL, would have recognized Sinden's talents and given him a break. What they did was invite him to camp and then ignore him.

My first direct contact with Harry was in 1973, my first year of coaching in Rochester, although I had played against him in different leagues for years. In those days we had none of our own players under contract, so the trick was to scrounge around the NHL and get some borderline big-leaguers on a lend-lease basis. Harry was one of the managers I went hustling to and he gave me three guys who helped right off the bat and I liked him for that.

Meanwhile, Harry had won a pair of Stanley Cups for the Bruins, first as a coach in 1970 and then as a manager in 1972. Tom Johnson was coach in '72, then Harry brought in Bep Guidolin to replace Johnson. And although Bep took the team to the finals, he and Harry did not see eye to eye on things, so he departed for Kansas City.

For reasons that I still can't fathom, Harry took a liking to me. Once, he invited me to Chicago for the Stanley Cup playoffs and didn't mention anything about coaching. My early impression of him was favourable. He had an earthy quality about him. When we returned to the hotel there was none of the formality of room service or such sophisticated trappings.

Old School Harry went to the corner grocery store and bought cheese, crackers, and all the beer we could carry and we had a picnic in the suite. I liked that.

The next time I saw Sinden was at the annual hockey meetings in Montreal. It was June 1974 and just about everybody connected with hockey, with the exception of Lord Stanley of Preston, showed up for the annual draft and general search for jobs. Guidolin had been dropped as Bruins' coach. The Bruins were looking for a replacement but I wasn't thinking about the job.

What interested me was Sinden. Somehow I had become intrigued by the man and his style. He seemed to be a cut or two above the run-of-the-mill hockey people. He was easily the classiest operator at the hockey convention.

One night Harry invited me out for a few beers. We talked about the draft, about the NHL generally, about players in particular, about life and sometimes, even, about the distant world outside of hockey. Sometime before the stroke of midnight, Harry leaned back and uttered the unexpected words: "How would you like to coach the Boston Bruins?"

I had the feeling of being ever so slightly electrocuted. Being knighted by Queen Elizabeth was about the only accomplishment that could be equated with an offer to coach in the NHL. And yet, when the feeling subsided I looked Sinden in the eye and wanted to say thanks, but no thanks!

"Look, Harry," I said, "I want a little time to think about it. Lemme talk to my wife."

There was a lot of thinking to be done and not much time in which to do it. My inclination, oddly enough, was to reject the offer. Rochester had become home to me; home in the literal and figurative sense. We had been living there for ten years and had grown to love the city, the people and the hockey community. More than that, I had found myself as a coach and general manager there.

Money was irrelevant in my decision, as it has always been when it comes to hockey matters. I made $4,500 a year for nine years as a player before I got a raise to $5,200. When I came to Rochester, Jack Riley, the boss, increased my salary to $6,000 because that was what the newest rookies were making and he didn't want a man with ten years of pro experience to be getting less than they were.

Another real obstacle to my leaving was the link I had forged with the Rochester Americans hockey club. When I had taken the job of coach and general manager I had said that I wanted to build a dynasty. I had meant it, and I knew that I was getting closer every day.

Better still, management in Rochester left me alone. This has always been vital to me—room to do things my way without the higher-ups interfering—and the Rochester owners knew it and respected my feelings. I never had to worry about them meddling in the team's business.

I had already been fired once in Rochester, in 1972, because I ignored some orders from the front office (since replaced) when they wanted me to play a couple of guys I knew were stiffs. After I came back under a new administration, I was allowed to turn the club around and the people of Rochester appreciated what I had done. Why, one summer three different civic organizations voted me "Citizen of the Year," and I wasn't even a citizen!

I had a good thing going in Rochester. The town was alive hockey-wise; the owners respected me and said that I could stay there as long as I wished. I could have played it safe and simply given Sinden a thanks-but-no-thanks.

Before I made any decision, I phoned my wife, Rose, and told her the situation. "It's your decision, Don," she said. But she also wanted to be sure I realized what a great deal I would be giving up. We had a nice, comfortable home. I was making $30,000-a-year, plus expenses and the use of a car. "You know," added Rose, "you could run for mayor of Rochester—and win."

But she reiterated that I had to make the ultimate decision and—great wife that she was, is and always will be—Rose said she would go along with whatever I chose to do. You have no idea how much easier that makes it for a man. After all, she could have said, "Enough with the travelling; I don't want to move again. We stay!" I knew a lot of other wives who would have said just that.

That night I sat alone in my hotel room, mulling over the options. I remember a pervasive feeling to play it safe and stay in Rochester. But the more I thought about it, the more I became convinced that staying would be the cowardly thing to do. Finally, I said to myself: "For cripes sake, Don. You always wanted to be in the NHL. How many chances do you get to coach the Boston Bruins?" Then, I thought of my dad and what he would have thought of me if I had rejected Harry's offer. *That* did it.

The next morning I met Harry for breakfast. I didn't say a word until we had ordered the bacon-and-eggs. Finally, I said, "Yeah, I'll coach the Bruins."

I was very matter-of-fact about it; so much so that Harry couldn't believe it. With that, he shot back: "Okay, how much do you want, $10,000?"

There was a brief pause. Then Harry burst out laughing and I sailed along with him.

"Harry," I said, "I know you'll be fair." I wasn't going to quibble. All I wanted was the chance to prove myself. I told him to give me what he thought I was worth and as many years as he wanted.

"I'll give you a three year deal," he replied, "at $40,000 a year."

We shook hands and I walked away with a gushing feeling of satisfaction welling within me. It was a good contract, as far as I was concerned, but there was a more important reason for my accepting it and, I'll bet, to this day nobody would guess why. You see, a lot of people think I decided to go to Boston because I had been buried in the minors for so long that I craved the big time and that I couldn't wait to handle superstars like Bobby Orr and Phil Esposito. No way.

I took the Bruins job for one reason and one reason only—Harry Sinden. He had been an excellent coach and I felt that I couldn't just walk into the job without getting some help from a real *NHL* pro. I believed implicitly in Harry's ability to help make me an even better leader than I had been. And I was right.

Another thing. I had a gut feeling of rapport with Harry that I had never experienced before with a boss. I sensed that we could share a special kinship.

There was a lot about us that was similar. We both had had a middle-class upbringing. We came from the same community. Sinden had suffered for years as a minor leaguer, much in the manner that I had. He knew what tough-going was all about. He had scratched and crawled to get to the top, and now I was there with him. Besides, he liked bagpipe music. I had been a tenor drummer in the Rochester pipe band. How could I not be a Harry Sinden fan after that?

As soon as we agreed on the deal I phoned Rose.

"I'm taking the Bruins' job," I said.

"Okay. What time does your flight get in?" was her reply.

That was Rose! Always taking things in stride. Can you imagine—for the first time in our lives we owned our own home, the children were going to school, and we had friends in Rochester. All this was gone and all she said was, "What time do you get in?" I have heard that some hockey wives leave their husbands because their intellectual lives aren't being fulfilled. I think the song "Stand By Your Man" was written for Rose. She is one in a million.

On the flight back to Rochester my mind was filled with conflicting thoughts. I kept saying to myself, "Hey, Don, you're coach of the Bruins." Then I began reflecting as the clouds rolled by. I was getting $10,000 more than I was getting in Rochester but I was going to suffer ten times more pressure. The cushy part of the job I was leaving kept intruding in my thoughts. I had been general manager. I could come and go as I pleased. I could get the players I wanted, not the ones someone else ordered me to get.

The real clincher, the episode that convinced me that I had done the right thing, occurred when I arrived home and told my nine-year-old son Timothy that I had accepted the Bruins' job.

Timothy said breathlessly, "You mean I'm going to meet Bobby Orr?" "Yeah, and so will I," said I, just as breathlessly.

If the truth be known, I was awed by the new job and I hadn't even started it yet. I signed the Bruins contract without even reading it; that's how much I trusted Harry. I didn't even have an agent or an attorney look it over for me. Rose was amused. "You know, Don," she said, "you should keep a rubber stamp handy for signing all contracts."

Sinden called a press conference in Boston to announce the deal. The story that I was taking the job broke while I was still in Rochester, but I flew down to Boston the next day where I was formally introduced in The Garden Room of Boston Garden. When I walked in, the first thing I noticed was the huge photo of Eddie Shore hanging on the wall, then the photos of Dit Clapper and other distinguished Bruins. As I entered the press conference, the pack of reporters and television people amazed me. I instantly got the feeling that they were taking a skeptical view of me, wondering who is this jerk up from the minors. To say the least, I was impressed by the turnout.

I was not so impressed by my debut up at the podium. I made "great" statements like, "How can we lose with the kind of great players we have on this team?" And, "If we lose, it'll be my fault." Wonderful. I started digging my own grave on the first day of the job.

Apparently, some members of the media were impressed. "If you like honesty and animation with your ice hockey," wrote Joe Gordon in the Quincy Massachusetts *Patriot-Ledger*, "you'll like Don Cherry."

Actually, I was the original Mr. Naiveté. I had no idea what was going on behind the scenes with the Bruins so, when I talked to the newspaper guys it was without a lot of the facts Harry had at his fingertips.

But more about that later. "I like a tough team," I told them, "and I know I have tough guys on this club and I'll bring out the toughness. They're going to be rough. Every team I've ever been with has been. We intimidated every club in the American League."

Someone asked a good question: did I anticipate having any trouble with the players? "A few," I said, "will probably try to take advantage but when they do I'll step on them and step on them hard."

It sounded good, but I hadn't even met the players yet. That would come just before training camp. In the meantime, my dealings were with Harry and they couldn't have been better. I could hardly wait until the phone rang. When he would say, "Don, Harry here," I would actually get a thrill. And when he told me that he had never considered anyone else for the coaching job I got an even bigger thrill.

The thrill was gone the minute I met the players. This happened at a pre-season bash the Bruins threw at a country club in suburban Boston. They pulled out all the stops; grills with flaming hors d'oeuvres, bloody marys, beer, everything. Starting out the season with a party seemed like a good idea; little did I know that the party would continue for six months. A couple of the players depressed me no end. One guy was so stiff he couldn't talk.

I felt like a jerk and I couldn't imagine how these guys would be able to get in shape eating and drinking the way they did.

All of a sudden it came to me; I was in trouble with this hockey team and I hadn't even coached it yet. I felt I was in trouble and I knew the club was in trouble and so did Harry. Even though I knew most of the guys were winners, some of them had outgrown hockey. Hockey had become a means to an end.

Some of the players were fat, and not only fat physically, but fat in the heart. I could see they had forgotten that hard work had brought them here in the first place. I could feel that the fat cat syndrome had seeped in. This wasn't a hockey club, it was a country club. Some of the guys loved everything about hockey. They loved the limelight, they loved the hours, they loved the adoration, they loved the pay. There was just one thing they didn't love and that was playing the game. We were all in trouble.

Harry's feeling about the partying was, as Al Jolson once said, "You ain't seen nuthin' yet." He knew what the problem was but I took a little longer to appreciate the enormity of it all. I was still a bit too awed and impressed by the big names. "You'll see what I mean," Harry insisted.

Still, Harry didn't put pressure on me in terms of the personnel; at least not in the beginning. I could not have asked for more support if my brother had been general manager of the Bruins. Every so often I would have to pinch myself to believe how well the Sinden-Cherry alliance was going. It was like a marriage made in heaven. I couldn't wait for the game to end just to have the pleasure of sitting down and talking hockey with the man. We usually agreed on *anything*.

Very early on I came to the understanding that Harry was bitter about some of the personnel. I think that he had been burned by some of the players in the past and had come to resent them. That's why he kept telling me that I'd find out what they were *really* like and it helps explain his general attitude toward them. But I give him credit for being democratic; he treated all players alike, even a superstar like Bobby Orr.

Interestingly, Harry and I never got really close, in the personal sense, although we spent a lot of time together during my first season. It was purely a hockey liaison. We didn't socialize together, and hardly ever visited each other's homes. That I left for Harry and Tom Johnson. Their relationship was airtight in every way. Johnson was Sinden's eyes and ears for the team whenever Harry wasn't around. There was a movie around at the time starring Sir Laurence Olivier called *Sleuth*. Well, the players called Tom SuperSleuth, so you can take it from there.

At first I had no problem with Johnson. He just stayed in the background, puffing his big cigar and, since I was getting on famously with Harry, there was no problem with Tom. My problem was with the hockey club. In Rochester, I could rule like Napoleon; I was coach *and* general manager. If a kid didn't follow orders he was benched. And if he still didn't follow orders he was gone. It was a simple formula; play Cherry's way, or don't play for Cherry's team. That formula didn't work in my rookie season with the Bruins. For starters, the team was loaded with fat cats.

Because the war with the WHA was going great guns, every big shot in the NHL knew damn well that if his team gave him any grief, all he had to do was jump to the WHA and make a bundle. You didn't need a Ph.D. in economics to realize that superstars like Bobby Hull and Gerry Cheevers were getting rich, quick, but so were a bunch of wimps who couldn't check their grandmothers or shoot a puck through a pane of glass.

We didn't play nearly as well as we should have that first year. It's easy to look back now and see my mistakes. I should have made the Bruins play my system instead of their wide open style, which is becoming more popular now.

We weren't tough enough. I remember in Detroit a player named Hank Nowak almost took Bobby Orr's head off with an elbow and nobody got upset.

On the subject of Orr, he was, as usual, absolutely fantastic. He had 46 goals and 85 assists that season. He was blocking shots, hitting, fighting. It certainly wasn't his fault we were second to Buffalo. But he was frustrated because he knew I wasn't doing my job. I wanted to put in a system that I knew would work, but some of the players came to me and said they couldn't play that way.

So I said to myself, "Maybe they're right. After all, they've won the Stanley Cup, they've been to the finals, maybe my way is wrong." I knew that way of thinking was wrong, but I went along with it anyway.

Anyway, as we went through the season a lot of players told me not to worry, to wait until the playoffs when they'd make their move. I waited, and I waited. I didn't want to rock any boats, at least not in my rookie season. I kept waiting, and then the playoffs came. We played Chicago in the first round, best of three series. The bell rang and I waited to see my thoroughbreds make their move. And what a move it was. The only thing that could plunge faster than the Bruins did is a supersonic elevator. One, two, three and we were out. I remember after the last game, one of the reporters said to Gillie Gilbert, "Gillie, Esposito was hot, he had 56 shots on him and you had only 18." And Gillie said, "But those 18, there were a lot of good ones in them." Can you imagine how many good ones there were in the 56?

The wipeout left me in a state of shock I had never experienced before. I felt our being ousted was my fault, which it was. Maybe I was just an upstart minor leaguer. I severely questioned my coaching ability, and what I had done to the one man who had confidence in me—Harry Sinden. While I felt badly for myself, I felt worse for Harry. I had let him down, and I told him so. We met after the series at the 3B's Restaurant. I said, "Look, Harry, I know I have two years left on my contract. Forget about 'em. I let you down. As far as I'm concerned you don't have to pay me for the next two years. You can get rid of me right now and I'll have no complaints."

He looked at me as if I was nuts. "Are you kidding? I had never even thought of firing you. But next year, be Don Cherry. You weren't this year." What better vote of confidence could I ask for than the boss saying, "You lost, but don't worry, you're my coach."

I knew we had the nucleus of a good team wih lots of heart. While I washed my car, I played a song by The Who, called "Won't Get Fooled Again." I'd play that record over and over, and I'd say to myself, "They will play my system or else."

One last thing proved to me that I would change the Bruins. The Stanley Cup finals were on television and one of my players came on. He was all tanned since he had just come back from Bermuda, and he was wearing gold beads and everything. The sportscaster asked him, "Why were the Bruins beaten out?" And the guy said, "We weren't mentally prepared." Well, that was my job as coach, and I said to myself, "You son of a bitch, you'll be prepared next year."

It was a tough grind changing the dressing room from a country club to a sweat-shop but gradually the team changed from an undisciplined, doing-it-any-way club, to a tough disciplined grind-you-down team that played just as hard on the road as it did at home, which showed character.

Everything had been going beautifully. We had been in first place for three straight seasons. Earlier, in the second season, Harry had made a dynamite trade, we finished with over a hundred points four seasons in a row, we made the finals, I was coach-of-the-year, and everything was lovely. Life was sweet.

My honeymoon with Harry didn't end abruptly, but rather deteriorated over a series of incidents that took place starting with the fifth season.

Let me say up front, that I was, at the very least, partly to blame for the rift developing. In other words, Harry and I would have stayed friends if I hadn't kept opening my mouth.

Perhaps the best example was The Case of the Phantom Pucks. You have to understand that every team in the league has its official crest laminated on the pucks used in the games. Every team, that is, except the Bruins. Our pucks were black on top, black on the bottom and black on the sides. These pucks looked as if they were on loan from the local street hockey league!

Needless to say, this amateurism seeped down to the players. The rookies, for example, would kid about it. "I only hope I don't score my first goal in Boston Garden," they'd tell me. "If I do, I'll have to put a blank puck on my mantlepiece." Even the fans who normally treasure the pucks that fly into the stands would throw them back at us. Who wants to keep a phantom puck no one knows about?

Everyone made fun of us over the pucks; the opposition, even the refs. I said to Leo Monahan of the *Boston Herald*, "We're being laughed at all around the league. The refs hold these pucks up and look at us and laugh before the games." This was a fatal mistake. Leo put that in the paper the next day, and Harry was really ticked off about it. That was the first straw.

The second straw involved a defenseman named Doug Halward who was the Bruins' first pick in the 1975 amateur draft. When Halward arrived at training camp in September 1975 he was a weak, skinny kid who weighed in at about 175 pounds. Up until then our first round picks had been disasters and this kid, physically at least, didn't look like any bargain to me.

What I wanted from that camp was a big, tough, strong defenseman and I found one—Mike Milbury. Now this kid was a natural. He had been born in Brighton, Massachusetts, and raised in Walpole, just outside of Boston. A graduate of Colgate University, he played football in addition to hockey. Grit could have been his middle name.

Earlier that summer, I had held a hockey school, and John Hoff, who had played with Milbury, mentioned Mike to me and said that he could play my style and that I'd really like him. Weeks later, when we were through in Boston, Harry, the scouts and I were talking about who to invite to camp and I said, "Isn't there a guy named Mulberry or something like that?" And they said, "Oh yeah, Milbury. Okay, we'll invite him too." That's how close Mike came to not being a Bruin.

Mike had spent a year in the minors at Rochester, had picked up 246 minutes in penalties and that, in itself, told me he was a battler. If I had any doubts they were removed in training camp. He wanted desperately to make the Bruins and showed it during the exhibition season. Mike had even worked on his biggest problem, turning into the corners.

I wasn't terribly upset when Mike tailed off in his last exhibition game before the season started. Admittedly, it was a real stinkeroo and he was pretty disturbed by his performance. Mike had got the flu just before the game, but he wanted to make the team so much that he hadn't told me. Consequently, he played a bad game. "Don't worry," I told him, "you've made the team. You've been my best defenseman."

Little did I know that Sinden was eagerly awaiting that bad game. I had no idea how Harry felt about the kid until I began making out my practice roster the next day. As I was pencilling in the names Harry walked over and told me to hold up, there were some names to be scratched because he was sending them down to the minors.

One by one—Doug Gibson, Gordie Clarke—he scratched names. Then, he came to Milbury. "He goes down, too." The words had a distant ring to them. I heard them but I couldn't be sure I heard them right.

When I realized that he did want to chuck Milbury I couldn't believe it. "Hold it," I said, "I don't want him sent down. He's been our best defenseman."

He looked at me, somewhat incredulously. Like, who is this person challenging Harry Sinden? "Milbury goes and Halward stays!"

"Wait a minute," I countered, firing my best shots. "Halward will be good eventually but he's weak now and he can't skate with us. He needs a year in the minors."

This time, Sinden stared at me with a look of finality. "Milbury goes to the minors. Halward stays—AND THAT'S FINAL." He wheeled and walked out of the room.

I was totally bewildered. Obviously, I had been under the mistaken impression that we had been buddies and that we could talk things over in a rational way; that Harry would, at least, hear my arguments and discuss them with reason. Stunned to the core, I sat staring at the dressing room wall when Milbury happened to walk in.

I didn't know what to say to the kid. Everybody on the team from Wayne Cashman to the stickboy, figured that Milbury had made the team. Finally I pulled myself together and took Mike aside. "You're goin' to Rochester, Mike."

He was incredulous. Tears began rolling down his cheeks. "Don," he said, "why?" I didn't have the answer.

Sinden knew deep down that Halward wasn't ready but he was the

Beyond
BLACK

Beyond
BLACK

Hilary Mantel

A JOHN MACRAE BOOK

Henry Holt and Company | New York

Henry Holt and Company, LLC
Publishers since 1866
175 Fifth Avenue
New York, New York 10010

Henry Holt® is a registered trademark of
Henry Holt and Company, LLC.

Library of Congress Cataloging-in-Publication Data

Mantel, Hilary, [date]
  Beyond black : a novel / Hilary Mantel.—1st ed.
     p.   cm.
  "A John Macrae book."
  ISBN-13: 978-0-8050-7356-0
  ISBN-10: 0-8050-7356-6
    1. Female friendship—Fiction. 2. Divorced women—Fiction. 3. Women mediums—
Fiction. 4. Spritualists—Fiction. 5. England—Fiction. I. Title.
PR6063.A438B49 2005
823'.914—dc22   2004063589

Henry Holt books are available for special
promotions and premiums. For details contact:
Director, Special Markets.

First Edition 2005

Designed by Paula Russell Szafranski

Printed in the United States of America

1   3   5   7   9   10   8   6   4   2

For Jane Haynes

"There are powers at work in this country about which we have no knowledge."

—H.M. the Queen
(attributed)

Beyond
BLACK

one

Travelling: the dank oily days after Christmas. The motorway, its wastes looping London: the margin's scrub grass flaring orange in the lights, and the leaves of the poisoned shrubs striped yellow-green like a cantaloupe melon. Four o'clock: light sinking over the orbital road. Teatime in Enfield, night falling on Potter's Bar. There are nights when you don't want to do it, but you have to do it anyway. Nights when you look down from the stage and see closed stupid faces. Messages from the dead arrive at random. You don't want them and you can't send them back. The dead won't be coaxed and they won't be coerced. But the public has paid its money and it wants results.

A sea-green sky: lamps blossoming white. This is marginal land: fields of strung wire, of treadless tyres in ditches, fridges dead on their backs, and starving ponies cropping the mud. It is a landscape running with outcasts and escapees, with Afghans, Turks and Kurds: with scapegoats, scarred with bottle and burn marks, limping from the cities with broken ribs. The life forms here are rejects, or anomalies: the cats tipped from speeding cars, and the Heathrow sheep, their fleece clotted with the stench of aviation fuel.

Beside her, in profile against the fogged window, the driver's face is set. In the back seat, something dead stirs, and begins to grunt and breathe. The car flees across the junctions, and the space the road encloses is the space inside her: the arena of combat, the wasteland, the place of civil strife behind her ribs. A heart beats, taillights wink. Dim lights shine from tower blocks, from passing helicopters, from fixed stars. Night closes in on the perjured ministers and burnt-out pedophiles, on the unloved viaducts and graffitied bridges, on ditches beneath mouldering hedgerows and railings never warmed by human touch.

Night and winter: but in the rotten nests and empty setts, she can feel the signs of growth, intimations of spring. This is the time of Le Pendu, the Hanged Man, swinging by his foot from the living tree. It is a time of suspension, of hesitation, of the indrawn breath. It is a time to let go of expectation, yet not abandon hope; to anticipate the turn of the Wheel of Fortune. This is our life and we have to lead it. Think of the alternative.

A static cloud bank, like an ink smudge. Darkening air.

It's no good asking me whether I'd choose to be like this, because I've never had a choice. I don't know about anything else. I've never been any other way.

And darker still. Colour has run out from the land. Only form is left: the clumped treetops like a dragon's back. The sky deepens to midnight blue. The orange of the streetlights is blotted to a fondant cerise; in pastureland, the pylons lift their skirts in a ferrous gavotte.

two

Colette put her head around the dressing room door. "All right?" she said. "It's a full house."

Alison was leaning into the mirror, about to paint her mouth on. "Could you find me a coffee?"

"Or a gin and tonic?"

"Yes, go on then."

She was in her psychic kit now; she had flung her day clothes over the back of a chair. Colette swooped on them; lady's maid was part of her job. She slid her forearm inside Al's black crepe skirt. It was as large as a funerary banner, a pall. As she turned it the right way out, she felt a tiny stir of disgust, as if flesh might be clinging to the seams.

Alison was a woman who seemed to fill a room, even when she wasn't in it. She was of an unfeasible size, with plump creamy shoulders, rounded calves, thighs and hips that overflowed her chair; she was soft as an Edwardian, opulent as a showgirl, and when she moved you could hear (though she did not wear them) the rustle of plumes and silks. In a small space, she seemed to use up more than her share of the oxygen; in return her skin breathed out moist perfumes, like a giant tropical flower. When you came into a room she'd left—her bedroom, her hotel room, her dressing room backstage—you felt her as a presence, a trail. Alison had gone, but you would see a chemical mist of hair spray falling through the bright air. On the floor would be a line of talcum powder, and her scent—*Je Reviens*—would linger in curtain fabric, in cushions, and in the weave of towels. When she headed for a spirit encounter, her path was charged, electric; when her body was out on stage, her face—cheeks glowing, eyes alight—seemed to float still in the dressing room mirror.

In the centre of the room Colette stooped, picked up Al's shoes. For a moment she disappeared from her own view. When her face bobbed back into sight in the mirror, she was almost relieved. What's wrong with me? she thought. When I'm gone I leave no trace. Perfume doesn't last on my skin. I barely sweat. My feet don't indent the carpet.

"It's true," Alison said. "It's as if you wipe out the signs of yourself as you go. Like a robot housekeeper. You polish your own fingerprints away."

"Don't be silly." Colette said. "And don't read my private thoughts." She shook the black skirt, as if shaking Alison.

"I often ask myself, let's see now, is Colette in the room or not? When you've been gone for an hour or two, I wonder if I've imagined you."

Colette looped the black skirt onto a hanger, and hung it on the back of the long mirror. Soon Al's big black overshirt joined it. It was Colette who had persuaded her into black. Black, she had said, black *and perfectly plain*. But Alison abhorred plainness. There must be something to capture the gaze, something to shiver, something to shine. At first glance the shirt seemed devoid of ornament, but a thin line of sequins ran down the sleeve, like the eyes of sly aliens, reflecting black within black. For her work onstage, she insisted on colour: emerald, burnt orange, scarlet. "The last thing you want, when you go out there," she explained, "is to make them think of funerals."

Now she pouted at herself in the glass. "I think that's quite nice, don't you?"

Colette glanced at her. "Yes, it suits you."

Alison was a genius with makeup. She had boxes full and she used it all, carrying it in colour-coded wash bags and cases fitted with loops for brushes and small-size bottles. If the spirit moved her to want some apricot eye shadow, she knew just which bag to dip into. To Colette, it was a mystery.

When she went out to get herself a new lipstick, she came back with one that, when applied, turned out to be the same colour as all the others she had, which was always, give or take, the colour of her lips.

"So what's that shade called?" she asked.

Alison observed herself, a cotton bud poised, and effected an invisible improvement to her underlip. "Dunno. Why don't you try it? But get me that drink first." Her hand moved for her lipstick sealant. She almost said, look out, Colette, don't tread on Morris.

He was on the floor, half sitting and half lying, slumped against the wall; his stumpy legs were spread out, and his fingers played with his fly buttons. When Colette stepped back she trampled straight over him.

As usual she didn't notice. But Morris did. "Fucking stuck-up cow," he said, as Colette went out. "White-faced fucking freak. She's like a bloody ghoul. Where did you get her, gel, a churchyard?"

Under her breath Alison swore back at him. In Colette's five years as her partner, he'd never accepted her; time meant little to Morris. "What would you know about churchyards?" she asked him. "I bet you never had a Christian burial. Concrete boots and a dip in the river, considering the people you mixed with. Or maybe you were sawed up with your own saw?"

Alison leaned forward again into the mirror, and slicked her mouth with the tiny brush from the glass tube. It tickled and stung. Her lips flinched from it. She made a face at herself. Morris chuckled.

It was almost the worst thing, having him around at times like these, in your dressing room, before the show, when you were trying to calm yourself down and have your intimate moments. He would follow you to the lavatory if he was in that sort of mood. A colleague had once said to her, "It seems to me that your guide is on a very low vibratory plane, very low indeed. Had you been drinking when he first made contact?"

"No," Al had told her. "I was only thirteen."

"Oh, that's a terrible age," the woman said. She looked Alison up and down. "Junk food, I expect. Empty calories. Stuffing yourself."

She'd denied it, of course. In point of fact she never had any money after school for burgers or chocolate, her mum keeping her short in case she used the money to get on a bus and run away. But she couldn't put any force into her denial. Her colleague was right, Morris was a low person. How did she get him? She probably deserved him, that was all there was to it. Sometimes she would say to him, Morris, what did I do to deserve you? He would rub his hands and chortle. When she had provoked him and he was in a temper with her, he would say, count your blessings, girl, you fink I'm bad but you could of had MacArthur. You could have had Bob Fox, or Aitkenside, or Pikey Pete. You could have had my mate Keef Capstick. You could of had Nick, and then where'd you be?

Mrs. Etchells (who taught her the psychic trade) had always told her, there are some spirits, Alison, who you already know from way back, and you just have to put names to the faces. There are some spirits that are spiteful and will do you a bad turn. There are others that are bloody buggering bastards, excuse my French, who will suck the marrow out your bones. Yes, Mrs. E, she'd said, but how will I know which are which? And Mrs. Etchells had said, God help you, girl. But God having business elsewhere, I don't expect he will.

Colette crossed the foyer, heading for the bar. Her eyes swept over the paying public, flocking in from the dappled street; ten women to every man. Each evening she liked to get a fix on them, so she could tell Alison what to expect. Had they prebooked, or were they queuing at the box office? Were they swarming in groups, laughing and chatting, or edging through the foyer in singles and pairs, furtive and speechless? You could probably plot it on a graph, she thought, or have some kind of computer programme: the demographics of each town, its typical punters and their networks, the location of the venue relative to car parks, pizza parlours, the nearest bar where young girls could go in a crowd.

The venue manager nodded to her. He was a worn little bloke coming up to retirement; his dinner jacket had a whitish bloom on it and was tight under the arms. "All right?" he said. Colette nodded, unsmiling; he swayed back on his heels, and as if he had never seen them before he surveyed the bags of sweets hanging on their metal pegs, and the ranks of chocolate bars.

Why can't men just *stand?* Colette wondered. Why do they have to sway on the spot and feel in their pockets and pat themselves up and down and suck their teeth? Alison's poster was displayed six times, at various spots through the foyer. The flyers around advertised forthcoming events: *Fauré's Requiem*, giving way in early December to *Jack and the Beanstalk*.

Alison was a Sensitive: which is to say, her senses were arranged in a different way from the senses of most people. She was a medium: dead people talked to her, and she talked back. She was a clairvoyant; she could see straight through the living, to their ambitions and secret sorrows, and tell you what they kept in their bedside drawers and how they had travelled to the venue. She wasn't (by nature) a fortune-teller, but it was hard to make people understand that. Prediction, though she protested against it, had become a lucrative part of her business. At the end of the day, she believed, you have to suit the public and give them what they think they want. For fortunes, the biggest part of the trade was young girls. They always thought there might be a stranger on the horizon, love around the corner. They hoped for a better boyfriend than the one they'd got—more socialized, less spotty: or at least, one who wasn't on remand. Men, on their own behalf, were not interested in fortune or fate. They believed they made their own, thanks very much. As for the dead, why should they worry about them? If they need to talk to their relatives, they have women to do that for them.

"G and T," Colette said to the girl behind the bar. "Large."

The girl reached for a glass and shoveled in a single ice cube.

"You can do better than that," Colette said. "And lemon."

She looked around. The bar was empty. The walls were padded to hip height with turquoise plastic leather, deep-buttoned. They'd been needing a damp cloth over them since about 1975. The fake wood tables looked sticky: the same applied.

The girl's scoop probed the ice bucket. Another cube slinked down the side of the glass, to join its predecessor with a dull tap. The girl's face showed nothing. Her full, lead-coloured eyes slid away from Colette's face. She mouthed the price.

"For tonight's artiste," Colette said. "On the house, I'd have thought!"

The girl did not understand the expression. She had never heard "on the house." She closed her eyes briefly: blue-veined lids.

Back through the foyer. It was filling up nicely. On the way to their seats, the audience had to pass the easel she had set up, with Al's superenlarged picture swathed in a length of apricot polyester that Al called "my silk." At first Colette had had trouble draping it, getting the loops just right, but now she'd got it pat—a twist of her wrist made a loop over the top of the portrait, another turn made a drift down one side, and the remainder spilled in graceful folds to whatever gritty carpet or bare boards they were performing on that night. She was working hard to break Al's addiction to this particular bit of kitsch. Unbelievably tacky, she'd said, when she first joined her. She thought instead of a screen on which Al's image was projected. But Al had said, you don't want to find yourself overshadowed by the special effects. Look, Col, I've been told this, and it's one bit of advice I'll never forget; remember your roots. Remember where you started. In my case, that's the village hall at Brookwood. So when you're thinking of special effects, ask yourself, can you reproduce it in the village hall? If you can't, forget it. It's me they've come to see, after all. I'm a professional psychic, not some sort of magic act.

The truth was, Al adored the photo. It was seven years old now. The studio had mysteriously disappeared two of her chins; and caught those big starry eyes, her smile, and something of her sheen, that inward luminescence that Colette envied.

"All right?" said the manager. "All humming along, backstage?" He had slid back the lid of the ice cream chest and was peering within.

"Trouble in there?" Colette asked. He closed the lid hastily and looked shifty, as if he had been stealing. "See you've got the scaffolding up again."

"C'est la vie," sighed the manager, and Colette said, "Yes, I dare say."

Alison kept out of London when she could. She would fight her way in as far as Hammersmith, or work the further reaches of the North Circular. Ewell and Uxbridge were on her patch, and Bromley and Harrow and Kingston-on-Thames. But the hubs of their business were the conurbations that clustered around the junctions of the M25, and the corridors of the M3 and M4. It was their fate to pass their evenings in crumbling civic buildings from the sixties and seventies, their exoskeletons in constant need of patching: tiles raining from their roofs, murals stickily ungluing from their walls. The carpets felt tacky and the walls exhaled an acrid vapour. Thirty years of freeze-dried damp had crystallized in the concrete, like the tiny pellets from which you boil up packet soup. The village hall was worse, of course, and they still played some of those. She had to liaise with village-idiot caretakers, and bark her shins and ankles hauling chairs into the semicircle Al favoured. She had to take the money on the door, tread the stage beforehand to detect comic squeaks, and pull out splinters; it was not unknown for Al to kick off her shoes partway through the first half, and commune barefoot with Spirit World.

"Is she all okay back there on her own?" asked the manager. "A large gin, that's the ticket. Anything else she needs? We could fill the place twice over, you know. I call her the consummate professional."

Backstage, Al was sucking an extra-strong mint. She could never eat before a show, and afterwards she was too hot, too strung-up, and what she needed to do was talk, talk it all out of her system. But sometimes, hours after she had put out the light, she would wake up and find herself famished and nauseous. She needed cake and chocolate bars then, to pad her flesh and keep her from the pinching of the dead, their peevish nipping and needle teeth. God knows, Colette said, what this eating pattern does to your insulin levels.

I'd really like my gin, she thought. She imagined Colette out there, doing battle for it.

Colette was sharp, rude and effective. Before they joined up, Al was thrust into all sorts of arrangements that she didn't want, and she was too shy to speak out if things didn't suit her. She never did sound checks unless the management told her to, and that was a mistake; you needed to insist on them. Before Colette, nobody had tested the lighting, or walked out onstage as her surrogate self, to judge the acoustics and the sight lines from the performer's point of view. Nobody had even checked underfoot, for nails or broken glass. Nobody made them take the high stool away—they were always putting out a high stool for her to perch on, not having realized she was a big girl. She hated having to hoist herself up, and teeter like an angel on a pinhead: getting her skirt trapped, and trying to drag it from under her bottom while keeping her balance: feeling the stool buck under her, threatening to pitch her off. Before Colette, she'd done whole shows standing, just leaning against the high stool, sometimes draping one arm over it, as if that were the reason why it was put there. But Colette just minced the management when she spotted a stool onstage. "Take it away, she doesn't work under those conditions."

Instead Colette asked for an armchair, wide, capacious. Here, ideally, Alison would begin the evening, relaxed, ankles crossed, steadying her breathing before her opening remarks. At the first hint of a contact, she would lean forward; then she would jump up and advance to the front of the stage. She would hang over the audience, almost floating above their heads, her lucky opals flashing fire as she reached out, fingers spread. She'd got the lucky opals mail-order but, if asked, she pretended they'd been left to her family by a Russian princess.

She had explained it all when Colette first joined her. Russia was favourite for ancestors, even better than Romany, nowadays; you didn't want to put anxiety in the clients' minds, about fly-tipping, head lice, illegal tarmac gangs, or motorhomes invading the Green Belt. Italian descent was good, Irish was excellent—though you must be selective. In the Six Counties hardly anywhere would do—too likely to crop up on the news. For the rest, Cork and Tipperary sounded too comic, Wicklow and Wexford like minor ailments, and Waterford was too dull.

"Al," Colette said, "from where do you derive your amazing psychic gifts tonight?"

Al said at once, in her platform voice, "From my old great-grandmother, in County Clare. Bless her."

Bless her and bless her, she said, under her breath. She looked away from the mirror so Colette wouldn't see her lips moving. Bless all my great-grandmothers, whoever and wherever they may be. May my dad rot in hell, whoever he may be; whatever hell is and wherever, let him rot in it; and let them please lock the doors of hell at night, so he can't be out and about, harassing me. Bless my mum, who is still earthside of course, but bless her anyway; wouldn't she be proud of me if she saw me in chiffon, each inch of my flesh powdered and perfumed? In chiffon, my nails lacquered, with my lucky opals glittering—would she be pleased? Instead of being dismembered in a dish, which I know was her first ambition for me: swimming in jelly and blood. Wouldn't she like to see me now, my head on my shoulders and my feet in my high-heeled shoes?

No, she thought, be realistic: she wouldn't give a toss.

• • •

Ten minutes to go. Abba on the sound system, "Dancing Queen." Glass of gin held in one hand, the bottle of tonic looped by her little finger, Colette peeped through a swing door at the back of the hall. Every seat was full and space was tight. They were turning people away, which the manager hated to do but it was fire regulations. How does it feel tonight? It feels all right. There'd been nights when she'd had to sit in the audience, so Alison could pick her out first and get the show going, but they didn't like doing that and they didn't need to do it often. Tonight she would be flitting around the hall with a microphone, identifying the people Al picked out and passing the mike along the rows so she could get clear answers out of them. We'll need three minimum to cover the space, she'd told the manager, and no comedians who trip over their own feet, please. She herself, fast and thin and practiced, would do the work of two.

Colette thought, I can't stand them now: the clients, the punters, the trade. She didn't like to be among them, for any purpose. She couldn't believe that she was ever one of them: lining up to listen to Al, or somebody like her. Booking ahead (all major cards accepted) or jostling in a queue by the box office: a tenner in her fist, and her heart in her mouth.

Alison twisted her rings on her fingers: the lucky opals. It wasn't nerves exactly, more a strange feeling in her diaphragm, as if her gut were yawning: as if she were making space for what might occur. She heard Colette's footsteps: my gin, she thought. Good-good. Carefully, she took the mint out of her mouth. The action left her lips sulky; in the mirror, she edged them back into a smile, using the nail of her third finger, careful not to smudge. The face does disarrange itself; it has to be watched. She wrapped the mint in a tissue, looked around, and looped it hesitantly towards a metal bin a few feet away. It fell on the vinyl.

Morris grunted with laughter. "You're bloody hopeless, gel."

This time, as Colette came in, she managed to step over Morris's legs. Morris squawked out, "Tread on me, I love it."

"Don't you start!" Al said. "Not you. Morris. Sorry."

Colette's face was thin and white. Her eyes had gone narrow, like arrow slits. "I'm used to it." She put the glass down by Alison's eyelash curlers, with the bottle of tonic water beside it.

"A splash," Al directed. She picked up her glass and peered into the fizzing liquid. She held it up to the light.

"I'm afraid your ice has melted."

"Never mind." She frowned. "I think there's someone coming through."

"In your G and T?"

"I think I caught just a glimpse. An elderly person. Ah well. There'll be no lolling in the old armchair tonight. Straight on with the show." She downed the drink, put the empty glass on the countertop with her strewn boxes of powder and eye shadow. Morris would lick her glass while she was out, running his yellow fissured tongue around the rim. Over the public address system, the call came to switch off cell phones. Al stared at herself in the mirror. "No more to be done," she said. She inched to the edge of her chair, wobbling a little at the hips. The manager put his face in at the door. "All right?" Abba was fading down: "Take a Chance on Me." Al took a breath. She pushed her chair back; she rose and began to shine.

She walked out into the light. The light, she would say, is where we come from, and it's to the light we return. Through the hall ran small detonations of applause, which she acknowledged only with a sweep of her thick lashes. She walked, slowly, right to the front of the stage, to the taped line. Her head turned. Her eyes searched, against the dazzle. Then she spoke, in her special platform voice. "This young lady." She was looking three rows back. "This lady here. Your name is—? Well, Leanne, I think I have a message for you."

Colette released her breath from the tight space where she held it.

Alone, spotlit, perspiring slightly, Alison looked down at her audience. Her voice was low, sweet, and confident, and her aura was a perfectly adjusted aquamarine, flowing like a silk shawl about her shoulders and upper arms. "Now Lee, I want you to sit back in your seat, take a deep breath, and relax. And that goes for all of you. Put on your happy faces—you're not going to see anything that will frighten you. I won't be going into a trance, and you won't be seeing spooks, or hearing spirit music." She looked around, smiling, taking in the rows. "So why don't you all sit back and enjoy the evening? All I do is, I just tune in, I just have to listen hard and decide who's out there. Now, if I get a message for you, please raise your hand, shout up—because if you don't, it's very frustrating for the spirits trying to come through. Don't be shy, you just shout up or give me a wave. Then my helpers will rush to you with the microphone—don't be afraid of it when it comes to you, just hold it steady and speak up."

They were all ages. The old had brought cushions for their bad backs; the young had bare midriffs and piercings. The young had stuffed their coats under their chairs, but their elders had rolled theirs and held them on their knees like swaddled babies. "Smile," Al told them. "You're here to enjoy yourselves, and so am I. Now, Lee my love, let me get back to you—where were we? There's a lady here called Kathleen, who's sending lots of love in your direction. Who would that be, Leanne?"

Leanne was a dud. She was a young lass of seventeen or so, hung about with unnecessary buttons and bows, her hair in twee little bunches, her face peaky. Kathleen, Al suggested, was her granny: but Leanne wouldn't own it because she didn't know her granny's name.

"Think hard, darling," Al coaxed. "She's desperate for a word with you."

But Lee shook her bunches. She said she didn't think she had a granny; which made some of the audience snigger.

"Kathleen says she lives in a field, at a certain amount of money . . . bear with me . . . Penny. Penny Meadow, do you know that address? Up the hill from the market—such a pull, she says, when you've got a bag full of potatoes." She smiled at the audience. "This seems to be before you could order your groceries online," she said. "Honestly, when you think how they lived in those days—we forget to count our blessings, don't we? Now Lee, what about Penny Meadow? What about Granny Kathleen walking uphill?"

Leanne indicated incredulity. *She* lived on Sandringham Court, she said.

"Yes, I know," Al said. "I know where you live, sweetheart, but this isn't anywhere around here, it's a filthy old place, Lancashire, Yorkshire, I'm getting a smudge on my fingers, it's grey, it's ash, it's something below the place you hang the washing—could it be Ashton-under-Lyne? Never mind," Alison said. "Go home, Leanne, and ask your mum what Granny was called. Ask her where she lived. Then you'll know, won't you, that she was here for you tonight."

There was a patter of applause. Strictly speaking, she hadn't earned it. But they acknowledged that she'd tried; and Leanne's silliness, deeper than average, had brought the audience over to her side. It was not uncommon to find family memory so short, in these towns where nobody comes from, these southeastern towns with their floating populations and their car parks where the centre should be. Nobody has roots here; and maybe they don't want to acknowledge their roots or recall their grimy places of origin and their illiterate foremothers up north. These days, besides, the kids don't remember back more than eighteen months—the drugs, she supposed.

She was sorry for Kathleen, panting and striving, her wheezy goodwill evaporating, unacknowledged; Penny Meadow and all the rows about seemed shrouded in a northern smog. Something about a cardigan, she was saying. A certain class of dead people was always talking about cardigans. The button off it, the pearl button, see if it's dropped behind the dresser drawer, that little drawer, that top drawer, I found a threepenny bit there once, back of the drawer, it gets down between the you-know, slips down the whatsit, it's wedged like—and so I took it, this threepence, and I bought me friend a cake with a walnut on top. Yes, yes, Al said, they're lovely, those kind of cakes: but it's time to go, pet. Lie down, Kathleen. You go and have a nice lie-down. I will, Kathleen said, but tell her I want her mum to look for that button. And by the way, if you ever see my friend Maureen Harrison, tell her I've been looking for her this thirty year.

Colette's eyes darted around, looking for the next pickup. Her helpers were a boy of seventeen, in a sort of snooker player's outfit, a shiny waistcoat and a skewed bow tie; and, would you believe it, the dozy little slapper from the bar. Colette thought, I'll need to be everywhere. The first five minutes, thank God, are no guide to the evening to come.

Look, this is how you do it. Suppose it's a slow night, no one in particular pushing your buttons; only the confused distant chitchat that comes from the world of the dead. So you're looking around the hall and smiling, saying, "Look, I want to show you how I do what I do. I want to show you it's nothing scary, it's just, basically, abilities that we all have. Now can I ask, how many of you," she pauses, looks around, "how many of you have sometimes felt you're psychic?"

After that it's according to, as Colette would say, the demographics. There are shy towns and towns where the hands shoot up, and of course as soon as you're onstage you can sense the mood, even if you weren't tipped off about it, even if you've never been in that particular place before. But a little word, a word of encouragement, a "don't hold back on me," and sooner or later the hands go up. You look around—there's always that compromise between flattering stage lighting and the need to see their faces. Then you choose a woman near the front, not so young as Leanne but not so old she's completely buggered up, and you get her to tell you her name.

"Gillian."

Gillian. Right. Here goes.

"Gill, you're the sort of woman—well"—she gives a little laugh and a shake of her head—"well, you're a bit of a human dynamo, I mean that's how your friends describe you, isn't it? Always on the go, morning, noon, and night, you're the sort of person, am I right, who can keep all the plates spinning? But if there's one thing, if there's one thing, you know, all your friends say, it's that you don't give enough time to yourself. I mean, you're the one everybody depends on, you're the one everybody comes to for advice, you're the Rock of Gibraltar, aren't you, but then you have to say to yourself, hang on, hang on a minute, who do I go to when I want advice? Who's there for Gilly, when it comes to the crunch? The thing is you're very supportive, of your friends, your family, it's just give give give, and you do find yourself, just now and then, catching yourself up and saying, hang on now, who's giving back to me? And the thing about you, Gillian—now stop me if you think I'm wrong—is that you've got so much to give, but the problem is you're so busy running round picking up after other people and putting their lives to rights, that you haven't hardly got any opportunity to develop your own—I mean your own talents, your own interests. When you think back, when you think back to what made you happy as a young girl, and all the things you wanted out of life—you see, you've been on what I call a Cycle of Caring, and it's not given you, Gill, it's not given you the opportunity to look within, to look beyond. You really are capable, now I'm not telling you this to flatter you, but you really are capable of the most extraordinary things if you put your mind to it, if you just give all those talents of yours a chance to breathe. Now am I right? Say if I'm not right. Yes, you're nodding. Do you recognize yourself?"

Gillian has of course been nodding since the first time Al paused for breath. In Alison's experience there's not a woman alive who, once past her youth, doesn't recognize this as a true and fair assessment of her character and potential. Or there may be such a woman, out in some jungle or desert, but these blighted exceptions are not likely to be visiting Alison's Evening of Psychic Arts.

She is now established as a mind reader; and if she can tell Gillian something about herself, her family, so much the better. But she's really done enough—Gillian's brimming with gratification—so even if nobody comes through from Spirit, she can just move right on to whoever is her next target. But long before this point Alison has become conscious of a background mutter (at times rising to a roar) situated not there in the hall but towards the back of her skull, behind her ears, resonating privately in the bone. And on this evening, like every other, she fights down the panic we would all feel, trapped with a crowd of dead strangers whose intentions towards us we can't know. She takes a breath, she smiles, and she starts her peculiar form of listening. It is a silent sensory ascent; it is like listening from a stepladder, poised on the top rung; she listens at the ends of her nerves, at the limit of her capacities. When you're doing platform work, it's rare that the dead need coaxing. The skill is in isolating the voices, picking out one and letting the others recede—making them recede, forcing them back if need be, because there are some big egos in the next world. Then taking that voice, the dead voice you've chosen, and fitting it to the living body, to the ears that are ready to hear.

So: time to work the room. Colette tensed, forward on her toes, ready to sprint with the mike. "This lady. I feel some connection with the law here. Do you have to see a solicitor?"

"Constantly," the woman said. "I'm married to one."

There was a yell of laughter. Al joined it. Colette smirked. She won't lose them now, she thought. Of course she wanted Al to succeed; of course I do, she told herself. They had a joint mortgage, after all; financially they were tied together. And if I quit working for her, she thought, how would I get another job? When it comes to YOUR LAST POSITION, what would I put on my CV?

• • •

"Who's got indigestion at the back?" Al's forehead was damp, the skin at the nape of her neck was clammy. She liked to have clothes with pockets so she could carry a folded cologne tissue, ready for a surreptitious dab, but you don't usually get pockets in women's clothes, and it looks stupid taking a handbag out on stage. "This lady," she said. She pointed; the lucky opals winked. "This is the one I'm speaking to. You're the one with the heartburn, I can feel it. I have someone here for you who's very happy in Spirit World, a Margo, Marje, can you accept that? A petite woman wearing a turquoise blouse, she was very fond of it, wasn't she? She says you'll remember."

"I do remember, I do," the woman said. She took the mike gingerly and held it as if it might detonate. "Marje was my aunt. She was fond of turquoise and also lilac."

"Yes,"—and now Al softened her voice—"and she was like a mother to you, wasn't she? She's still looking out for you, in Spirit World. Now tell me, have you seen your GP about that indigestion?"

"No," the woman said. "Well, they're so busy."

"They're well paid to look after you, my love."

"Coughs and colds all around you," the woman said. "You come out worse than you went in—*and* you never see the same doctor twice."

There was an audible smirk from the audience, a wash of fellow feeling. But the woman herself looked fretful. She wanted to hear from Marje: the dyspepsia she lived with every day.

"Stop making excuses." Al almost stamped her foot. "Marje says, why are you putting it off? Call the surgery tomorrow morning and book yourself in. There's nothing to be frightened of."

Isn't there? Relief dawned on the woman's face; or an emotion that would be relief, when it clarified; for the moment she was tremulous, a hand on her ribs, folded in on herself as if to protect the space of the pain. It would take her some time to give up thinking it was cancer.

Now it's the glasses ploy. Look for a woman in middle age who isn't wearing glasses and say, have you had your eyes tested recently? Then the whole world of optometry is at your command. If she had an eye test last week, she'll say, yes, as a matter of fact I have. They'll applaud. If she says no, not recently, she'll be thinking, but I know I ought to . . . and you say, get it checked, I've a feeling you need a new prescription. As for the woman who says she wears no glasses ever: oh, my love, those headaches of yours! Why don't you just pop along to Boots? I can see you, a month from now, in some really pretty squarish frames.

You could ask them if they need to see the dentist, since everybody does, all the time; but you don't want to see them flinch. You're giving them a gentle nudge, not a pinch. It's about impressing them without scaring them, softening the edges of their fright and disbelief.

"This lady—I see a broken wedding ring—did you lose your husband? He passed quite recently? And very recently you planted a rosebush in his memory."

"Not exactly," the woman said. "I placed some—in fact it was carnations—"

"Carnations in his memory," said Al, "because they were his favourite, weren't they?"

"Oh, I don't know," said the woman. Her voice slid off the mike; she was too worried to keep her head still.

"You know, aren't men funny?" Al threw it out to the audience. "They just don't like talking about these things; they think it means they're oversensitive or something—as if we'd mind. But I can assure you, he's telling me now, carnations were his favourite."

"But where *is* he?" the woman said, still off the mike. She wasn't going to quarrel about the flowers; she was pressed against the back of her seat, almost hostile, on the verge of tears.

Sometimes they waited for you afterwards, the punters, at the back exit, when you were running head down for the car park. In the ghastly lights behind the venue, in the drizzle and the rain, they'd say, when you gave me the message I didn't know, I didn't understand, I couldn't take it in. "I know it's difficult," Al would say, trying to soothe them, trying to help them, but trying, for God's sake, to get them off her back; she would be sweating, shaking, desperate to get into the car and off. But now, thank God, she had Colette to manage the situation; Colette would smoothly pass over their business card, and say, "When you feel ready, you might like to come for a private reading."

Now Alison fished around in the front rows for somebody who'd lost a pet and found a woman whose terrier, on an impulse three weeks ago, had dashed out of the front door into the traffic. "Don't you listen," she told the woman, "to people who tell you animals have no souls. They go on in spirit, same as we do."

Animals distressed her, not cats but just dogs: their ownerless whimper as they padded though the afterlife on the trail of their masters. "And has your husband gone over too?" she asked, and when the woman said yes, she nodded sympathetically but pulled her attention away, throwing out a new question, changing the topic: "Anybody over here got blood pressure?"

Let her think it, that dog and master are together now; let her take comfort, since comfort's what she's paid for. Let her assume that Tiddles and his boss are together in the Beyond. Reunion is seldom so simple; and really it's better for dogs—if people could just grasp it—not to have an owner waiting for them, airside. Without a person to search for, they join up in happy packs, and within a year or two you never hear from them individually: there's just a joyful corporate barking, instead of that lost whine, the sore pads, the disconsolate drooping head of the dog following a fading scent. Dogs had figured in her early life—men, and dogs—and much of that life was unclear to her. If you knew what the dogs were up to, she reasoned, if you knew what they were up to in Spirit World, it might help you work out where their owners were now. They must be gone over, she thought, most of those men I knew when I was a child; the dogs, for sure, are in spirit, for years have passed and those kinds of dogs don't make old bones. Sometimes in the supermarket she would find herself standing in Pets, eyeing the squeaky toys, the big tough chews made for big friendly jaws; then she would shake herself and move slowly back towards organic vegetables, where Colette would be waiting with the cart, cross with her for vanishing.

She will be cross tonight, Al thought, smiling to herself: I've slipped up again about the blood pressure. Colette has nagged her, don't talk about blood pressure, talk about hypertension. When she'd argued back—"They might not understand me"—Colette lost her temper and said, "Alison, without blood pressure we'd all be dead, but if you want to sound like something from the remedial stream, don't let me get in your way."

Now a woman put her hand up, admitted to the blood pressure. "Carrying a bit of weight, aren't we, darling?" Al asked her. "I've got your mum here. She's a bit annoyed with you—well no, I'm pitching it a bit high—*concerned* would be more like it. You need to drop a stone, she's saying. Can you accept that?" The woman nodded, humiliated. "Oh, don't mind what *they* think." Al swept her hand over the audience; she gave her special throaty chuckle, her woman-to-woman laugh. "You've no need to worry about what anybody here's thinking, we could most of us stand to lose a few pounds. I mean, look at me, I'm a size twenty and not ashamed of it. But your mum now, your mum, she says you're letting yourself go, and that's a shame, because you know you're really—look at you, you've got such a lot going for you, lovely hair, lovely skin—well excuse me, but it seems to me your mum's a plainspoken lady, so excuse me if I offend anybody, she's saying, get up off your bum and go to the gym."

This is Al's public self: a little bit jaunty and a little bit crude, a bit of a schoolmistress and a bit of a flirt. She often speaks to the public about "my wicked sense of humour," warning them not to take offence; but what happens to her sense of humour in the depth of the night, when she wakes up trembling and crying, with Morris crowing at her in the corner of the room?

Colette thought, you are a size 26 and you *are* ashamed of it. The thought was so loud, inside her own head, that she was amazed it didn't jump out into the hall.

"No," Al was saying, "please give the mike back to this lady, I'm afraid I've embarrassed her and I want to put it right." The woman was reluctant, and Al said to her neighbour, "Just hold that mike steady under her chin." Then Alison told the fat woman several things about her mother, which she'd often thought but not liked to admit to. "Oh, and I have your granny. Your granny's coming through. Sarah Anne? Now she's an old soul," Al said. "You were five when she passed, am I right?"

"I'm not sure."

"Speak up, my love."

"Small. I was small."

"Yes, you don't remember much about her, but the point is she's never left you, she's still around, looking after the family. And she likes those cabinets you've got—I can't quite make this out—a new kitchen, is it?"

"Oh, my God. Yes," the woman said. "Yes." She shifted in her seat and turned bright red.

Al chuckled, indulging her surprise. "She's often with you in that kitchen. And by the way, you were right not to go for the brushed steel, I know they tried to talk you into it, but it's so over and done with, there's nothing worse than a dated kitchen when you come to sell, and besides it's such a harsh look at the heart of the home. Sarah Anne says, you won't go wrong with light oak."

They burst into applause: the punters, the trade. They are deeply appreciative of information about their kitchen fittings; they marvel at your uncanny knowledge of where they position their bread bin. This is how you handle them; you tell them the small things, the personal things, the things no one else could really know. By this means you make them drop their guard; only then will the dead begin to speak. On a good night, you can hear the scepticism leaking from their minds, with a low hiss like a tyre deflating.

Someone in uniform was trying to get through. It was a policeman, young and keen, with a flushed face; he was eager for promotion. She worked the rows, but no one would own him. Perhaps he was still earthside, employed at the local station; you did get these crossed wires, from time to time. Something to do with radio frequencies, perhaps?

"This lady, have you got ear trouble? Or ear trouble somewhere in the family?" Slowly, the barmaid lurched across the hall in her platform shoes, the mike held out at arm's length.

"What?" the woman said.

"Ear trouble."

"The boy next door to me plays football," the woman said. "He's done his knee up. He was getting in trim for the World Cup. Not that he's playing in it. Only in the park. Their dog died last year, but I don't think it had ear trouble."

"No, not your neighbour," Al insisted. "You, someone close to you."

"I haven't got anyone close to me."

"What about throat trouble? Nose trouble? Anything in the ENT line at all? You have to understand this," Al said, "when I get a message from Spirit World, I can't give it back. I can't pick and choose. Think of me as your answering machine. Imagine if people from Spirit World had phones. Now your answering machine, you press the button and it plays your messages back. It doesn't wipe some out, on the grounds that you don't need to know them."

"And it records the wrong numbers, too," said a pert girl near the front. She had her friends with her; their sniggers ruffled adjacent rows.

Alison smiled. It was for her to make the jokes; she wouldn't be upstaged. "Yes, I admit we record the wrong numbers. And we record the nuisance calls, if you like to put it that way. I sometimes think they have telesales in the next world, because I never sit down with a nice cup of coffee without some stranger trying to get through. Just imagine—double glazing salesman . . . debt collectors . . ."

The girl's smile faded. She tensed.

Al said, "Look, darling. Let me give you a word of advice. Cut up that credit card. Throw away those catalogues. You can break these spending habits—well, you must, really. You have to grow up and exercise some self-control. Or I can see the bailiffs in, before Christmas."

Al's gaze rested, one by one, on those who had dared to snigger; then she dropped her voice, whipped her attention away from the troublemaker, and became confidential with her audience.

"The point is this. If I get a message I don't censor it. I don't ask, do you need it? I don't ask, does it make sense? I do my duty, I do what I'm here for. I put it out there, so the person it applies to can pick it up. Now people in Spirit World can make mistakes. They can be wrong, just like the living. But what I hear, I pass on. And maybe, you know, what I tell you may mean nothing to you at the time. That's why I sometimes have to say to you, stay with that: go home: live with it. This week or next week, you'll go, oh, I get it now! Then you'll have a little smile, and think, she wasn't such a fool, was she?" She crossed the stage; the opals blazed.

"And then again, there are some messages from Spirit World that aren't as simple as they seem. This lady, for example—when I speak about ear trouble, what I may be picking up is not so much a physical problem—I might be talking about a breakdown in communication." The woman stared up at her glassily. Al passed on.

"Jenny's here. She went suddenly. She didn't feel the impact, it was instantaneous. She wants you to know."

"Yes."

"And she sends her love to Peg. Who's Peg?"

"Her aunt."

"And to Sally, and Mrs. Moss. And Liam. And Topsy."

Jenny lay down. She'd had enough. Her little light was fading. But wait, here's another—tonight she picked them up as if she were vacuuming the carpet. But it was almost nine o'clock, and it was quite usual to get onto something serious and painful before the interval. "Your little girl, was she very poorly before she passed? I'm getting—this is not recent, we're going back now, but I have a very clear—I have a picture of a poor little mite who's really very sick, bless her."

"It was leukemia," her mother said.

"Yes, yes, yes," Al said, swiftly agreeing, as if she had thought of it first: so that the woman would go home and say, she told me Lisa had leukemia, she knew. All she could feel was the weakness and the heat, the energy of the last battle draining away: the flickering pulse at the hairless temple, and the blue eyes, like marbles under translucent lids, rolling into stillness. Dry your tears, Alison said. All the tears of agony you've shed, the world doesn't know, the world can't count them; and soberly, the woman agreed: nobody knows, she said, and nobody can count. Al, her own voice trembling, assured her, Lisa's doing fine airside, the next world's treated her well. A beautiful young woman stood before her—twenty-two, twenty-three—wearing her grandmother's bridal veil. But whether it was Lisa or not, Al could not say.

Eight-fifty, by Colette's watch. It was time for Al to lighten up. You have to start this process no less than eight minutes before the end of the first half. If the interval catches you in the middle of something thrilling and risky, they simply don't want to break; but she, Al, she needed the break, to get back there, touch base with Colette, gulp a cold drink and redo her face. So she would begin another ward round now, picking up a few aches and pains. Already she was homing in on a woman who suffered from headaches. Don't we all, Colette thought. It was one of the nets Al could safely cast. God knows, her own head ached. There was something about these summer nights, summer nights in small towns, that made you feel that you were seventeen again, and had chances in life. The throat ached and clogged then; there was tightness behind her eyes, as if unshed tears had banked up. Her nose was running, and she hadn't got a tissue . . . Al had found a woman with a stiff left knee and was advising her on traditional Chinese medicine; it was a diversion, but they'd go away disappointed if she didn't throw in some jargon about meridians and ley lines and chakras and feng shui. Gently, soothingly, she was bringing the first part of the evening to a close; and she was having her little joke now, asking about the lady standing at the back, leaning against the wall there, the lady in beige with a bit of a sniffle.

It's ridiculous, Colette thought, she can't possibly see me from where she's standing. She just, somehow, she must just simply know that at some point in the evening I cry.

"Never mind, my dear," Al said, "a runny nose is nothing to be ashamed of. Wipe it on your sleeve. We're not looking, are we?"

You'll pay for it later, Colette thought, and so she will; she'll have to regurgitate or else digest all the distress she's sucked in from the carpet and the walls. By the end of the evening she'll be sick to her stomach from other people's chemotherapy, feverish and short of breath; or twitching and cold, full of their torsions and strains. She'll have a neck spasm, or a twisted knee, or a foot she can hardly put on the floor. She'll need to climb in the bath, moaning, amid the rising steam of aromatherapy oils from her special travel pack, and knock back a handful of painkillers, which, she always says, she should be allowed to set against her income tax.

Almost nine o'clock. Alison looked up, to the big double doors marked EXIT. There was a little green man above the door, running on the spot. She felt like that little green man. "Time to break," she said. "You've been lovely." She waved to them. "Stretch your legs, and I'll see you in fifteen."

Morris was sprawled in Al's chair when she came into her dressing room. He had his dick out and his foreskin pushed back, and he'd been playing with her lipstick, winding it up to the top of the tube. She evicted him with a dig to his shin from her pointed toe; dropped herself into the vacated chair—she shuddered at the heat of it—and kicked off her shoes. "Do yourself up," she told him. "Button your trousers, Morris." She spoke to him as if he were a two-year-old who hadn't learned the common decencies.

She eased off the opals. "My hands have swelled up." Colette watched her through the mirror. Al's skin was bland and creamy, flesh and fluid plumping it out from beneath. "Is the air-conditioning working?" She pulled at bits of her clothing, detaching them from the sticky bits of herself.

"As if carnations were anybody's favourite!" Colette said.

"What?" Al was shaking her hands in the air, as if they were damp washing.

"That poor woman who was just widowed. You said roses, but she said carnations, so then you said carnations."

"Colette, could you try to bear in mind, I've talked to about thirty people since then?"

Alison held her arms in a U above her head, her naked fingers spread. "Let the fluid drain," she said. "Anything else, Colette? Let's have it."

"You always say, oh, make a note, Colette, keep your eyes open, listen and tell me what goes right and what goes wrong. But you're not willing to listen, are you? Perhaps it's you who's got the hearing problem."

"At least I haven't got a sniffle problem."

"I can never understand why you take your shoes off, and your rings off, when you've got to force them back on again."

"Can't you?" Al sipped her black-currant juice, which she brought with her in her own carton. "What *can* you understand?" Though Al's voice was lazy, this was turning into a nasty little scrap. Morris had lain down across the doorway, ready to trip up anyone who came in.

"Try thinking yourself into my body," Al suggested. Colette turned away and mouthed *no, thank you.* "It's hot under the lights. Half an hour and I'm fit to drop. I know you've been running around with the mike, but it's easier on the feet to be moving than standing still."

"Is it really? How would you know that?"

"It's easy, when you're thin. Everything's easier. Moving. Thinking. Deciding what you'll do and what you won't. You have choices. You can choose your clothes. Choose your company. I can't." Al drank the end of her carton, with a little sound of sucking and bubbling. She put it down, and squashed the tip of the straw, judiciously, with her forefinger.

"Oh, and the kitchen units," Colette said.

"What's your problem? I was right."

"It's just telepathy," Colette said.

"*Just?*"

"Her granny didn't tell you."

"How can you be sure?"

She couldn't, of course. Like the punters out there, she could entertain simultaneously any number of conflicting opinions. They could believe in Al and not believe in her, both at once. Faced with the impossible, their minds, like Colette's, simply scuttled off in another direction.

"Look," Alison said, "do we have to go through this every time? I would have thought we'd been on the road together for long enough now. And we've been making the tapes, haven't we? Writing this book you say we're writing? I'd have thought I'd answered most of your questions by now."

"All except the ones that matter."

Al shrugged. A quick dab of Rescue Remedy under the tongue, and then she began to repaint her lips. Colette could see the effort of concentration needed; the spirits were nagging in her ear, wanting to stake out their places for the second half.

"You see, I'd have imagined," she said, "that sometimes, once in a while, you'd feel the urge to be honest."

Alison gave a little comic shiver, like a character in a pantomime. "What, with the punters? They'd run a mile," she said. "Even the ones with the blood pressure would be up and charging out the door. It'd kill them." She stood up and pulled down her skirt, smoothing the creases over her hips. "And what would that do but make more work for me?"

"Your hem's up at the back," Colette said. Sighing, she sank to her knees and gave the satin a tug.

"I'm afraid it's my bottom that does it," Al said. "Oh, dear." She turned sideways to the mirror and resettled the skirt at what passed for her waistline. "Am I okay now?" She held up her arms, stamped her feet in her high heels. "I could have been a flamenco dancer," she said. "That would have been more fun."

"Oh, surely not," Colette said. "Not more fun than this?" She nudged her own head at the mirror and smoothed down her hair. Damp, it lay on her head like strings of white licorice.

The manager put his head around the door. "All right?" he said.

"Will you stop saying that?" Colette turned on him. "No, not all right. I want you out there for the second half; that girl from the bar is useless. And turn the bloody air-conditioning up, we're all melting." She indicated Alison. "Especially her."

Morris rolled lazily onto his back in the doorway and made faces at the manager. "Bossy cow, ain't she?"

"So sorry to disturb your toilette," the manager said, bowing to Alison.

"Okay, okay, time to move." Colette clapped her hands. "They're out there waiting."

Morris grabbed Al's ankle as she stepped over him. She checked her stride, took a half pace backwards, and ground her heel into his face.

The second half usually began with a question-and-answer session. When Colette first joined Al she had worried about this part of the evening. She waited for some sceptic to jump up and challenge Al about her mistakes and evasions. But Al laughed. She said, those sort of people don't come out at night, they stay at home watching *Question Time* and shouting at the TV.

Tonight they were quick off the mark. A woman stood up, wreathed in smiles. She accepted the microphone easily, like a professional. "Well, you can guess what we all want to know."

Al simpered back at her. "The royal passing."

The woman all but curtseyed. "Have you had any communication from Her Majesty the Queen Mother? How is she faring in the other world? Has she been reunited with King George?"

"Oh, yes," Alison said. "She'll be reunited."

In fact, the chances are about the same as meeting somebody you know at a main line station at rush hour. It's not 14 million to one, like the national lottery, but you have to take into account that the dead, like the living, sometimes like to dodge and weave.

"And Princess Margaret? Has she seen HRH her daughter?"

Princess Margaret came through. Al couldn't stop her. She seemed to be singing a comic song. Nothing derails an evening so fast as royalty. They expect to make the running, they choose the topic, they talk and you're supposed to listen. Somebody, perhaps the princess herself, was pounding a piano, and other voices were beginning to chime in. But Alison was in a hurry; she wanted to get to a man—the evening's first man—who'd got his hand up with a question. Ruthless, she gave the whole tribe the brush-off: Margaret Rose, Princess Di, Prince Albert, and a faint old cove who might be some sort of Plantagenet. It was interesting for Al that you got so many history programmes on TV these days. Many a night she'd sat on the sofa, hugging her plump calves, pointing out people she knew. "Look, isn't that Mrs. Pankhurst?" she'd say. "I've never seen her in that hat."

The manager—pretty quick around the room now Colette had given him a rocket—had got the mike across the hall. The man had risen to his feet. Poor old bloke, he looked shaky. "I've never done this before," he said.

"Take it steady," Al advised. "No need to rush, sir."

"Never been to one of these," he said. "But I'm getting on a bit myself, now, so . . ."

He wanted to know about his dad, who'd had an amputation before he died. Would he be reunited with his leg, in Spirit World?

Al could reassure him on the point. In Spirit World, she said, people are healthy and in their prime. "They've got all their bits and whatsits. Whenever they were at their happiest, whenever they were at their healthiest, that's how you'll find them in Spirit World."

The logic of this, as Colette had often pointed out, was that a wife could find herself paired with a preadolescent for a husband. Or your son could, in Spirit World, be older than you. "You're quite right, of course," Al would say blithely. Her view was, believe what you want, Colette: I'm not here to justify myself to you.

The old man didn't sit down; he clung, as if he were at sea, to the back of the chair in the row ahead. He was hoping his dad would come through, he said, with a message.

Al smiled. "I wish I could get him for you, sir. But again it's like the telephone, isn't it? I can't call them; they have to call me. They have to want to come through. And then again, I need a bit of help from my spirit guide."

It was at this stage in the evening that it usually came out about the spirit guide. "He's a little circus clown," Al would say. "Morris is the name. Been with me since I was a child. I used to see him everywhere. He's a darling little bloke, always laughing, tumbling, doing his tricks. It's from Morris that I get my wicked sense of humour."

Colette could only admire the radiant sincerity with which Al said this: year after year, night after bloody night. She blazed like a planet, the lucky opals her distant moons. For Morris always insisted, he insisted that she give him a good character, and if he wasn't flattered and talked up, he'd get his revenge.

"But then," Al said to the audience, "he's got his serious side too. He certainly has. You've heard, haven't you, of the tears of a clown?"

This led to the next, the obvious question: how old was she when she first knew about her extraordinary psychic gifts?

"Very small, very small indeed. In fact I remember being aware of presences before I could walk or talk. But of course it was the usual story with a Sensitive child—Sensitive is what we call it, when a person's attuned to Spirit—you tell the grown-ups what you see, what you hear, but they don't want to know, you're just a kiddie, they think you're fantasizing. I mean, I was often accused of being naughty when I was only passing on some comment that had come to me through Spirit. Not that I hold it against my mum, God bless her, I mean she's had a lot of trouble in her life—and then along came me!" The trade chuckled en masse, indulgent.

Time to draw questions to a close, Alison said; because now I'm going to try to make some more contacts for you. There was applause. "Oh, you're so lovely," she said. "Such a lovely, warm and understanding audience! I can always count on a good time whenever I come in your direction. Now I want you to sit back, I want you to relax, I want you to smile, and I want you to send some lovely positive thoughts up here to me . . . and let's see what we can get."

Colette glanced down the hall. The manager seemed to have his eye on the ball, and the vague boy, after shambling about aimlessly for the first half, was now at least looking at the trade instead of up at the ceiling or down at his own feet. Time to slip backstage for a cigarette? It was smoking that kept her thin: smoking and running and worrying. Her heels clicked in the dim narrow passage, on the composition floor.

The dressing room door was closed. She hesitated in front of it. Afraid, always, that she'd see Morris. Al said there was a knack to seeing Spirit. It was to do with glancing sideways, not turning your head: extending, Al said, your field of peripheral vision.

Colette kept her eyes fixed in front of her; sometimes the rigidity she imposed seemed to make them ache in their sockets. She pushed the door open with her foot, and stood back. Nothing rushed out. On the threshold she took a breath. Sometimes she thought she could smell him; Al said he'd always smelled. Deliberately, she turned her head from side to side, checking the corners. Al's scent lay sweetly on the air: there was an undernote of corrosion, damp, and drains. Nothing was visible. She glanced into the mirror, and her hand went up automatically to pat her hair.

She enjoyed her cigarette in the corridor, wafting the smoke away from her with a rigid palm; careful not to set off the fire alarm. She was back in the hall in time to witness the dramatic highlight—which was always, for her, some punter turning nasty.

Al had found a woman's father, in Spirit World. "Your daddy's still keeping an eye on you," she cooed.

The woman jumped to her feet. She was a small aggressive blonde in a khaki vest, her cold bluish biceps pumped up at the gym. "Tell the old sod to bugger off," she said. "Tell the old sod to stuff himself. Happiest day of my life when that fucker popped his clogs." She knocked the mike aside. "I'm here for my boyfriend that was killed in a pileup on the sodding M25."

Al said, "There's often a lot of anger when someone passes. It's natural."

"Natural?" the girl said. "There was nothing natural about that fucker. If I hear any more about my bastard dad I'll see you outside and sort you out."

The trade gasped, right across the hall. The manager was moving in, but anyone could see he didn't fancy his chances. Al seemed quite cool. She started chatting, saying anything and nothing—now, after all, would have been a good time for a breakthrough ditty from Margaret Rose. It was the woman's two friends who calmed her; they waved away the vague boy with the mike, dabbed at her cheeks with a screwed-up tissue, and persuaded her back into her seat, where she muttered and fumed.

Now Alison's attention crossed the hall and rested on another woman, not young, who had a husband with her: a heavy man, ill at ease. "Yes, this lady. You have a child in Spirit World."

The woman said politely, no, no children. She said it as if she had said it many times before; as if she were standing at a turnstile, buying admission tickets and refusing the half-price.

"I can see there are none earthside, but I'm talking about the little boy you lost. Well, I say little boy. Of course, he's a man now. He's telling me we have to go back to . . . back a good few years, we're talking here thirty years and more. And it was hard for you, I know, because you were very young, darling, and you cried and cried, didn't you? Yes, of course you did."

In these situations, Al kept her nerve; she'd had practice. Even the people at the other side of the hall, craning for a view, knew something was up and fell quiet. The seconds stretched out. In time, the woman's mouth moved.

"On the mike, darling. Talk to the mike. Speak up, speak out, don't be afraid. There isn't anybody here who isn't sharing your pain."

Am I, Colette asked herself. I'm not sure I am.

"It was a miscarriage," the woman said. "I never—I never saw—they didn't say and so I didn't—"

"Didn't know it was a little boy. But," Al said softly, "you know now." She turned her head to encompass the hall: "You see, we have to recognize that it wasn't a very compassionate world back then. Times have changed, and for that we can all be thankful. I'm sure those nurses and doctors were doing their best, and they didn't mean to hurt you, but the fact is, you weren't given a chance to grieve."

The woman hunched forward. Tears sprang out of her eyes. The heavy husband moved forward, as if to catch them. The hall was rapt.

"What I want you to know is this." Al's voice was calm, unhurried, without the touch of tenderness that would overwhelm the woman entirely; dignified and precise, she might have been querying a grocery bill. "That little boy of yours is a fine young man now. He knows you never held him. He knows that's not your fault. He knows how your heart aches. He knows how you've thought of him"—Al dropped her voice—"always, always, without missing a day. He's telling me this, from Spirit. He understands what happened. He's opening his arms to you, and he's holding you now."

Another woman, in the row behind, began to sob. Al had to be careful, at this point, to minimize the risk of mass hysteria. *Women*, Colette thought: as if she weren't one. But Alison knew just how far she could take it. She was on form tonight; experience tells. "And he doesn't forget your husband," she told the woman. "He says hello to his dad." It was the right note, braced, unsentimental: "Hello, Dad." The trade sighed, a low mass sigh. "And the point is, and he wants you to know this, that though you've never been there to look after him, and though of course there's no substitute for a mother's love, your little boy has been cared for and cherished, because you've got people in Spirit who've always been there for him—your own grandma? And there's another lady, very dear to your family, who passed the year you were married."

She hesitated. "Bear with me, I'm trying for her name. I get the colour of a jewel. I get a taste of sherry. Sherry, that's not a jewel, is it? Oh, I know, it's a glass of port. Ruby. Does that name mean anything to you?"

The woman nodded, again and again and again: as if she could never nod enough. Her husband whispered to her, "Ruby, you know—Eddie's first wife?" The mike picked it up. "I know, I know," she muttered. She gripped his hand. Her fluttering breath registered. You could almost hear her heart.

"She's got a parcel for you," Al said. "No, wait; she's got two."

"She gave us two wedding presents. An electric blanket *and* some sheets."

"Well," Al said, "if Ruby kept you so warm and cosy, I think you can trust her with your baby." She threw it out to the audience. "What do you say?"

They began to clap: sporadically, then with gathering force. Weeping broke out again. Al lifted her arm. Obedient to a strange gravity, the lucky opals rose and fell. She'd saved her best effect till last.

"And he wants you to know, this little boy of yours who's a fine young man now, that in Spirit he goes by the name you chose for him, the name you had planned to give him . . . if it—if he—if he was a boy. Which was"—she pauses—"correct me if I'm wrong—which was Alistair."

"Was it?" said the heavy husband: he was still on the mike, though he didn't know it. The woman nodded.

"Would you like to answer me?" Al asked pleasantly.

The man cleared his throat, then spoke straight into the mike. "Alistair. She says that's right. That was her choice. Yes."

Unseeing, he handed the mike to his neighbour. The woman got to her feet, and the heavy man led her away as if she were an invalid, her handkerchief held over her mouth. They exited, to a fresh storm of applause.

"Steroid rage, I expect," Al said. "Did you see those muscles of hers?" She was sitting up in her hotel bed, dabbing cream on her face. "Look, Col, as you quite well know, everything that *can* go wrong for me out there *has* gone wrong at some time. I can cope. I can weather it. I don't want you getting stressed."

"I'm not stressed. I just think it's a landmark. The first time anybody's threatened to beat you up."

"The first time while you've been with me, maybe. That's why I gave up working in London." Al sat back against the pillows, her eyes closed; she pushed the hair back from her forehead, and Colette saw the jagged scar at her hairline, dead white against ivory. "Who needs it? A fight every night. And the trade pawing you when you try to leave, so you miss the last train home. I like to get home. But you know that, Col."

But she doesn't like night driving, either; so when they're outside the ring of the M25, there's nothing for it except to put up somewhere, the two of them in a twin room. A bed-and-breakfast is no good because Al can't last through till breakfast, so for preference they need a hotel that will do food through the night. Sometimes they take prepacked sandwiches, but it's joyless for Al, sitting up in bed at 4 A.M., sliding a finger into the plastic triangle to fish out the damp bread. There's a lot of sadness in hotel rooms, soaked up by the soft furnishings: a lot of loneliness and guilt and regret. A lot of ghosts too: whiskery chambermaids stumping down the corridors on their bad legs, tippling night porters who've collapsed on the job, guests who've drowned in the bath or suffered a stroke in their beds. When they check into a room, Alison stands on the threshold and sniffs the atmosphere, inhales it: and her eyes travel dubiously around. More than once, Colette has shot down to reception to ask for a different room. "What's the problem?" the receptionists will say (sometimes adding *madam*) and Colette, stiff with hostility and fright, will say, "Why do you need to know?" She never fails in her mission; challenged, she can pump out as much aggression as the girl in the khaki vest.

What Alison prefers is somewhere new-built and anonymous, part of some reliable chain. She hates history: unless it's on television, safe behind glass. She won't thank you for a night in a place with beams. "Sod the inglenooks," she once said, after an exhausting hour tussling with an old corpse in a sheet. The dead are like that; give them a cliché and they'll run to it. They enjoy frustrating the living, spoiling their beauty sleep. They enjoyed pummelling Al's flesh and nagging at her till she got earache; they rattled around in her head until some nights, like tonight, it seemed to quiver on the soft stem of her neck. "Col," she groaned, "be a good girl, rummage around in the bags and see if you can find my lavender spray. My head's throbbing."

Colette knelt on the floor and rummaged as directed. "That woman at the end, the couple, the miscarriage—you could have heard a pin drop."

Al said, *"See a pin and pick it up, and all the day you'll have good luck.* My mum told me that. I never do, though—see a pin. Or find money in the street."

That's because you're too fat to see your feet, Colette thought. She said, "How did you do that thing with the name? When you were going on about mother love I nearly puked, but I have to hand it to you, you got there in the end."

"Alistair? Well, of course, if he'd been called John, you wouldn't be giving me any credit. You'd have said it was one of my lucky guesses." She sighed. "Look, Colette, what can I tell you? The boy was standing there. He knew his own name. People do."

"The mother, she must have been thinking his name."

"Yes, yes, I could have picked it out of her head. I know that's your theory. Mind reading. Oh, God, Colette," Al slid down inside the covers. She closed her eyes. Her head dropped back against the pillows. "Think that, if you find it easier. But you will admit I sometimes tell people things they've yet to find out."

She hated that phrase of Al's: *Think that, if you find it easier.* As if she were a child and couldn't be told the truth. Al only seemed dense—it was part of her act. The truth was, she listened to Radio Four when they were on the road. She'd got a vocabulary, though she didn't use it on the trade. She was quite a serious and complicated person, and deep, deep and sly: that was what Colette thought.

Al seldom talked about death. At first when they started working together, Colette had thought the word would slip out, if only through the pressure of trying to avoid it. And sometimes it did; but mostly Al talked about passing, she talked about spirit, she talked about passing into Spirit World; to that eventless realm, neither cold nor hot, neither hilly nor flat, where the dead, each at their own best age and marooned in an eternal afternoon, pass the ages with sod-all going on. Spirit World, as Al describes it to the trade, is a garden, or to be more accurate, a public place in the open air: litter-free like an old-fashioned park, with a bandstand in a heat haze in the distance. Here the dead sit in rows on benches, families together, on gravelled paths between weedless beds, where heat-sozzled flowers bob their heads, heavy with the scent of eau-de-cologne: their petals crawling with furry, intelligent, stingless bees. There's a certain nineteen-fifties air about the dead, or early sixties perhaps, because they're clean and respectable and they don't stink of factories: as if they came after white nylon shirts and indoor sanitation but before satire, certainly before sexual intercourse. Unmelting ice cubes (in novelty shapes) chink in their glasses, for the age of refrigeration has come. They eat picnics with silver forks, purely for pleasure, because they never feel hunger or gain weight. No wind blows there, only a gentle breeze, the temperature being controlled at a moderate 71 degrees Fahrenheit; these are the English dead, and they don't have centigrade yet. All picnics are share and share alike. The children never squabble or cut their knees, for whatever happened to them earthside, they are beyond physical damage now. The sun shall not strike them by day nor the moon by night; they have no red skin or freckles, none of the flaws that make the English so uncouth in summer. It's Sunday, yet the shops are open, though no one needs anything. A mild air plays in the background, not quite Bach, possibly Vaughan Williams, quite like the early Beatles too; the birds sing along, in the verdant branches of the seasonless trees. The dead have no sense of time, no clear sense of place; they are beyond geography and history, she tells her clients, till someone like herself tunes in. Not one of them is old or decrepit or uselessly young. They all have their own teeth: or an expensive set of implants, if their own were unsightly. Their damaged chromosomes are counted and shuffled into good order; even the early miscarriages have functioning lungs and a proper head of hair. Damaged livers have been replaced, so their owners live to drink another day. Blighted lungs now suck at God's own low-tar blend. Cancerous breasts have been rescued from the surgeons' bin, and blossom like roses on spirit chests.

Al opened her eyes. "Col, are you there? I was dreaming that I was hungry."

"I'll ring down for a sandwich, shall I?"

She considered. "Get me ham on brown. Whole wheat. Dab of mustard—French, not English. Dijon—tell them cupboard on the left, third shelf. Ask them for—do they do a cheese plate? I'd like a slice of Brie and some grapes. And some cake. Not chocolate. Coffee maybe. Walnuts. It has walnuts on top. Two at the rim and one in the centre."

In the night Al would be out of bed, her large outline blocking the light that leaked in from the hotel forecourt; it was the sudden darkness that woke Colette, and she would stir and see Al outlined, in her chiffon and lace, against the glow from the bedside lamp. "What's the matter, what do you need?" Colette would murmur: because you didn't know what was happening, it could be trivial, but then again. . . .Sometimes Al wanted chocolate out of her bag, sometimes she was facing the pangs of birth or the shock of a car crash. They might be awake for minutes or hours. Colette would slide out of bed and fill the plastic kettle, jerking its cord into its socket. Sometimes the water remained unboiled and Al would break off from her travail and say, "Plug switched on at the socket, Col?" and she would hiss, yes, yes, and shake the bloody thing so that water slapped out of the spout; and quite often, that would make it go: so temper, Al said, was just as good as electricity.

Then, while Al rolled towards the bathroom to retch over the bowl, she would forage for dusty tea bags and eventually they would sit side by side, their hands wrapped around the hotel cups, and Al would mutter, "Colette, I don't know how you do it. All your patience. These broken nights."

"Oh, you know," she'd joke. "If I'd had kids . . ."

"I'm grateful. I might not show it. But I am, sweetheart. I don't know where I'd be now, if we'd never met."

At these times, Colette felt for her; she was not without feeling, though life had pushed her pretty far in that direction. Al's features would be softened and blurred; her voice would be the same. She would have panda eyes from the night's makeup, however diligent she'd been with the cotton-wool pads; and there was something childlike about her, as she made her apologies for the way she made her living. For the bad nights Colette carried brandy, to ward off fresh nausea and bouts of pain. Crouching to slide a hand into her overnight bag, she'd think, Al, don't leave me, don't die and leave me without a house and a job. You're a silly cow, but I don't want to do this world on my own.

So, after a night more or less broken, they would fight back to wakefulness, somewhere around seven-thirty, side by side in their twin beds. Whatever had happened during the night, however many times she had been up and down, Colette's sheets were still tucked in tight, as if her body were completely flat. Al's bed looked, more often than not, as if there had been an earthquake in it. On the floor by their slippers they would find last night's room-service plates, with a pallid half tomato and some crumbled potato crisps; cold sodden tea bags in a saucer, and strange grey-white fragments, like the ghosts of boiled water, floating in the bottom of the kettle. Colette would put on breakfast TV to swamp the traffic noise beyond the window, the sigh of tyres, the rumble of distant aircraft approaching Luton—or Stanstead, if they had headed east. Al would lever herself, groaning, from the wreck of her bed, and begin the complex business of putting her persona in place; then she would go down for her breakfast. Colette would kick the remnants of room service out into the corridor, begin picking up after them and packing their bags. Al brought her own towelling robe, and now it was damp and perfumed after her bath, and bulked out the case; hotel robes didn't fit her, she would have needed to tie two together in some sort of Siamese twin arrangement. She always travelled with two or three pairs of scissors, and her own sewing kit; as if she were afraid that she might begin to unravel.

Colette would pack these items away; then she would put the lucky opals in the case, count the bracelets, fit the makeup brushes snugly into their tabs and crevices, retrieve the hairpiece from where it was lying; pull from the closet her own insignificant crease-free outfits, flop them over her arm and drop them into her bag. She could not eat breakfast; it was because, when she had been with her husband Gavin, breakfast had been prime time for rows. She would forage for more tea, though often the allocation of room supplies was so mean that she'd be left with the Earl Grey. Sipping it, she would raise the window blind, on Home Counties rain or vapid sunshine. Al would tap on the door to be let in—there was only ever the one key, in these places—and come in looking fat, full of poached eggs. She would cast a critical eye over the packing, and begin, because she was ashamed of it, to haul her bed into some sort of shape, dragging up the blankets from the floor and sneezing gently as she did so.

Colette would reach into her bag and flip over the antihistamines. "Water," Al would say, sitting down, as if exhausted, among the poor results of her labour. Then, "Steal the shower caps," she would say, "because you can't get them these days, you know, and they're only good for twice."

So Colette would go back into the bathroom to pocket the shower cap supplies; they left the shampoos and the slivers of soap, they weren't cheap or petty in that way at all. And her mind would be running, it's 8:30 A.M. and Morris not here, steal all shower caps, check behind bathroom door, 8:31 and he's not here, out of bathroom looking cheerful, throw stolen shower caps into bag, switch off TV say are we right then; 8:32 and Al stands up, 8:32 she wanders to the mirror; 8:33 she is dropping the sodden tea bags from the saucer into the used cups, Al she says, what are you doing, can we not get on the road please—and then she will see Al's shoulders tense. It's nothing she's done, nothing she's said: it's the banging and cursing, audible only to Al, that tells her they have been rejoined by Morris.

It was one of the few blessings Colette could count, that he didn't always stay the night when they were away. The lure of strange towns was too much for him, and it was her job to provide him with a strange town. To stray up to a five-mile range from their lodging didn't seem to bother him. On his bent, tough little legs, he was a good walker. But reservations at room-only motor lodges were not his favourite. He grumbled that there was nothing to do, stranded somewhere along the motorway, and he would sit in the corner of their room being disgusting. Al would shout at him for picking his feet; after that, she would go quiet and look furious, so Colette could only guess what he might be doing. He grumbled also if to get to his evening out he had to take a bus ride or find himself a lift. He liked to be sure, he said, that if need be he could get back to her within twenty minutes of the pubs' closing. "What does he mean, if need be?" she'd asked. "What would happen if you were separated from Morris? Would you die?" Oh no, Al said; he's just a control freak. I wouldn't die, neither would he. Though he has already, of course. And it seemed that no harm came to him on the nights when he would fall in with some other lowlifes and drift off with them, and forget to come home. All next day they'd have to put up with him repeating the beery jokes and catchphrases he had picked up.

When she'd first joined Al, she'd not understood about Morris. How could she? It wasn't within the usual range of experience. She had hoped he'd just lurch off one night and not come back; that he'd have an accident, get a blow on the head that would affect his memory, so he'd not be able to find his way back to them. Even now, she often thought that if she could get Al out of a place on the dot of 8:30, they'd outsmart him; hurtle back onto the motorway and leave him behind, cursing and swearing and walking around all the cars in the car parks, bending down and peering at the number plates. But somehow, try as she might, they could never get ahead of him. At the last moment, Al would pause, as she was hauling her seat belt over her bulk. "Morris," she would say, and click the belt's head into its housing.

If Morris were earthside, she had once said to Al, and you and he were married, you could get rid of him easily enough; you could divorce him. Then if he bothered you, you could see a solicitor, take out an injunction. You could stipulate that he doesn't come within a five-mile radius, for example. Al sighed and said, in Spirit World it's not that simple. You can't just kick out your guide. You can try and persuade him to move on. You can hope he gets called away, or that he forgets to come home. But you can't leave him; he has to leave you. You can try and kick him out. You might succeed, for a while. But he gets back at you. Years may go by. He gets back at you when you're least expecting it.

So, Colette had said, you're worse off than if you were married. She had been able to get rid of Gavin for the modest price of a do-it-yourself divorce; it had hardly cost more than it would to put an animal down. "But he would never have left," she said. "Oh, no, he was too cosy. I had to do the leaving."

The summer they had first got together, Colette had said, maybe we could write a book. I could make notes on our conversations, she said. You could explain your psychic view of the world to me, and I could jot it down. Or I could interview you, and tape it.

"Wouldn't that be a bit of a strain?"

"Why should it be? You're used to a tape recorder. You use one every day. You give tapes of readings to clients, so what's the problem?"

"They complain, that's the problem. There's so much crap on them."

"Not your predictions?" Colette said, shocked. "They don't complain about those, surely?"

"No, it's the rest of the stuff—all the interference. People from Spirit, chipping in. And all the whizzes and bangs from airside. The clients think we've had a nice cosy chat, one to one, but when they listen back, there are all these blokes on the tape farting and spitting, and sometimes there's music, or a woman screaming, or something noisy going on in the background."

"Like what?"

"Fairgrounds. Parade grounds. Firing squads. Cannon."

"I've never come across this," Colette said. She was aggrieved, feeling that her good idea was being quashed. "I've listened to lots of tapes of psychic consultations, and there were never more than two voices on them."

"That doesn't surprise me." Al had sighed. "My friends don't seem to have this problem. Not Cara, or Gemma, or any of the girls. I suppose I've just got more active entities than other people. So the problem would be, with the tapes, could you make the words out?"

"I bet I could if I stuck at it." Colette thrust her jaw out. "Your pal Mandy's done a book. She was flogging it when I went down to see her in Hove. Before I met you."

"Did you buy one?"

"She wrote in it for me. Natasha, she put. *Natasha, Psychic to the Stars.*" Colette snorted. "If she did it, we can."

Al said nothing; Colette had already made it clear she had no time for Mandy, and yet Mandy—Natasha to the trade—was one of her closest psychic sisters. She's always so smart, she thought, and she's got the gift of the gab, and she knows what I go through, with Spirit. But already Colette was tending to push other friendships out of her life.

"So how about it?" Colette said. "We could self-publish. Sell it at the Psychic Fayres. What do you think? Seriously, we should give it a go. Anybody can write a book these days."

three

Colette joined Alison in those days when the comet Hale-Bopp, like God's shuttlecock, blazed over the market towns and dormitory suburbs, over the playing fields of Eton, over the shopping malls of Oxford, over the traffic-crazed towns of Woking and Maidenhead: over the choked exit roads and the junctions of the M4, over the superstores and out-of-town carpet ware-houses, the nurseries and prisons, the gravel pits and sewage works, and the green fields of the Home Counties shredded by diggers. Native to Uxbridge, Colette had grown up in a family whose inner workings she didn't under-stand, and attended a comprehensive school where she was known as Mon-ster. It seemed, in retrospect, a satire on her lack of monster qualities; she had in fact no looks at all, good or bad, yes or no, pro or con. In her school pho-tographs, her indefinite features seemed neither male nor female, and her pale bobbed hair resembled a cowl.

Her shape was flat and neutral; fourteen passed, and nothing was done in the breast department. About the age of sixteen, she began to signal with her pale eyes and say, I'm a natural blonde, you know. In her English classes she was praised for her neat handwriting, and in maths she made, they told her, consistent progress. In religious studies she stared out of the window, as if she might see some Hindu deities squatting on the green mesh of the boundary fence. In history, she was asked to empathize with the sufferings of cotton mill operatives, plantation slaves, and the Scots foot soldiers at Flodden; it left her cold. Of geography, she had simply no idea at all; but she learned French quickly, and spoke it without fear and with the accent native to Uxbridge.

She stayed on after sixteen, because she didn't know what she would do or where she would go once she left the classroom; but once her virginity was lost, and her elder sister moved out, leaving her with a room and a mirror of her own, she felt more definite, more visible, more of a presence in the world. She left school with two indifferent A-levels, didn't think of university. Her mind was quick, shallow, and literal, her character assertive.

She went to a secretarial college—there were still secretaries then—and became competent in shorthand, typing, and simple bookkeeping. When the PC came along, she adjusted without difficulty, assimilating successively WordStar, WordPerfect, and Microsoft Word. To her second job, in marketing, she brought her spreadsheet skills (Microsoft Excel and Lotus 1-2-3), together with PowerPoint for her presentation packages. Her third job was with a large charity, as an administrator in the fund-raising section. Her mail-merging was beyond reproach; it was indifferent to her whether she used dBase or Access, for she had mastered both. But though she had all the e-skills necessary, her telephone manner was cold and faintly satirical. It was more appropriate, her supervisor noted in her annual review, for someone selling time-shares. She was hurt; she had meant to do some good in the world. She left the charity with excellent references, and took a post with a firm of event organizers. Travel was involved, usually at the back of the plane, and fourteen-hour days in cities she never got to see. Sometimes she had to think hard: had she been to Geneva? Was Barcelona the place where her travel iron blew up, or was that Dundee?

It was at an event she met Gavin. He was an itinerant software developer whose key card wouldn't work, standing at the reception desk of a hotel in La Défense, entertaining the staff by his sad efforts in Franglais. His tie was in his pocket; his suit hanger, slung over his left shoulder, skewed his jacket away from his shirt and tugged his shirt away from his skin. She noticed the black chest hairs creeping out of the open top button, and the beads of sweat on his forehead. He seemed the very model of a man. She stood at his elbow and chipped in, sorting out the problem. At the time he seemed grateful. Only later did she realize it was the worst thing she could have done: introducing herself at the moment of his humiliation. He would rather have slept in the corridor than be rescued by some bint wearing a photograph of herself pinned over her left tit. All the same, he asked her to meet him after he'd showered and have a drink in the bar. "Well, Colette"—he read her name off her badge. "Well, Colette, you're not a bad-looking girl."

Gavin had no sense of humour about himself, and neither did she. So there was a thing, a thing they had in common. He had relatives in Uxbridge, it turned out, and like her he had no interest in getting beyond the hotel bar and into the city. She didn't sleep with him till the final night of the conference, because she didn't want to seem cheap; but she walked back in a daze to her own room, and stared at herself in the full-length mirror, and said, Colette, you're not a bad-looking girl. Her skin was a matt beige. Her beige hair flipped cheekily at chin level, giving her a surrogate smile. Her teeth were sound. Her limbs were straight. Her hips were small. Straight-cut silk trousers covered her tough cyclist's legs. Her bosom was created by a garment with two curved underwires, and boosted by padding that slid into a pocket so you could remove it; but why would anyone want to do that? Without taking her eyes from her own image, she cupped her hands beneath her breasts. Gavin would have the whole of her: all that was hers to give.

They saw a converted flat in Whitton, and thought it might be a good investment. It was leasehold, of course; otherwise, Colette would have done the conveyancing herself, from a DIY guide. As it was, she rang around the solicitors and beat them down to a price, making sure she got their best offers in writing. Once they had moved into the flat, Gavin said, let's split the bills. Kids, he said, were not his priority at this time in his life. She got an IUD fitted, as she didn't trust the Pill; against the workings of nature, some mechanical contrivance seemed called for. Later he would say, you're unnatural, you're cold, I wanted kids but you went off and got this lump of poisoned plastic stuck up you, and you didn't tell me. This was not strictly true; she had cut out an article about the topic from a trade mag passed to her by an ex-colleague who worked for a medical supplies company, and she had put it in the back pocket of his briefcase, where she had thought he might see it.

They got married. People did. It was the tag end of the Thatcher/Major years and people held a wedding to show off. They didn't have friends, so they invited everybody they knew. The wedding took six months to plan. When she woke up on the day, she had an urge to run downstairs, and howl in the streets of Whitton. Instead she pressed her frock and climbed into it. She was alone in the flat; Gavin was on his stag night, and she wondered what she would do if he didn't turn up: marry herself? The wedding was designed to be exhausting, to wring value from each moment they had paid for. So they could recover, she had booked ten days in the Seychelles: sea view, balcony, private taxi transfer, and fruit in room on arrival.

Gavin turned up just in time, his eyes pouched and his skin grey. After the registrar, they went out to a hotel in Berkshire with a trout steam running through the grounds and fishing flies in glass cases on the walls of the bar, and French windows leading onto a stone terrace. She was photographed against the stone balustrade, with Gavin's little nieces pawing her skirts. They had a marquee, and a band. They had gravlax with dill sauce, served on black plates, and a chicken dish that tasted, Gavin said, like an airline dinner. The Uxbridge people on both sides came, and never spoke to each other. Gavin kept belching. A niece was sick, luckily not on Colette's dress, which was hired. Her tiara, though, was bought: a special order to fit her narrow skull. Later she didn't know what to do with it. Space was tight in the flat in Whitton, and her drawers were crammed with packets of tights, which she bought by the dozen, and with sachets and scent balls to perfume her knickers. When she reached in amongst her underwear, the faux pearls of the tiara would roll beneath her fingers, and its gilt lattices and scrolls would remind her that her life was open, unfolding. It seemed mercenary to advertise it in the local paper. Besides, Gavin said, there can't be two people with a head shaped like yours.

The pudding at their wedding breakfast was strawberries and meringue stacked up in a tower, served on frosted glass platters sprinkled with little green flecks, which proved to be not chopped mint leaves but finely snipped chives. Uxbridge ate it with a stout appetite; after all, they'd already done raw fish. But Colette—once her suspicion was verified by a tiny taste at the tip of her tongue—had flown out in her tiara, cornered the duty manager, and told him she proposed to sue the hotel in the small claims court. They paid her off, as she knew they would, being afraid of the publicity; she and Gavin went back there gratis for their anniversary dinner, and enjoyed a bottle of house champagne. It was too wet that night to walk by the trout stream: a lowering, misty evening in June. Gavin said it was too hot, and walked out onto the terrace as she was finishing her main course. By then the marriage was over, anyway.

It was no particular sexual incompatibility that had broken up her marriage: Gavin liked it on Sunday mornings, and she had no objection. Neither was there, as she learned later, any particular planetary incompatibility. It was just that the time had come in her relationship with Gavin when, as people said, she could see no future in it.

When she arrived at this point, she bought a large-format softback called *What Your Handwriting Reveals*. She was disappointed to find that your handwriting can't shed any light on your future. It only tells of character, and your present and your past, and her present and her past she was clear about. As for her character, she didn't seem to have any. It was because of her character that she was reduced to going to bookshops.

The following week she returned the handwriting book to the shop. They were having a promotional offer—bring it back if it doesn't thrill. She had to tell the boy behind the counter why, exactly, it didn't; I suppose, she said, after so many years of word processing, I have no handwriting left. Her eyes flickered over him, from his head downwards, to where the counter cut off the view; she was already, she realized, looking for a man she could move on to. "Can I see the manager?" she asked, and amiably, scratching his barnet, the boy replied, "You're looking at him." "Really?" she said. She had never seen it before: a manager who dressed out of a dumpster. He gave her back her money, and she browsed the shelves, and picked up a book about tarot cards. "You'll need a pack to go with that," the boy said, when she got to the cash desk. "Otherwise you won't get the idea. There are different sorts, shall I show you? There's Egyptian tarot. There's Shakespeare tarot. Do you like Shakespeare?"

As if, she thought. She was the last customer of the evening. He closed up the shop and they went to the pub. He had a room in a shared flat. In bed he kept pressing her clit with his finger, as if he were inputting a sale on the cash machine: saying, Helen, is that all right for you? She'd given him a wrong name, and she hated it, that he couldn't see through to what she was really called. She'd thought Gavin was useless: but honestly! In the end she faked it, because she was bored and she was getting cramp. The Shakespeare boy said, Helen, that was great for me too.

It was the tarot that started her off. Before that she had been just like everybody, reading her horoscope in the morning paper. She wouldn't have described herself as superstitious or interested in the occult in any way. The next book she bought—from a different bookshop—was *An Encyclopedia of the Psychic Arts.* Occult, she discovered, meant hidden. She was beginning to feel that everything of interest was hidden. And none of it in the obvious places; don't, for example, look in trousers.

She had left that original tarot pack in the boy's room, inadvertently. She wondered if he had ever taken it out and looked at the pictures; whether he ever thought of her, a mysterious stranger, a passing Queen of Hearts. She thought of buying another set, but what she read in the handbook baffled and bored her. Seventy-eight cards! Better employ someone qualified to read them for you. She began to visit a woman in Isleworth, but it turned out that her specialty was the crystal ball. The object sat between them on a black velvet cloth; she had expected it to be clear, because that's what they said, crystal-clear, but to look into it was like looking into a cloud bank or into drifting fog.

"The clear ones are glass, dear," the Sensitive explained. "You won't get anything from those." She rested her veined hands on the black velvet. "It's the flaws that are vital," she said. "The flaws are what you pay for. You will find some readers who prefer the black mirror. That is an option, of course."

Colette raised her eyebrows.

"Onyx," the woman said. "The best are beyond price. The more you look—but you have to know how to look—the more you see stirring in the depths."

Colette asked straight out and heard that her crystal ball had set her back 500 pounds. "And then only because I have a special friend." The psychic gained, in Colette's eyes, a deal of prestige. She was avid to part with her 20 pounds for the reading. She drank in everything the woman said, and when she hit the Isleworth pavement, moss growing between its cracks, she was unable to remember a word of it.

She consulted a palmist a few times, and had her horoscope cast. Then she had Gavin's done. She wasn't sure that his chart was valid, because she couldn't specify the time of his birth. "What do you want to know that for?" he'd said, when she asked him. She said it was of general interest to her, and he glared at her with extreme suspicion.

"I suppose you don't know, do you?" she said. "I could ring your mum."

"I very much doubt," he'd said, "that my mother would have retained that piece of useless information, her brain being somewhat overburdened in my opinion with things like where is my plastic washball for my Persil, and what is the latest development in bloody *EastEnders*."

The astrologer was unfazed by her ignorance. "Round it up," he said, "round it down. Twelve noon is what we use. We always do it for animals."

"For animals?" she'd said. "They have their horoscope done, do they?"

"Oh, certainly. It's a valuable service, you see, for the caring owner who has a problem with a pet. Imagine, for instance, if you kept falling off your horse. You'd need to know, is this an ideal pairing? It could be a matter of life or death."

"And do people know when their horse was born?"

"Frankly, no. That's why we have a strategy to approximate. And as for your partner—if we say noon that's fine, but we then need latitude and longitude—so where do we imagine Hubby first saw the light of day?"

Colette sniffed. "He won't say."

"Probably a Scorpio ascendant there. Controls by disinformation. Or could be Pisces. Makes mysteries where none needed. Just joking! Relax and think back for me. His mummy must have dropped a hint at some point. Where exactly did the dear chap pop out, into this breathing world scarce half made up?"

"He grew up in Uxbridge. But you know, she might have had him in hospital."

"So it could have been anywhere along the A40?"

"Could we just say, London?"

"We'll put him on the meridian. Always a wise choice."

After this incident, she found it difficult to regard Gavin as fully human. He was standardized on zero degrees longitude and twelve noon, like some bucking bronco, or a sad mutt with no pedigree. She did call his mum, one evening when she'd had a half bottle of wine and was feeling perverse.

"Renee, is that you?" she said.

Renee said, "How did you get my name?"

"It's me," she said, and Renee replied. "I've got replacement windows, and replacement doors. I've got a conservatory and the loft conversion's coming next week. I never give to charity, thank you, and I've planned my holiday for this year, and I had a new kitchen when you were last in my area."

"It's about Gavin," she said. "It's me, Colette. I need to know when he was born."

"Take my name off your list," her mother-in-law said. "And if you must call me, could you not call during my programme? It's one of my few remaining pleasures." There was a pause, as if she were going to put the receiver down. Then she spoke again. "Not that I need any others. I've had my suite recovered. I have a spa bath already. And a case of vintage wine. And a stair lift to help me keep my independence. Have you got that? Are you taking notice? Bugger off."

Click.

Colette held the phone. Daughter-in-law of fourteen months, spurned by *his* mother. She replaced the receiver, and walked into the kitchen. She stood by the double sink, mastering herself. "Gavin," she called, "do you want peas or green beans?"

There was no answer. She stalked into the sitting room. Gavin, his bare feet on the sofa arm, was reading *What Car?*

"Peas or green beans?" she asked.

No reply.

"*Gavin!*" she said.

"With wot?"

"Cutlets."

"What's that?"

"Lamb. Lamb chops."

"Okay," he said. "Whatever. Both."

"You can't." Her voice shook. "Two green veg, you can't."

"Who says?"

"Your mother," she said; she felt she could say anything, as he never listened. "When?"

"Just now on the phone."

"My mother was on the phone?"

"Just now."

"Bloody amazing." He shook his head and flicked over a page.

"Why? Why should it be?"

"Because she's dead."

"What? Renee?" Colette sat down on the sofa arm: later, when she told the story, she would say, well, at that point, my legs went from under me. But she would never be able to recapture the sudden fright, the weakness that ran through her body, her anger, her indignation, the violent exasperation that possessed her. She said, "What the hell do you mean, she's dead?"

"It happened this morning. My sis rang. Carole."

"Is this a joke? I need to know. Is this a joke? Because if it is, Gavin, I'll kneecap you."

Gavin raised his eyebrows, as if to say, why would it be funny?

"I didn't suggest it was," she said at once: why wait for him to speak? "I asked if it was *your idea* of a joke."

"God help anybody who made a joke around here."

Colette laid her hand on her rib cage, behind which something persistently fluttered. She stood up. She walked into the kitchen. She stared at the ceiling. She took a deep breath. She came back. "Gavin?"

"Mm?"

"She's really dead?"

"Mm."

She wanted to hit him. "How?"

"Heart."

"Oh, God! Have you no feeling? You can sit there, going peas or beans—"

"You went that," he said reasonably.

"Weren't you going to tell me? If I hadn't said, your mother was on the phone—"

Gavin yawned. "What's the hurry? I'd have told you."

"You mean you might just have mentioned it? When you got around to it? When would that have been?"

"After the food." She gaped at him. He said, with some dignity, "I can't mention when I'm hungry."

Colette bunched her fingers into fists, and held them at chest height. She was short of breath, and the flutter inside her chest had subdued to a steady thump. At the same time an uneasy feeling filled her, that anything she could do was inadequate; she was performing someone else's gestures, perhaps from an equivalent TV moment where news of a sudden death is received. But what are the proper gestures when a ghost's been on the phone? She didn't know. "Please. Gavin," she said. "Put down *What Car?* Just . . . look at me, will you? Now tell me what happened."

"Nothing." He threw the magazine down. "Nothing happened."

"But where was she? Was she at home?"

"No. Getting her shopping. In Safeway. Apparently."

"And?"

Gavin rubbed his forehead. He seemed to be making an honest effort. "I suppose she was pushing her trolley."

"Was she on her own?"

"Dunno. Yes."

"And then?"

"She fell over."

"She didn't die there, did she? In the aisle?"

"Nah, they got her to the hospital. So no worries about the death certificate."

"What a relief," she said grimly.

Carole, it seemed, was proposing to get the bungalow on the market as soon as possible, with Sidgewick and Staff, who for sole agency charged 2 percent on completion, and promised unlimited colour advertising and national tie-ins. "There should be a good payout," he said. "The place is worth a few quid."

That was why, he explained, he was reading the new edition of *What Car?* Renee's will would bring him nearer to what he most coveted in life, which was a Porsche 911.

"Aren't you upset?" she asked him.

He shrugged. "We've all got to go, haven't we? What's it to you? It's not as if you ever bothered with her."

"And she lived in a bungalow, Renee?"

" 'Course she did." Gavin picked up his magazine and rolled it up in his hands, as if she were a wasp and he was going to swat her. "We went over for our lunch, that Sunday."

"No, we didn't. We never went."

"Only because you kept cancelling us."

It was true. She'd hoped she could keep Renee at arm's length; the wedding reception had proved her to have a coarse joke habit and slipping false teeth. The teeth weren't all that was false. "She told me," she said to Gavin, "that she had a stair lift installed. Which, if she lived in a bungalow, she couldn't have."

"When? When did she tell you that?"

"On the phone just now."

"Hello? Hello? Anyone at home?" Gavin asked. "Are you ever stupid? I told you she's dead."

Alerted by the mutiny on her face, he rose from the sofa and slapped her with *What Car?* She picked up the Yellow Pages and threatened to take out his eye. After he had slunk off to bed, hugging his expectations, she went back into the kitchen and grilled the cutlets. The peas and green beans she fed to the waste disposal; she hated vegetables. She ate the lamb with her fingers, her teeth scraping the bone. Her tongue came out, and licked the last sweetness from the meat. She couldn't work out what was worse, that Renee had answered the phone after she was dead, or that she had answered the phone on purpose to lie to her and tell her to bugger off. She threw the bones down the waste disposal too, and rejoiced as the grinder laboured. She rinsed her fingers and wiped them on a kitchen roll.

In the bedroom, she inspected Gavin, spread-eagled across the available space. He was naked and snoring; his mag, rolled, was thrust under his pillow. That, she thought, is how much it means to him: the death of his only mother. She stood frowning down at him; her toe touched something hard and cold. It was a glass tumbler, lolling on its side, melted ice dribbling from its mouth onto the carpet. She picked it up. The breath of spirits hit her nostrils, and made her flinch. She walked into the kitchen and clicked the tumbler down on the draining board. In the dark tiny hall, she hauled Gavin's laptop from its case. She lugged it into the sitting room and plugged it into the mains. She copied the files she thought might interest her, and erased his crucial data for tomorrow. In terms of life documentation, Gavin was less than some animal. He routinely misled her: but was it any wonder? What sort of upbringing could he have had, from a woman with false teeth who told lies after she was dead?

She left the machine humming, and went back into the bedroom. She opened the wardrobe and went through Gavin's pockets. The word "rifled" came to her: "she rifled through his pockets." He stirred once or twice in his sleep, reared up, snorted, collapsed back onto the mattress. I could kill him, she thought, as he lies here, or just maim him if I liked. She found a bunch of credit card receipts in his knicker drawer; her index finger shuffled through them. She found newspaper ads for sex lines: *Spicy lesbo chicks!*

She packed a bag. Surely he would wake? Drawers clicked, opening and shutting. She glanced over her shoulder. Gavin stirred, made a sort of whinny, and settled back again into sleep. She reached down to unplug her hair dryer, wrapped the flex around her hand, and stood thinking. She was entitled to half the equity in the flat; if he would embrace the car loan, she would continue paying off the wedding. She hesitated for a final moment. Her foot was on the wet patch the ice had left. Automatically she plucked a tissue from an open box and blotted the the carpet. Her fingers squeezed, the paper reduced itself to wet pulp. She walked away, brushing her hands together to jettison it.

Gavin's screen saver had come up. Colette slotted a floppy into his drive, and overwrote his programs. She had heard of women who, before departing, scissored up their husband's clothes. But Gavin's clothes, in their existing state, were punishment enough. She had heard of women who performed castration; but she didn't want to go to jail. No, let's see how he gets on without his bits and bytes, she thought. With one keystroke, she wrecked his operating system.

She went down to the south coast to see a noted psychometrist, Natasha. She didn't know then, of course, that Natasha would figure in her later life. At the time, it was just another hope she grappled with, a hope of making sense of herself; it was just another item in her strained monthly budget.

The flat was two blocks back from the sea. She parked with difficulty and at some distance. She wasted time looking for the street numbers. When she found the right door she rang the bell and spoke into the intercom: "I'm your eleven-thirty."

Without a word, the psychic buzzed her up; but she thought she had heard a cough, stifling a little laugh. Her cheeks burned. She ran up three flights and as soon as Natasha opened the door she said, "I'm not late."

"No, dear. You're my eleven-thirty."

"You really ought to tell your clients where to park."

The psychic smiled tightly. She was a sharp little bleached blonde with a big jaw, common as a centrefold. "What?" she said. "You think I should exercise my powers and keep a space free?"

"I meant you should send a map."

She turned to lead the way: tight high bottom in the kind of jeans that acts as a corset. She's too old, Colette thought, for denim; shouldn't somebody tell her?

"Sit there," Natasha said precisely, dipping her false nail.

"The sun's in my eyes," Colette said.

"Diddums," said Natasha.

A sad-eyed icon drooped at her, from a cheap gilt frame on the wall; a mist washed up from the sea. She sat and flipped open her shoulder bag: "Do you want the cheque now?"

She wrote it. She waited for the offer of a cup of herb tea. It didn't come. She almost had hopes of Natasha; she was nasty, but there was a businesslike briskness about her that she'd never found in any psychic so far.

"Anything to give me?" Natasha said.

She dived into her bag and passed over her mother's wedding ring.

Natasha twirled it around her forefinger. "Quite a smiley lady."

"Oh, smiley," Colette said. "I concede that." She passed over a pair of cuff links that had belonged to her dad.

"Is that the best you can manage?"

"I don't have anything else of his."

"Sad," Natasha said. "Can't have been much of a relationship, can it? I sense that men don't warm to you, somehow." She sat back in her chair, her eyes far away.

Colette waited, respectfully silent.

"Well, look, I'm not getting much from these." She jiggled the cuff links in her hand. "They're definitely your dad's, are they? The thing is, with cuff links, with dads, they get them for Christmas and then it's, 'Oh, thanks, thanks a bunch, just what I always needed!'"

Colette nodded. "But what can you do? What can you get, for men?"

"Bottle of Scotch?"

"Yes, but you want something that will last."

"So he stuffs them in a drawer? Forgets he's got them?"

She wanted to say, *why* do you think men don't warm to me? Instead she opened her bag again. "My wedding ring," she said. "I suppose you didn't think I'd been married?"

Natasha held out a flat, open palm. Colette placed the ring on it. "Oh dear," Natasha said. "Oh dear oh dear."

"Don't worry, I've already left."

"Sometimes you've got to cut your losses," Natasha agreed. "Well, sweetie, what else can I tell you?"

"It's possible I might be psychic myself," Colette said casually. "Certain, really. I dialled a number and a dead person answered."

"That's unusual." Natasha's eyes flitted sideways, in a calculating way. "Which psychic line offers that service?"

"I wasn't calling a psychic line. I was calling my mother-in-law. It turned out she was dead."

"So what gave you the idea?"

"No—no, look, you have to understand how it happened. I didn't know she was dead when I rang. I didn't know till afterwards."

"So she was dead when you called? But you didn't realize?"

"Yes."

"So she came over from beyond?"

"Yes."

"What did she say to you?"

"She said she'd got a stair lift. It was a lie."

"Well, perhaps she's got one in Spirit?"

Colette considered. Renee had said there was no comfort she lacked. "I'm not really bothered about that aspect, about what she said, only that she picked the phone up. That she answered. At first that was what bothered me, about the stair lift—that she didn't even say the truth—but then when I thought about it, her saying anything seemed to be the most surprising. . . . Well, you know."

Colette's voice died in her throat. She was not used to speaking her thoughts. Life with Gavin had discouraged her.

"Nothing like that's ever happened to me before, but I think it proves I must have a gift. I'm a bit bored with my job and I wouldn't mind a change. I wondered about this, you know? If there's much money in it."

Natasha laughed. "Well, if you think you could stand the pace. You have to train."

"Oh do you? It's not enough to be able to do it?"

"Look," Natasha said, "I don't want to sound hostile, but isn't it possible that you're being a bit naïve? I mean you've got a good career now, I can see that. So why waste it? You'd need to build up your psychic skills. You can't expect to start cold at your age."

"I beg your pardon?" Colette said. "At my age?"

"I started at twelve," Natasha said. "You're not telling me you're twelve, are you?" With one hand, she lazily shuffled her cards together. "Want me to see what I get?" She began to lay out a spread, her nails clicking on the back of each card. "Look, if you're going to work with higher powers, it will happen. Nothing will stop it. But you'll get the here-and-now sorted, if you'll heed my advice." She looked up. "Letter *M* comes to mind."

Colette thought. "I don't know anyone of that letter." She thought, *M* for *Man?*

"Someone coming into your life. Not yet. An older bloke. Not too keen on you at first, I must say."

"But then?"

"All's well that ends well," Natasha said. "I suppose."

She had walked away, disappointed; when she got back to her car, she had been ticketed. After that she had gone for crystal healing, and had some private Reiki sessions. She arranged to meet Gavin in a new bar called Peppermint Plaza. He arrived before her, and when she walked in he was sitting on a pale green leather-look banquette, a bottle of Mexican lager planted in front of him, leafing through *Thames Valley Autotrader*.

"Renee's money not come through yet?" she asked. She slid into the seat opposite. "When it does, you could use some of it to buy me out of the flat."

"If you think I'm giving up the chance of a decent car, then no way," said Gavin. "If I don't get the Porsche this is what I'm getting, I'm getting this

Lancia." He flopped the magazine down on the table. "There's one here." He turned the picture around obligingly so it was the right way up for her. "Re-carro seats. Full spec. Seriously speedy."

"Put it on the market then. The flat. If you can't buy me out."

"You said that. You said it before. I said, yes. I agree. So don't go on about it. Okay?"

There was a silence. Colette looked around. "Quite nice here. Quiet."

"Bit girly."

"That's probably why I like it. Being a girl." Her knees touched his, under the table. She tried to pull her chair away, but it was bolted to the floor.

Gavin said, "I want fifty percent of the bills till the flat's sold."

"I'll pay half the monthly service charge." Colette pushed his magazine back across the table. "I won't pay half the utilities."

"What's that, utilities?"

"Gas and electric. Why should I pay to keep you warm?"

"I'll tell you what, you stuffed me with a huge sodding phone bill. You can pay that."

"It's your phone too."

"Yeah, but I'm not on it all night, blah-bloody-blah to some bint I've sat next to all day and I'll be seeing again the next morning. And it's not me phoning premium-rate lines to what's it called, bloody predictionists, bloody psychic lines at a quid a minute?"

"Actually, sex lines are premium rate too."

"Oh well, you would know about that, wouldn't you?" Gavin gathered up his car magazine, as if to shield it from her. "You're not normal."

She sighed. She couldn't summon up the energy to say, "I beg your pardon, not normal, what do you mean?" Any abstraction, indirection, or allusion was wasted on Gavin, and in fact even the most straightforward form of communication—other than a poke in the eye—was a challenge to his attention span. There hadn't, so far as she'd understood, been any dispute between them about what they did in the bedroom—it had seemed fairly straightforward stuff, though she was fairly ignorant and limited, she supposed, and Gavin, certainly, he was fairly ignorant and limited. But after the marriage is over, maybe that's what men do; they decide it was the sex that was wrong, because it's something they can communicate over a drink, something they

can turn into a story, snigger over; it's an explanation they can give themselves, for what would otherwise remain the complete mystery of human relationships. There were other mysteries, which loomed large to her and
hardly loomed at all for Gavin: what are we here for, what will happen next?
It was no use trying to explain to him that without the fortune-tellers she had
become afraid to act at all; that she liked to know that things were her fate,
that she didn't like life to be arbitrary. It was no use telling him either that she
thought she might be psychic herself. The incident of the posthumous phone
call, if it had ever sunk into his mind, had been chemically erased by the
vodka he had drunk the night she moved out; this was lucky for her, because
when next day he found his computer trashed he thought he had only himself
to blame.

"Don't you want to ask anything?" she asked. "Like where I'm living?"

"So where are you living, Colette?" he said sarcastically.

"With a friend."

"Jesus, you've got a friend?"

"But from next week I've arranged a house share in Twickenham. I'll have
to start paying rent, so I need the flat to be sold."

"All we need is a buyer."

"No, all we need is a seller."

"What?"

"Put it on the market."

"I have. Last week."

"Oh, for God's sake." She slammed her glass down. "Why didn't you just
come out and say that?"

"I would if I could get a word in edgewise. Besides, I thought you'd get a
tip-off from the spirits. I thought they'd say, a strange man is walking around
your bedroom with a steel measure."

Colette threw herself back in her seat; but it was strangely curved, and
pushed her forward again, so her diaphragm was against the table's edge. "So
how much did they suggest?" He told her. "That's far too low. They must
think you're an idiot. And they could be right. Leave it, Gavin, leave it. I'll get
on to it tomorrow. I'll phone them myself."

"They said, realistic price for a quick sale."

"More likely they've got a mate lined up, who they're selling it on to."

"That's your trouble." Gavin scratched his armpit. "You're paranoid."

"You don't know what you're talking about. You use words without any idea what they mean. All you know is stupid jargon out of car mags. Recarro seats. Spicy lesbo chicks. That's all you know."

Gavin turned down his mouth and shrugged. "So. You want anything?"

"Yes. I want my life back."

"From the flat."

"I'll make a list."

"Anything you want now?"

"The kitchen knives."

"Why?"

"They're good ones. Japanese. You don't want them. You won't cook."

"I might want to cut something."

"Use your teeth."

He took a pull on his lager. She finished her spritzer.

"If that's all?" she said. She gathered her bag and her jacket. "I want everything in writing, about the flat. Tell the agents, all the paperwork must be copied to me. I want full consultation at every point." She stood up. "I'll be ringing every two days to check on progress."

"I'll look forward to that."

"Not you. The agent. Have you got their card?"

"No. Not on me. Come back and get it."

Alarm flared inside her. Was he intending to mug her, or rape her? "Send it to me," she said.

"I don't have your address."

"Send it to the office."

When she got to the door it occurred to her that it might have been his single, clumsy effort at reconciliation. She glanced back. His head was down, and he was leafing through his magazine again. No chance, anyway. She would rather take out her appendix with nail scissors than go back to Gavin.

The encounter, though, had bruised her. Gavin was the first person, she thought, that I was ever really frank and honest with; at home, there wasn't much premium on frankness, and she'd never had a girlfriend she was really close to, not since she was fifteen. She'd opened her heart to him, such as it was. And for what? Probably, when she opened her heart, he hadn't even been listening. The night of Renee's death she had seen him as he truly was: callow and ignorant and not even ashamed of it, not even asking her why she was so panicked, not even appreciating that his mother's death woudn't, by itself, have affected her like that: but shouldn't it have affected him? Had he even bothered to go to the crematorium, or had he left it all to Carole? When she thought back to that night, which (she now knew) was the last night of her marriage, a peculiar disjointed, unstrung sensation occurred in her head, as if her thoughts and her feelings had been joined together by a zip, and the zip had broken. She had not told Gavin that in the days after she walked out, she had twice dialled Renee's home number, just to see what would happen. What happened was nothing, of course. The phone rang in the empty house—bungalow—whatever.

It put a dent in her belief in her psychic powers. She knew, of course—her recollection was sharp if Gavin's wasn't—that the woman on the phone had at no point actually identified herself. She hadn't said she wasn't Renee, but she hadn't agreed that she was, either. It was just possible that she had misdialled, and that she had been talking to some irate stranger. If pushed, she would have said it was her ma-in-law, but it was true that she didn't know her voice all that well, and the woman had lacked the trademark lisp that was caused by Renee's slipping teeth. Was that significant? It could be. Nothing else of a psychic nature seemed to manifest. She moved into the Twickenham house share and discovered that it made her unhappy to live with women younger than herself. She'd never thought of herself as a romantic, God knows, but the way they talked about men was near-pornographic, and the way they belched and put their feet on the furniture was like Gavin over again. She didn't have to sleep with them, but that was the only difference. Every morning the kitchen was strewn with Häagen-Dazs tubs, and lager cans, and polystyrene trays from lo-fat microwave dinners, with a scraping of something beige and jellified left in the bottom.

So where was she going in life? What was she for? No man with the initial *M* had come into her life. She was stagnating, and struck by how quickly a temporary situation can become desolating and permanent. Soon she needed her fortune told more than ever. But her regular clairvoyant, the one she trusted most, lived in Brondesbury, which was a long way for her to travel, and kept cats, to which she developed an allergy. She got herself a train timetable, and began to work her way out, each weekend, from the London suburbs to the dormitory towns and verdant conurbations of Berkshire and Surrey. So it came about that one Saturday afternoon in spring, she saw Alison perform in Windsor, at the Victoria Room in the Harte and Garter.

It was a two-day Psychic Extravaganza. She had not prebooked, but because of her general beigeness and her inoffensive manner, she was good at queue-jumping. She had sat modestly in the third row, her whippy body crouching inside her blouson jacket, her khaki-coloured hair pushed behind her ears. Alison had fingered her right away. The lucky opals flashed fire in her direction. "I'm getting a broken wedding ring. It's this lady here in beige. Is it you, darling?"

Mutely, Colette held up her hand, the tight gold band intact. She had started wearing it again, she hardly knew why; maybe just to spite Natasha in Hove, to show that a man had warmed to her, at least once.

Impatience crossed Alison's face: then her smile wiped the expression away. "I know you still wear his ring. Maybe he thinks of you; maybe you think of him?"

"Only with hatred," Colette said.

Al said, "Whatever. But you're on your own for now, darling." Al had held out her arms to the audience. "I see images, I can't help it. For a marriage, I see a ring. For a separation, a divorce, I see a ring that's broken. The line of the break is the line of the crack in this young girl's heart."

There was a murmur of sympathy from the audience. Colette nodded soberly, acknowledging what was said. Natasha had said much the same, when she held the wedding ring, as if in tweezers, between those dodgy false nails of hers. But Natasha had been a spiteful little slag, and the woman on the platform seemed to have no spite in her; Natasha had implied she was too old for new experiences, but Alison spoke as if she had her life before her. She spoke as if her feelings and thoughts could be mended; she imagined popping into the dry cleaners and getting the broken zip replaced, the zip that joined her thought to her feelings and joined her up inside.

This was Colette's introduction to the metaphorical side of life. She realized that she hadn't comprehended half that the fortune-tellers had said to her. She might as well have stood in the street in Brondesbury ripping up tenners. When they told you something, you were supposed to look at it all ways up; you were supposed to hear it, understand it, feel all around its psychological dimensions. You weren't supposed to fight it but to let the words sink into you. You shouldn't query and quibble and try and beat the psychic out of her convictions; you should listen with your inner ear and you should accept it, exactly what she said, if the feeling it gave you checked in with your feeling inside. Alison was offering hope and hope was the feeling she wanted to have, hope of redemption from the bathroom bickering of the house share, from finding other women's bras stuffed under a sofa cushion when she flopped down after work with the *Evening Standard*: and from the sound of her housemates rutting at dawn.

"Listen," Alison said. "What I want to say to you is, don't shed tears. The fact is, you barely started with this man. He didn't know what marriage was. He didn't know how to make an equal relationship. He liked—gadgets, am I right? Hi-fi, cars, that stuff; that was what he related to."

"Oh yes," Colette chirped up. "But then wouldn't it be true of most men?" She stopped herself. "Sorry," she said.

"True of most men?" Al queried gently. "I'll give you that. The point is, though, was it true of him? Was it true that at the great highlights of your life, he was thinking about sports seats and sound systems? But look, darling, there is a man for you. A man who will be in your life for years and years to come." She frowned. "I want to say—oh, you know, *for better or worse*—but you've been married, chuck, so you know all that."

Colette took a deep breath. "Does he have the initial *M*?"

"Don't prompt me, dear," Al said. "He's not in your life yet, but he's coming into it."

"So I don't know him now?"

"Not yet."

Oh, good, Colette thought; she had just done a quick mind scan of the men she already knew. "Will I meet him at work?"

Alison closed her eyes. "Sort of," she offered. She frowned. "More *through* work, than *at* work. Through work, is how I'd put it. First you'll be sort of colleagues, then it'll get closer. You'll have a—what's the word?—a long association. It may take a bit of time to get close. He has to warm to you." She chuckled. "His dress sense is a bit lacking, but I expect you'll soon fix that, darling." Alison smiled around at the audience. "She'll just have to wait and see. Exciting, isn't it?"

"It is." Colette nodded. She kept up an inner monologue. It is, it is. I have hope, I have hope. I will get a salary rise—no, not that. I will get a place of my own—no, not that. I must, I had better, I ought to look around for a new job, I ought to shake my life up and open myself to opportunities. But whatever I do, something will happen. I am tired. I am tired of taking care of myself. Something will happen that is out of my hands.

Alison did a few other things that night at the Harte and Garter. She told a depressed-looking woman that she'd be going on a cruise. The woman at once straightened her collapsed spine and revealed in an awestruck voice that she had received a cruise brochure by the morning post, which she had sent for because her silver wedding was coming up shortly, and she thought it was time they exported their happiness somewhere other than the Isle of Wight.

"Well I want to say to you," Alison had told her, "that you will be going on that cruise; yes you will." Colette marvelled at the way Alison could spend the woman's money. "And I'll tell you something else; you're going to have a lovely time. You're going to have the time of your life."

The woman sat up even straighter. "Oh, thank you, thank you!" she said. She seemed to take on a sort of glow. Colette could see it even though she was four rows away. It encouraged her to think that somebody could hand over a fiver at the door and get so much hope in return. It was cheap, compared to what she was paying in Brondesbury and elsewhere.

After the event, Colette walked to the Riverside station in the chilly evening air. The sun made a red channel down the centre of the Thames. Swans were bobbing in the milky water near the banks. Over towards Datchet, outside the pub called the Donkey House, some French exchange students were dipping one of their number in the water. She could hear their excited cries; they warmed her heart. She stood on the bridge and waved to them with a big sweep of her arm, as if she were bringing a light aircraft in to land.

I won't come back tomorrow, she thought. I will, I won't, I will.

The next morning, Sunday, her journey was interrupted by engineering works. She had hoped to be first in the queue but that was not to be. As she stepped out of the station, there was a burst of sunshine. The High Street was crammed with coaches. She walked uphill towards the castle and the Harte and Garter. The great Round Tower brooded over the street, and at its feet, like a munching worm, wound a stream of trippers gnawing at burgers.

It was eleven o'clock and the Extravaganza was in full spate. The tables and stands were set up in the hall where the medium had done the demonstration the night before. Spiritual healing was going on in one corner, Kirlian photography in another, and each individual psychic's table, swathed in chenille or fringed silk, bore her stock-in-trade of tarot pack, crystal ball, charms, incense, pendulums, and bells—plus a small tape machine so the client could have a record of her consultation.

Almost all the psychics were women. There were just two men, lugubrious and neglected: Merlin and Merlyn, according to their name cards. One had on his table a bronze wizard, waving a staff, and the other had what appeared to be a shrunken head on a stand. There was no queue at his table. She wandered up.

"What's that?" she mouthed, pointing. It was difficult to make yourself heard; the roar of prediction rose into the air and bounced around in the rafters.

"My spirit guide," the man said. "Well, a model of him."

"Can I touch it?"

"If you must, dear."

She ran her fingers over the thing. It wasn't skin but leather, a sort of leather mask bound to a wooden skull. Its brow was encircled by a cord into which were stuck the stumps of quills. "Oh, I get it," she said. "He's a Red Indian."

"Native American," the man corrected. "The actual model is a hundred years old. It was passed on to me by my teacher, who got it from his teacher. Blue Eagle has guided three generations of psychics and healers."

"It must be hard if you're a bloke. To know what to put on your table. That doesn't look too poncey."

"Look, do you want a reading, or not?"

"I don't think so," Colette said. To hear a psychic at all, you would almost have to be cheek to cheek, and she didn't fancy such intimacy with Blue Eagle's mate. "It's a bit sordid," she said. "This head. Off-putting. Why don't you chuck it and get a new model?" She straightened up. She looked around the room. "Excuse me," she said, shouting over a client's head to a wizened old bat in a shawl, "excuse me, but where's the one who did the dem last night? Alison?"

The old woman jerked her thumb. "Three down. In the corner there. Mind, she knows how to charge. If you hang on till I'm finished here, I can do you psychometry, cards, and palms, thirty quid all in."

"How very unprofessional," Colette said coldly.

Then she spotted her. A client, beaming, rose from the red leatherette chair, and the queue parted to let her through. Colette saw Alison, very briefly, put her face in her hands: before raising it, smiling, to the next applicant for her services.

Even Sundays bring their ebb and flow: periods of quiet and almost peace, when sleep threatens in the overheated rooms, and then times of such confusion—the sunlight strikes in, sudden and scouring, lighting up the gewgaws on the velvet cloth—and within the space of two heartbeats, the anxiety is palpable, a baby crying, the incense choking, the music whining, more fortune-seekers pressing in at the door and backing up those inside against the tables. There is a clatter as a few Egyptian perfume bottles go flying; Mrs. Etchells, three tables down, is jawing on about the joys of motherhood; Irina is calming a sobbing adolescent with a broken engagement; the baby, wound up with colic, twisting in the arms of an unseen mother, is preying on her attention as if he were entangled in her gut.

Alison looked up and saw a woman of her own age, meagrely built, with thin fair hair lying flat against her skull. Her features were minimal, her figure that of an orphan in a storm. A question jumped into Al's head: how would this play if you were a Victorian, if you were one of those Victorian cheats? She knew all about it; after all, Mrs. Etchells, who had trained her, almost went back to those days. In those days the dead manifested in the form of muslin, stained and smelly from the psychic's body cavities. The dead were packed within you, so you coughed or vomited them, or drew them out of your generative organs. They blew trumpets and played portable organs;

they moved the furniture; they rapped on walls; they sang hymns. They offered bouquets to the living, spirit roses bound by scented hands. Sometimes they proffered inconveniently large objects, like a horse. Sometimes they stood at your shoulder, a glowing column made flesh by the eyes of faith. She could see it easily, a picture from the past: herself in a darkened parlour, her superb shoulders rising white out of crimson velvet, and this straight flat creature at her elbow, standing in the half-light: her eyes empty as water, impersonating a spirit form.

"Would you like to come and sit?"

Not fair! the queue said. Not her turn!

"Please be patient," Alison said sweetly. "I think someone's trying to come through for this lady, and I daren't keep Spirit World waiting."

The queue fell back, murmuring. She sat down before her, the pallid meek being, like a sacrifice drained of blood. Al searched her for clues. Probably never known the joys of motherhood? Fair bet, with those tits. Oh, wait, didn't I see her last night? Near the front, third row, left of centre, no? Broken wedding ring. Man with the gadgets. Career girl, of sorts. Not much of a career, though. Drifting. Anxious. Pains in her gut. Tension at the back of her neck, a big dead hand squeezing her spine.

On her left, Mrs. Etchells was saying, "Going on hols, are we? I see an aeroplane." Irina was saying, yes, yes, yes, you are very sad now, but by October zey are coming, four men in a truck, and building your home extension.

Alison held out her hand to Colette. Colette put her hand in it, turned up. The narrow palm was drained of energy, almost corpselike.

I would have liked that, Al thought, all that Victorian fuss and frippery, the frocks, the spirit pianos, the men with big beards. Was she seeing herself, in a former life, in an earlier and possibly more lucrative career? Had she been famous, perhaps, a household name? Possibly; or possibly it was wish fulfillment. She supposed she had lived before, but she suspected there wasn't much glamour attached to whatever life she'd led. Sometimes when her mind was vacant she had a fleeting vision, low-lit, monochrome, of a line of women hoeing, bending their backs under a mud-coloured sky.

Well, now. . . . She scrutinized Colette's palm, picking up her magnifying glass. The whole hand was bespattered with crosses, on the major lines and between them. She could see no arches, stars, or tridents. There were several worrying islands in the heart line, little vacant plots. Perhaps, she thought, she sleeps with men whose names she doesn't know.

The pale client's voice cut through. She sounded common and sharp. "You said somebody was coming through for me."

"Your father. He recently passed into Spirit."

"No."

"But there's been a passing. I'm getting six, the number six. About six months back?"

The client looked blank.

"Let me jog your memory," Alison said. "I would be talking about Guy Fawkes Night, or maybe the run-up to Christmas. Where they say, only forty shopping days left, that sort of thing." Her tone was easy; she was used to people not remembering the deaths in their family.

"My uncle died last November. If that's what you mean."

"Your uncle, not your father?"

"Yes, my uncle. For Christ's sake, I should know!"

"Bear with me," Alison said easily. "You don't by any chance have some-thing with you? Something that belonged to your dad?"

"Yes." She had brought the same props she had given to the psychic in Hove. "These were his."

She handed over the cuff links. Alison cupped them in her left palm, rolled them around with her right forefinger. Golf balls. Though he didn't play golf. Still, people don't know what to buy for men, do they? She tossed them up and caught them again. "No way," she said. "Look, can you accept this? The bloke who owned these was not your dad. He was your uncle."

"No, it was my uncle that *died*." The client paused. "He died in November. My dad died about—I don't know, ages ago—" She put her hand to her mouth. "Oh," she said. "Run it past me again, will you?" Grant her this: she wasn't slow on the uptake.

"Let's just see if we can unknot this," Al said. "You say these are your fa-ther's cuff links. I say, no, though they may have belonged to the man you *called* your father. You say your uncle passed last November, and your father passed years ago. But I say, your uncle has been a long time in Spirit, but your dad passed in the autumn. Now, are you with me?"

The client nodded.

"You're sure you're with me? I mean, I don't want you to think I'm slandering your mum. But these things happen, in families. Now your uncle's name is—?"

"Mike."

"Mike, and your dad's—Terry, right? So you think. But the way I see it, Terry's your uncle and Uncle Mike's your dad."

Silence. The woman shifted in her chair. "He was always hanging about, Mike, when I was little. Always round the house."

"*Chez vous,*" Al said. "Well, he would be."

"It explains a lot. My flat hair, for one thing."

"Yes, doesn't it?" Alison said. "When you finally get it sorted out, who's who in your family, it does explain a lot." She sighed. "It's a shame your mum's passed, so you can't ask her what was what. Or why. Or anything like that."

"She wouldn't have told me. Can't you tell me?"

"My guess is, Terry was a quiet type, whereas Uncle Mike, he was a bit of a boyo. Which was what your mum liked. Impulsive, that's how I'd describe her, if I was pushed. You too, maybe. But only in—not in your general affairs but only in what we call—er—matters of partnership."

"What does that mean?"

"It means that when you see a bloke you like you go straight after him." Like a whippet after a hare, she thought. "You say to yourself, no, I must do strategy, play it cool, but you don't heed your own advice, you're very much—how shall I say it?—bed on the first date. Well, why not? I mean, life's too short."

"I can't do this. I'm sorry." The client half rose.

Alison put her hand out. "It's the shock. About your dad. It takes a bit of getting used to. I wouldn't have broken it to you like that if I didn't think you could take it. And straight talking—I think you can take that too."

"I can take it," Colette said. She sat down again.

"You're proud," Al said softly. "You won't be bested."

"That describes me."

"If Jack and Jill can do it, you can do it."

"That's true."

"You don't suffer fools gladly."

"I don't."

It was an old Mrs. Etchells line; she was probably using it right now, three tables down: "You don't suffer fools gladly, dear!" As if the client were going to come back at you "Fools! I love 'em! Can't get enough! I go out round the streets, me, looking for fools to ask them home to dinner!"

Alison sat back in her chair. "The way I see you now, you're dissatisfied, restless."

"Yes."

"You've reached a place in your life where you don't much want to be."

"Yes."

"You're ready and willing to move on."

"Yes."

"So do you want to come and work for me?"

"What?"

"Can you type, drive, anything like that? I need a sort of, what do they call it? Girl Friday."

"This is a bit sudden."

"Not really. I felt I knew you when I saw you from the platform last night."

"The platform?"

"The platform is what we call any kind of stage."

"Why?"

"I don't know. It's historical, I suppose."

Colette leaned forward. She locked her fists together between her knees. Alison said, "If you come into the front bar in about an hour, we can get a coffee."

Colette cast a glance at the long queue behind her.

"Okay, say an hour and a quarter?"

"What do you do, put up a CLOSED sign?"

"No, I just put them on divert, I say, go see Mrs. Etchells three tables down."

"Why? Is she good?"

"Mrs. Etchells? *Entre nous*, she's rubbish. But she taught me. I owe her."

"You're loyal?"

"I hope so."

"Is that her? Wrinkly old bag with a charm bracelet on? Now I'll tell *you* something. She's not loyal to you."

She spelled it out: "She tried to poach me, tried to catch me as I was look-ing about for you: cards, crystal, and psychometry thrown in, thirty quid."

Alison blushed, a deep crimson blush. "She said that? Thirty quid?"

"Fancy you not knowing."

"My mind was somewhere else." She laughed shakily. "Voilà. You've al-ready earned your money, Colette."

"You know my name?"

"It's that certain something French about you. *Je ne sais quoi.*"

"You speak French?"

"Never till today."

"You mustn't mind-read me."

"I would try not to."

"An hour and a quarter?"

"You could get some fresh air."

On Windsor Bridge, a young boy was sitting on a bench with his Rottweiler at his feet. He was eating an ice-cream cone and holding another out to the dog. Passersby, smiling, were collecting to watch. The dog ate with civil, swirling motions of his tongue. Then he crunched the last of his cornet, swarmed up onto the bench and laid his head lovingly on the boy's shoulder. The boy fed him the last of his own ice cream, and the crowd laughed. The dog, encouraged, licked and nibbled the boy's ears, and the crowd went ohh, feech, yuk, how sweet!

The dog jumped down from the bench. Its eyes were steady and its paws huge. For two pins, or the dog equivalent, it would set itself to eat the crowd, worrying each nape and tossing the children like pancakes.

Colette stood and watched until the crowd had dispersed and she was alone. She crossed the bridge and edged down Eton High Street, impeded by tourists. I am like the dog, she thought. I have an appetite. Is that wrong? My mum had an appetite. I realize it now, how she talked in code all those years. No wonder I never knew what was what and who was who. Nor surprising her aunts were always exchanging glances, saying things like I wonder where Colette gets her hair from, I wonder where she gets her brains? The man she'd called her father was distinguished by the sort of stupidity that made him squalid. She had a mental picture of him, sprawled before the television scratching his belly. Perhaps, when she'd bought him the cuff links, she'd been hoping to improve him. Her Uncle Mike, on the other hand—who was really her father—was a man whose wallet was always stuffed. Hadn't he been round every week flashing his fivers and saying, here, Angie, get something nice for little Colette? He'd paid, but he hadn't paid enough; he'd paid as an uncle, but not as a dad. I'll sue the bastard, she thought. Then she remembered he was dead.

She went into the Crown and Cushion and got a pineapple juice, which she took into a corner. Every few minutes she checked her watch. Too early, she started back across the bridge.

Alison was sitting in the front room of the Harte and Garter with a cafetière and two cups. She had her back to the door, and Colette paused for a moment, getting a view of her: she's *huge*, she thought, how can she go around like that? As she watched, Alison's plump smooth arm reached for the coffee and poured it into the second cup.

Colette sat down. She crossed her legs. She fixed Alison with a cool stare. "You don't mind what you say, do you? You could have really upset me, back there."

"There was a risk." Alison smiled.

"You think you're a good judge of character."

"More often than not."

"And my mum. I mean, for all you know, I could have burst into tears. I could have collapsed."

Not a real risk, Al thought. At some level, in some recess of themselves, people know what they know. But the client was determined to have her moment.

"Because what you were saying, really, is that she was having an affair with my uncle under my dad's nose. Which isn't nice, is it? And she let my dad think I was his."

"I wouldn't call it an affair. It was more of a fling."

"So what does that make her? A slag."

Alison put down her coffee cup. "They say don't speak ill of the dead." She laughed. "But why not? They speak ill of you."

"Do they?" Colette thought of Renee. "What are they saying?"

"A joke. I was making a joke. I see you think I shouldn't."

She took from Colette the thimble-sized serving of milk she was fumbling with, flicked up the foil with her nail, and tipped the milk into Colette's coffee.

"Black. I take it black."

"Sorry."

"Another thing you didn't know."

"Another."

"This job you were talking about—" Colette broke off. She narrowed her eyes and looked speculatively at Al, as if she were a long way off.

Al said, "Don't frown. You'll stay like that one day. Just ask me what you need to ask."

"Don't you know?"

"You asked me not to read your mind."

"You're right. I did. Fair's fair. But can you shut it off like that? Shut it off and then just turn it on when you want it?"

"It's not like that. I don't know how I can explain. It's not like a tap."

"Is it like a switch?"

"Not like a switch."

"It's like—I suppose—is it like somebody whispering to you?"

"Yes. More like that. But not exactly whispering. I mean, not in your ear."

"Not in your ear." Colette stirred her coffee round and round.

Al picked up a paper straw of brown sugar, pinched off the end, and dropped it into Colette's cup. "You need the energy," she explained. Colette, frowning, continued to stir.

"I have to get back soon," Al said. "They're building up in there."

"So if it's not a switch—"

"About the job. You could sleep on it."

"And it's not a tap—"

"You could ring me tomorrow."

"And it's not somebody whispering in your ear—"

"My number's on the leaflet. Have you got my leaflet?"

"Does your spirit guide tell you things?"

"Don't leave it too long."

"You said he was called Morris. A little bouncing circus clown."

"Yes."

"Sounds a pain."

"He can be."

"Does he live with you? In your house? I mean, if you call it 'live'?"

"You might as well," Al said. She sounded tired. "You might as well call it 'live' as call it anything." She pushed herself to her feet. "It's going to be a long afternoon."

"Where *do* you live?"

"Wexham."

"Is that far?"

"Just up into Bucks."

"How do you get home, do you drive?"

"Train and then a taxi."

"By the way, I think you must be right. About my family."

Al looked down at her. "I sense you're wavering. I mean, about my offer. It's not like you to be indecisive. More like you to take the plunge."

"I'm not quite sure what you'd want me to do. I'm used to a job description."

"We could work one up. If that's what's worrying you. Write your own, why not? You'll soon see what needs to be done." Alison was rummaging for something in her bag. "I may not be able to pay as much as your last job. But then, when you've looked at my books, you'll be able to tell me what I can afford. And also, it's a quality-of-life thing, isn't it? I should think the schedule will be more relaxed than in your last job. You'd have more leisure." Then she said, as if she were embarrassed, "You wouldn't get rich out of me. I'm no good for lottery numbers or anything like that."

"Can you hang on for a minute?" Colette said. "I need to know more."

"They'll be waiting."

"Make them wait."

"Yes, but not too long. Or Mrs. Etchells will catch them." Al had found a tube of mints in her bag. She proffered it to Colette. "Keeps the mind alert," she said. "What I need, you see, is someone to keep the diary straight and make sure I don't double-book. Liaise with the management, wherever I'm on the platform. Book hotels. Do the accounts. It would be good to have someone to answer the phone. If I'm with a client, I can't always break off."

"You don't have an answering machine?"

"The clients would rather hear a human voice. Anyway, I'm not very good with electrical things."

"So how do you do your washing? In a tub?"

"No, the fact is—" Alison looked down. She looked harried. "I can see there's a lot I'm going to have to explain to you," she said.

The truth was, it emerged, that whatever message Alison left on her machine was liable to become corrupted. Other messages, quite different ones, would overlay it. Where did they come from? "There's no simple answer to that," Alison said. She checked her watch. "I meant to eat but I've been talking."

"I'll bring you a sandwich in, shall I?"

"I never eat when I'm reading. It's not professional. Oh, well. Do me no harm to be hungry, will it? I'll hardly waste away." She patted her tummy, smiled miserably. "Look, about the travelling, I do travel a lot, and I used to drive, but I don't anymore. I think if I had a friend with me, I could manage, so we could split it, you see."

"You need a navigator?"

"It's not so much that." What Alison needed, she explained—picking again at the sugar straws, opening them and putting them down—was a warm living body beside her, as she drove from town to town, fayre to fayre, and from one Psychic Extravaganza to another. Otherwise, a spirit would come and sit in the passenger seat, and natter on while she tried to negotiate an unfamiliar one-way system. "Do you know Bracknell? Bracknell's hell. All those roundabouts."

"What's to stop the spirits from climbing in the back seat instead? Or have you got a two-door?"

Alison looked at her for a long moment. Colette thought she was actually going to answer the question. "Look, Colette," she said softly. She had got four straws lined up now, and she moved them about, delicately, with one finger: changing the pattern, shuffling and reshuffling. "Look, it doesn't matter if you're a bit sceptical. I understand. I'd be sceptical myself. All you need to realize is that it doesn't matter what you think, it doesn't matter what I think—what happens, happens all the same. The only thing is, I don't do tests, I don't do tricks for people to try to prove myself, because I don't need to prove anything. Do you see?"

Colette nodded.

Alison raised a finger to a girl who was serving and pointed to the cafetière. "A refill for you," she explained. "I can see you're bitter. Why shouldn't you be? Life hasn't treated you well. You've worked hard and had no reward. You've lost your home. And you've lost a lot of your money, haven't you?"

Colette's eyes followed the trail of brown sugar curling across the table; like an initial, trying to form itself. "You seem to know a lot about me."

"I laid out a spread for you. After you'd gone."

"A spread?"

"The tarot cards."

"I know. Which spread?"

"Basic Romany."

"Why that?"

"I was in a hurry."

"And what did you see?"

"I saw myself."

Al got up and headed back towards the main hall, handing a ten-pound note to a girl as she passed, pointing to the table she had just left. That's far too much, Colette thought, two pots of coffee, ten pounds, what is she thinking? She felt a flare of indignation, as if it were her own cash that had been spent. She drank all the coffee, so as not to be wasteful, tipping the pot so its muddy grounds shifted. She went to the LADIES, and as she washed her hands she watched herself in the mirror. Maybe no mind-reading in it, she thought. No psychic tricks needed, or information from spirit guides. She did look like a woman who had lost her money: lost her lottery ticket in life, lost her dad and lost her home.

That summer they laughed a lot. They acted as if they were in love, planning for each other treats and nice things to eat and surprising each other with thoughtful gifts. Alison gave Colette a voucher for a day spa in Windsor; I won't come, she said cheerfully, I don't want some foul-breathed anorexic lecturing me about my cellulite, but you enjoy yourself, Colette. Colette dropped into Caleys and bought a warm throw, soft mohair and the colour of crushed raspberries; lovely, Al said that evening, just what I need, something to cover me up.

Colette took over most of the driving, finding that she didn't mind at all. "Change the car," she said to Alison, and they went out to a showroom that very afternoon. They picked one because they liked the colour and the upholstery; she imagined herself, putting two fingers up to Gavin, and when the salesman tried to talk car sense they just giggled at each other. "The truth is, they're all the same these days," she said loudly. "I don't know much, I but I do know that."

Al wasn't interested, she just wanted it done with; but when the salesman tried to trap her into a finance deal, she slapped him down smartly. She agreed on a delivery date, wrote a cheque; Colette was impressed by her style. When they got home she rummaged through Al's wardrobe and threw out the worst bits of Lurex. She tried to smuggle the "silk" out, in a black bin liner, but Al went after the plastic bag and retrieved it, drawing it out and looping it around her arm. "Nice try," she said to Colette. "But I'm sticking with it, please."

Colette's education in the psychic trade was brisk and no-nonsense. Al's absurd generosity to the waitress in the coffee shop might represent one side of her nature, but she was businesslike in her own way. She wouldn't be taken for a ride, she knew how to charge out every minute of her time, though her accounts, kept on paper, were a mess. Having been a credulous person so recently, Colette was now cynical and sneery. She wondered how long it would be before Al initiated her into some fraud. She waited and waited. By mid-August she thought, what fraud could there be? Al doesn't have secret wires tapping into people's thoughts. There's no technology in her act. All she does is stand onstage and make weak jokes. You may say Al's a fake because she has to be, because nobody can do what she claims to do. But there it is; she doesn't make claims, she demonstrates. And when you come down to it she can deliver the goods. If there is a fraud, it's a transparent one; so clear that no one can see it.

Al hadn't even been registered for VAT when Colette had come on board as her business brain. As for income tax, her allowances were all over the place. Colette went to the tax office in person. The official she saw admitted to a complete ignorance of a medium's trade; she was poised to take advantage of it. "What about her clothes," she said, "her stage outfits? Her outfits for meeting her clients. She has to look good, it's a professional obligation."

"Not one we recognize, I'm afraid," the young woman said.

"Well, you should! As you ought to know, being the size you are yourself, decent clothes in large sizes don't come cheap. She can't get away with the tat you find on the High Street. It's got to be specialist shops. Even her bras— well, I don't need to spell it out."

"I'm afraid it's all dual purpose," the woman said. "Underwear, outerwear, whatever; it's not just specific to her trade, is it?"

"What? You mean, she could pop to the postbox in it? Do the dusting? In one of her stage outfits?"

"If she liked. I'm trying to envisage—you didn't bring pictures, did you?"

"I'll drop some in."

"That might be a help. So we could work out what sort of class of item we're dealing with—you see, if it were, well, a barrister's wig, say, or protective clothing, say, boots with steel toe caps, for example—"

"So are you telling me they've made special rules about it? For mediums?"

"Well, no, not specifically for—what you say your partner does. I'm just going by the nearest cases I can envisage. At this stage." The woman looked restless. "I suppose you might classify it as show business. Look, I'll pass it up for consideration. Take it under advisement."

Colette wished—wished very strongly, most sincerely—that she had Al's powers, just for sixty seconds. So that a whisper, a hiss, a flash, so that something would overtake her, some knowledge, insight, some piece of special information, so that she could lean across the desk and tell the woman at the tax office something about her private life, something embarrassing: or something that would make the hair stand up on the back of her neck. For the moment, they agreed to differ. Colette undertook to keep a complete record of Al's expenditure on stage outfits. She lost no time, of course, in computerizing their accounts. But the thought nagged at her that a record kept in figures was not quite enough.

Hence her good idea, about writing a book. How hard could it be? Al made tape recordings for her clients, so wasn't it logical, in the larger world, to tape-record Al? Then all she would need to do would be transcribe, edit, tighten up here and there, make some chapter headings. . . . Her mind moved ahead, to costings, to a layout, to a photographer. Fleetingly, she thought of the boy in the bookshop, who'd sold her the tarot pack. If I'd been self-employed then, she thought, I could have set those cards against tax. Those days seemed distant now: leaving the boy's bed-sit at 5 A.M. in the rain. Her life with Gavin had receded; she remembered things he had, like his calculator, and his diver's watch, but not necessarily the evil things he had done. She remembered her kitchen—the scales, the knives—but not anything she cooked there. She remembered her bed, and her bed linen; but not sex. I can't keep on losing it, she thought, losing chunks of my life, years at a time. Or who will I be when I'm old? I should write a book for me too. I need a proof of some sort, a record of what goes down.

The tape recorder worked well on the whole, though sometimes it sounded as if Alison had a bag over her head; Colette's questions, always, were piercingly clear. But when they played the tapes back, they found that, just as Al had foreseen, other items had intruded. Someone speaking, fast and urgent, in what might be Polish. A twittering, like small birds in a wood: nightingales, Alison said unexpectedly.

Once, a woman's irate voice cut through Alison's mutter: "Well, you're in for it now. You've started so you may as well finish. It's no use asking for your money back, sunshine. The trade doesn't work that way."

COLETTE: When you were a child, did you ever suffer a severe blow to the skull?
ALISON: Several . . . Why, didn't you?

four

COLETTE: It's Tuesday and I'm just—it's ten-thirty in the evening and—Al, can you come a bit closer to the mike? I'm just resuming where we left off last night—now, Alison, we've sort of addressed the point about the trivia, haven't we? Still, you might like to put your answer on the tape.

ALISON: I have already explained to you that the reason we get such trivial information from Spirit is—

COLETTE: All right, there's no need to sound like a metronome. Monotone. Can't you sound a bit more natural?

ALISON: If the people who've passed—is that okay now?

COLETTE: Go on.

ALISON: If the people who've passed were to give you messages about angels and, you know, spiritual matters, you'd think it was a bit vague. We wouldn't have any way of checking on them. But if they give you messages about your kitchen units, you can say if they're right or wrong.

COLETTE: So what you're mainly worried about is convincing people?

ALISON: No.

COLETTE: What then?

ALISON: I don't feel I have to convince anybody, personally. It's up to them whether they come to see me. Their choice. There's no compulsion to believe anything they don't want. . . . Oh, Colette, what's that? Can you hear it?

COLETTE: Just carry on.

ALISON: It's snarling. Somebody's let the dogs out?

COLETTE: What?

ALISON: I can't carry on over this racket.

(*click*)

COLETTE: Okay, trying again. It's eleven o'clock and we've had a cup of tea—

ALISON: —and a chocolate chip cookie—

COLETTE: —and we're resuming. We were talking about the whole issue of proof, and I want to ask you, Alison, have you ever been scientifically tested?

ALISON: I've always kept away from that. You see, if you were in a laboratory wired up, it's as good as saying, we think you're some sort of confidence trick. Why should people come through from Spirit for other people who don't believe in them? You see, most people, once they've passed, they're not really interested in talking to this side. The effort's too much for them. Even if they wanted to do it, they haven't got the concentration span. You say they give trivial messages, but that's because they're trivial people. You don't get a personality transplant when you're dead. You don't suddenly get a degree in philosophy. They're not interested in helping me out with proof.

COLETTE: On the platform you always say, you've had your gift since you were very small.

ALISON: Yes.

COLETTE: (*whispering*) Al, don't do that to me. I need a proper answer on the tape. Yes, you say it, or yes, it's true?

ALISON: I don't generally lie on the platform. Well, only to spare people.

COLETTE: Spare them what? (*pause*) Al?

ALISON: Can you move on?

COLETTE: Okay, so you've had this gift—

ALISON: If you call it that.

COLETTE: You've had this ability since you were small. Can you tell us about your childhood?

ALISON: I could. When you were little, did you have a front garden?

COLETTE: Yes.

ALISON: What did you have in it?

COLETTE: Hydrangeas, I think.

ALISON: We had a bathtub in ours.

When Alison was young she might as well have been a beast in the jungle as a girl growing up outside Aldershot. She and her mum lived in an old terraced house with a lot of banging doors. It faced a busy road, but there was open land at the back. Downstairs there were two rooms, and a lean-to with a flat roof, which was the kitchen. Upstairs were two bedrooms, and a bathroom, which had a bath tub in it so there was no actual need for the one in the garden. Opposite the bathroom was the steep short staircase that led up to the attic.

Downstairs, the front room was the place where men had a party. They came and went with bags inside which bottles rattled and chinked. Sometimes her mum would say, better watch ourselves tonight, Gloria, they're bringing spirits in. In the back room, her mum sat smoking and muttering. In the lean-to, she sometimes absently opened cans of carrots or butterbeans, or stood staring at the grill pan while something burned on it. The roof leaked, and black mould drew a drippy wavering line down one corner.

The house was a mess. Bits were continually falling off it. You'd get left with the door handle in your hand, and when somebody put his fist through a window one night it got mended with cardboard and stayed like that. The men were never willing to do hammering or operate a screwdriver. "Never do a hand's turn, Gloria!" her mother complained.

As she lay in her little bed at night the doors banged, and sometimes the windows smashed. People came in and out. Sometimes she heard laughing, sometimes scuffling, sometimes raised voices and a steady rhythmic pounding. Sometimes she stayed in her bed till daylight came, sometimes she was called to get up for one reason and another. Some nights she dreamed she could fly; she passed over the ridge tiles, and looked down on the men about

their business, skimming over the waste ground, where vans stood with their
back doors open, and torchlight snaked through the smoky dark.

Sometimes the men were there in a crowd, sometimes they swarmed off
and vanished for days. Sometimes at night just one or two men stayed and
went upstairs with her mum. Then next day the bunch of them were back
again, tee-heeing beyond the wall at men's private jokes. Behind the house
was a scrubby field, with a broken-down caravan on blocks; sometimes there
was a light in it. Who lives in there? she asked her mum, and her mum
replied, What you don't know won't hurt you, which even at an early age Alison knew was untrue.

Beyond the caravan was a huddle of leaning corrugated sheds and a line of
lockup garages to which the men had the keys. Two white ponies used to
graze in the field, then they didn't. Where have the ponies gone? she asked
her mum. Her mum replied, to the knackers, I suppose.

She said, Who's Gloria? You keep talking to her. Her mum said, Never
you mind.

"Where is she?" she said. "I can't see her. You say, yes Gloria, no Gloria,
want a cuppa, Gloria? Where is she?"

Her mum said, "Never mind Gloria, you'll be in Kingdom Come. Because
that's where I'm going to knock you if you keep this up."

Her mum would never stay in the house if she could help it: pacing, smoking, smoking, pacing. Desperate for a breath of air, she would say, "Come on,
Gloria," shrug on her coat and flee down the road to the minimart; and because she did not want the trouble of washing or dressing Alison, or having
her underfoot whining for sweeties, she would take her up to the top of the
house and lock her in the attic. "She can't come to any harm up there," she
would reason, out loud to Gloria. "No matches, so she can't set the house on
fire. Too small to climb out the skylight. Nothing sharp up here the like of
which she is drawn to, such as knives or pins. There's really no damage she
could come to."

She put an old rug up there for Alison to sit on, when she played with her
blocks and animals. "Quite a little palace," she said. There was no heating,
which again was a safety factor, there being no outlets for Alison to put her
fingers into. She could have an extra cardigan instead. In summer the attic
was hot. Midday rays streamed fiercely down, straight from the sky to the

dusty rug. They lit up the corner where the little lady used to fade up, all dressed in pink, and call out to Alison in a timid Irish voice.

Alison was perhaps five years old when the little lady first appeared, and in this way she learned how the dead could be helpful and sweet. She had no doubt that the little lady was dead, in every meaningful sense. Her clothes were feltlike and soft to the touch, and her pink cardigan was buttoned right up to the first fold of her chin. "My name is Mrs. McGibbet, darlin'," she said. "Would you like to have me round and about? I thought you might like to have me with you, round and about."

Mrs. McGibbet's eyes were blue and round and startled. In her cooing voice, she talked about her son, who had passed over before her, met with an accident. They'd never been able to find each other, she said, I never could meet up with Brendan. But sometimes she showed Alison his toys, little miniature cars and tractors, neatly boxed. Once or twice she faded away and left the toys behind. Mum just stubbed her toe on them. It was as if she didn't see them at all.

Mrs. McGibbet was always saying, "I wouldn't want, my darlin', to come between a little girl and her mother. If that were her mother coming up the stair now, coming up with a heavy tread, no, I wouldn't want to put myself forward at all." When the door opened she faded away: leaving sometimes an old doll collapsed in the corner where she had sat. She chuckled as she fell backwards, into the invisible place behind the wall.

Al's mum forgot to send her to school. "Good grief," she said, when the man came around to prosecute her, "you mean to say she's that age already?"

Even after that, Al was never where she should be. She never had a swimsuit, so when it was swimming she was sent home. One of the teachers threatened she'd be made to swim in her knickers next week, but she went home and mentioned it, and one of the men offered to go down there and sort it out. When Al went to school next day she told the teacher, Donnie's coming down; he says he'll push a bottle up your bleeding whatnot, and—I don't think it's very nice, miss—ram it in till your guts come out your mouf.

After that, on swimming afternoon, she was just sent home again. She never had her rubber-soled shoes for skipping and hopping or her eggs and basin for mixing a cake, her times tables or her poem or her model mosque made out of milk-bottle tops. Sometimes when she came home from school one of the men would stop her in the hall and give her 50 pence. She would run up to the attic and put it away in a secret box she had up there. Her mother would take it off her if she could, so she had to be quick.

One day the men came with a big van. She heard yapping and ran to the window. Three blunt-nosed brindle dogs were being led towards the garages. "Oh, what are their names?" she cried. Her mother said, "Don't you go calling their names. Dogs like that, they'll chew your face off. Isn't that right, Gloria?"

She gave them names anyway: Blighto, Harry and Serene. One day Blighto came to the house and bumped against the back door. "Oh, he's knocking," Al said. She opened the door though she knew she shouldn't, and tried to give him half her wafer biscuit.

A man came shooting out of nowhere and hauled the dog off her. He kicked it into the yard while he got Alison up off the floor. "Emmie, sort it!" he yelled, then wrapped his hands in an old jersey of her mum's and went out and pummelled the dog's face, dragging it back to the sheds and twisting its neck as he dragged. He came back in shouting, "I'll shoot the fucker, I'll strangle that bastard dog." The man, whose name was Keith, wept when he saw how the dog had ripped at her hairline. He said, Emmie, she ought to go to Casualty, that needs stitching. Her mum said she couldn't be sitting in a queue all afternoon.

The man washed her head at the kitchen sink. There wasn't a cloth or a sponge so he put his hand on the back of her neck, pressed her down over the plastic bowl, and slapped the water up at her. It went in her eyes, so the bowl blurred. Her blood went in the bowl but that was all right; it was all right because the bowl itself was red. "Stay there, darling," he said, "just keep still," and his hand lifted from her nape as he bent to rummage in the cupboard at his feet. Obedient, she bent there; blood came down her nose too and she wondered why that was. She heard the chinking noise as Keith tossed the empties out from under the sink. Em, he said, you not got any disinfectant in here? Give us a rag for Christsakes, tear up a sheet, I don't know, and her mother said, use your hankie or ain't you got none? In the end her mother came up behind her with the used dish towel and Keith ripped it out of her hand. "There you go, there you go, there you go," he kept saying, dabbing away, sighing the words between his teeth.

She felt faint with pain. She said, "Keef, are you my dad?"

He wrung the cloth between his hands. "What you been telling her, Emmie?" Her mother said, "I've not been telling her nothing, you ought to know by now she's a bloody little liar. She says she can hear voices in the wall. She says there are people up in the attic. She's got a screw loose, Gloria says."

Keith moved: she felt a sudden sick cold at her back as he pulled away, as his body warmth left her. She reared up, dripping water and dilute pink blood. Keith had crossed the room and pinned her mother up against the wall. "I told you, Emmie, if I told you once I told you a dozen times, I do not want to hear that name spoken." And the dozen times, Keith reinforced, by the way he gave her mum a little bounce, raising her by her hair near the scalp and bobbing her down again. "Gloria's buggered off back to Paddyland," he said [bounce]. "That's all [bounce] you bloody [bounce] know about it, do you [bounce] understand [bounce] that? Do I bloody [bounce-bounce-bounce-bounce] make myself [bounce] crystal-clear? You just [bounce] forget you ever [bounce] set eyes."

"She's all right, is Gloria," said her mum, "she can be a good laugh," and the man said, "Do you want me to give you a slap? Do you want me to give you a slap and knock your teeth out?"

Alison was interested to see this happen. She had had many kinds of slap, but not that kind. She wiped the water from her eyes, the water and blood, till her vision cleared. But Keith seemed to get tired of it. He let her mother go and her legs went from under her; her body folded and slid down the wall, like the lady in the attic who could fold herself out of sight.

"You look like Mrs. McGibbet," Al said.

Her mother twitched, as if her wires had been pulled; she squeaked up from the floor. "Who's speaking names now?" she said. "You wallop her, Keith, if you don't want names spoken. She's always speaking names." Then she screamed a new insult that Al had never heard before.

"You poxy little poxer, you got blood on your chin. Where've you got that from? You poxy little poxer."

Al said, "Keef, does she mean me?"

Keith wiped his sweating forehead. It made you sweat, bouncing a woman a dozen times by the short hair of her head. "Yes. No," he said. "She means to say poxy little boxer. She can't talk, sweetheart, she don't know who she's talking to; her brain's gone, what she ever had of it."

"Who's Gloria?" she asked. Keith made a hissing through his teeth. He tapped one fist into his opposite palm. For a moment she thought he was going to come after her, so she backed up against the sink. The cold edge of it dug into her back; her hair dripped, blood and water, down her T-shirt. Later she would tell Colette, I was never so frightened as then; that was my worst moment, one of the worse ones anyway, that moment when I thought Keef would knock me to Kingdom Come.

But Keith stepped back. "Here," he said. He thrust the dish towel into her hand. "Keep at it," he said. "Keep it clean."

"Can I stay off school?" she said, and Keith said, yes, she'd better. He gave her a pound note and told her to yell out if she saw a dog loose again.

"And will you come and save me?"

"Somebody'll be about."

"But I don't want you to strangle it," she said, with tears in her eyes. "It's Blighto."

The next time she recalled seeing Keith was a few months later. It was night, and she should have been in bed as nobody had called her out. But when she heard Keith's name she reached under her mattress for her scissors, which she always kept there in case they should be needed. She clutched them in one hand; with the other she held up the hem of the big nightie that was lent her as a special favour from her mum. When she came scrambling down the stairs, Keith was standing just inside the front door; or at least some legs were, wearing Keith's trousers. He had a blanket over his head. Two men were supporting him. When they took off the blanket she saw that every part of his face looked like fatty mince, oozing blood. ("Oh, this mince is fatty, Gloria!" her mother would say.) She called out to him, "Keef, that needs stitching!" and one of the men swooped down on her and wrenched the scissors out of her hand. She heard them strike the wall, as the man flung them; looming above her, he pushed her into the back room and slammed the door.

Next day a voice beyond the wall said, "Hear Keef got mashed up last night. Tee-hee. As if he ain't got troubles enough."

She believed she never saw Keith again, but she might have seen him and just not recognized him; it didn't seem as if he'd have much left by way of original features. She remembered how, the evening of the dog bite, once her head had stopped bleeding, she had gone out to the garden. She followed the furrows dug by the dog's strong hind legs, as Keith dragged him away from the house, and Blighto twisted to look back. Not until it rained hard did the ruts disappear.

At that time Alison was saving up for a pony. One day she went up to the attic to count her money. "Ah dear," said Mrs. McGibbet, "the lady your mother has been up here, darlin', raiding your box that was your own peculiar property. The coins she's tipped into her open purse, and the one single poor note she has tucked away in her brassiere. And not a thing I could do to stop her, my rheumatics being aggravated by the cold and damp, for by the time I was up and out of my corner, she had outstripped me."

Alison sat down on the floor. "Mrs. McGibbet," she said, "can I ask you a question?"

"You surely can. And why should you have to ask if you can ask, I ask myself?"

"Do you know Gloria?"

"Do I know Gloria?" Mrs. McGibbet's eyelids fell over her bright blue eyes. "Ah, you've no business asking."

"I think I saw her. I think I can see her these days."

"Gloria is a cheap hoor, what else should she be? I never should have given her the name, for it put ideas in her head that was above her station. Go on the boat then, heedless and headstrong, she would go on the boat. Get off at Liverpool with all its attendant vices and then where will she go but via a meat lorry to the dreadful metropolis with its many occasions of sin. End up dead, dead and haunting about in a British army town, in a dirty house with a bath in the front garden, and her own mother a living witness to every hoor's trick that she can contrive."

After that, when she got 50 pence from the men, she took it straight down to the minimart and bought chocolate, which she ate on the way home.

• • •

When Alison was eight years old, or maybe nine or ten, she was playing out-side one day, a greyish sticky day in late summer. She was alone, of course: playing horses, neighing occasionally, and progressing at a canter. The rough grass of their back plot was worn in patches, like the pile on the rug that made the attic into a little palace.

Something drew her attention, and she stopped in her paces, and glanced up. She could see men going to and fro from the garages, carrying boxes.

"Hi-ya!" she said. She waved to them. She was sure they were men she knew.

But then a minute later she thought they were men she didn't know. It was hard to tell. They kept their faces turned away. A sick feeling crept over her. Silent, faces downcast, the men moved over the tussocky grass. Silent, faces downcast, they passed the boxes. She couldn't judge the distance from herself to them; it was as if the light had grown more thick and dense. She took a step forward, but she knew she should not. Her dirty nails dug into the palms of her hands. Sick came up into her throat. She swallowed it and it burned. Very slowly, she turned her head away. She took one plodding step towards the house. Then another. Air thick as mud clotted around her ankles. She had some idea of what was in the boxes, but as she stepped inside the house it slipped clear from her mind, like a drug slipping from a syringe and deep into a vein.

Her mother was in the lean-to, nattering away to Gloria. "Excuse me, will you," she said affably, "while I just see if this child wants a clip around the ear?" She turned around and glared at her daughter. "Look at you," she said. "Wash your face, you're all running in sweat, you bloody turn me up. I was never like that at your age, I was a neat little thing, I had to be, I wouldn't have made a living if I'd gone about like that. What's the matter with you, you're green, girl, look at yourself in the mirror, have you been stuffing your-self with them Rolo again? If you're going to chuck up, go outside and do it."

Alison did as she was told and looked at herself in the mirror. She didn't recognize the person she saw there. It was a man, with a check jacket on and a tie skew-whiff; a frowning man with a low hairline and a yellowish face. Then she realized that the door was open, and that the men were piling in behind her. "Fuck, Emmie, got to wash me hands!" one of them shouted.

She ran. For always, more or less, she was afraid of the men. On the stairs to the attic she doubled up and let brown liquid run out of her mouth. She hoped her mother would think it was the cat, Judy, who was responsible. She toiled on upwards and swung open the door. Mrs. McGibbet was sitting, already formed, in her corner. Her stumpy legs in their thick stockings stuck out in front of her, wide apart, as if she had been punched and knocked down. Her eyes were no longer startled, but blank as if their blinds had been drawn.

She did not greet Alison: no "How's my darlin' girl today?" She just said, in a distracted mutter, "There's an evil thing you wouldn't want to see at all. There's an evil thing you wouldn't want to see. . . ." She faded with rapidity; there was a scrabbling noise beneath the floorboards, and she was gone.

Mrs. McGibbet never came back after that day. She missed her, but she realized that the old lady was too frightened to return. Al was a child and hadn't got the option of leaving. Now there was no appeal or relief from Gloria and her mum, and the men in the front room. She went out to play at the back as seldom as possible; even the thought of it made thick spit come up into her mouth. Her mother berated her for getting no fresh air. If she was forced to play out—which happened sometimes, with the door locked after her—she made it a rule never to raise her eyes as far as the sheds and the lockup garages, or the belt of woodland beyond them. She could not shake off the atmosphere of that afternoon, a peculiar suspension, like a breath held: the men's averted faces, the thunderous air, the dying grass, her mother's outgust of tobacco smoke, the yellow face in the mirror where she expected to see her own, the man's need to wash his hands. As for what was in the cardboard boxes, she hoped not to think about it; but sometimes the answer turned up, in dreams.

COLETTE: So . . . are you going to tell me?
ALISON: I might, if I was quite sure I knew.
COLETTE: Only *might*?
ALISON: I don't know if I could speak it out.
COLETTE: Drugs, could it have been? Or didn't they have drugs in those days?
ALISON: God Almighty, of course they had drugs, do you think I come out of the Ark? They've always had drugs.
COLETTE: So?

ALISON: It was a funny district, you see, the army camps all around, these squaddies coming and going, I mean it was a big area for, well, women like my mum and the sort of men she knew, there was a lot of illegal gambling, there were women and boys who were on the game, there were all sorts of—

COLETTE: So come on, what do you think was in the boxes? (*pause*) Bits of Gloria?

ALISON: No. Surely not? Keef said she'd gone home to Ireland.

COLETTE: You didn't believe that, did you?

ALISON: I didn't believe it or not believe it.

COLETTE: But she did disappear?

ALISON: Not from our house, she didn't. Yes Gloria, no, Gloria, have a cuppa Gloria.

COLETTE: I'm quite interested in this because it suggests your mum was mad or something—but let's just keep to the point about the disappearance—was anything reported?

ALISON: I was eight. I didn't know what was reported.

COLETTE: Nothing on TV?

ALISON: I'm not sure we had a TV. Well, yes, we did. Several. I mean the men used to bring them in under their arms. Just, we never had an aerial. That was us. Two bathtubs, no TV aerial.

COLETTE: Al, why do you make such silly jokes all the time? You do it when you're on the platform. It's not appropriate.

ALISON: Personally I think the use of humour's very important when you're dealing with the public. It puts them at their ease. Because they're scared, when they come in.

COLETTE: I was never scared. Why do they come if they're scared?

ALISON: Most people have a very low fright threshold. But it doesn't stop them being curious.

COLETTE: They should toughen up.

ALISON: I suppose we all should. (*sighs*) Look, Colette—you come from Uxbridge. Oh, I know you say, Uxbridge not Knightsbridge, but it's a place where you had hydrangeas, right? Well, that's not like where I come from. I suppose if you had a crime in Uxbridge, if you had somebody disappear, the neighbours would notice.

COLETTE: So what are you saying?

ALISON: People went missing all the time, round our way. There was wasteland. There was army land, there was miles of it. There was heath land and just generally these acres where anything . . . could have. . . .

COLETTE: Did the police ever come round?

ALISON: The police came round regularly, I mean there was no surprise in that.

COLETTE: So what did you do?

ALISON: My mother would say, down on the floor. The police would flap the letter box. They'd shout through, is that Mrs. Emmeline Cheetham?

COLETTE: Was that her name?

ALISON: Yes, Emmeline. It's nice, isn't it?

COLETTE: I mean Cheetham, that's not your name.

ALISON: I changed it. Think about it.

COLETTE: Oh, yes. . . . Al, does this mean you might have previous identities?

ALISON: Past lives?

COLETTE: No . . . For God's sake, I'm just talking about other names, other names by which you may have been known to the Revenue. I mean you must have worked before you became self-employed, so you must have tax records in the name of Cheetham, with some other district. I wish you'd mentioned this before!

ALISON: I want to go to the loo.

COLETTE: Because I don't think you have any idea how embattled I am. About your tax. And I can do without any complication of this nature.

ALISON: So could you turn the tape off?

COLETTE: Oh, cross your legs, you can hang on for two minutes. Just to get us back on track—we are concluding our conversation about the mysterious boxes Alison saw when she was eight—

ALISON: Or maybe nine, or ten.

COLETTE: —and these boxes were being carried by people she didn't know, men, and towards the back of her house, yes?

ALISON: Yes, towards the back, that's right. Down towards the fields. The open ground. And no, I don't know what was in them. Oh God, Colette, can you switch off? I really need the loo. And Morris is making such a racket. I don't know what was in those boxes, but sometimes I feel as if it's me. Does that make sense to you?

COLETTE: I think the big question is, will it make sense to our readers?

(*click*)

When Alison was at school, she had to keep My Diary. She was allowed to crayon what she did every day, as well as put words. She put about Keith and his face getting mashed. About the dog Blighto and the drag of his claws in the mud.

"Do we really want to know about this, Alison?" her teacher said.

Her mother was invited in to see the headmaster, but when she lit up he tapped the NO SMOKING sign perched on top of the typewriter on his desk.

"Yes, I can read," Emmeline said proudly, as she puffed away.

"I really think—" said he, and her mother said, "Look, you asked me here, so you've got to put up with it, is that right?" She tapped her ash into his wire in-tray. "You got a complaint about Alison, is that it?"

"It's not a question of complaint," the headmaster said.

"Oh, good," said her mum. "Because my daughter's as good as gold. So if you had any complaint, it'd be up to you to get it sorted. Otherwise I'd have to get you sorted, wouldn't I?"

"I'm not sure you quite grasp, Mrs. Cheetham—"

"I dare say," Al's mum said. "We know where your sort get off, smacking little girls' bottoms, I mean you wouldn't do it otherwise, it's not a man's job, is it?"

"Nothing of that kind—" the headmaster began.

Alison began to cry loudly.

"Shut it," her mother said casually. "So I'm just telling you, I don't like people writing to me. I don't like stuff coming through my door. Any more of it, and you'll be picking your teeth out of your typewriter." She took one last draw on her cigarette and dropped the stub on the carpet tiles. "I'm only saying."

• • •

By the time Al was in Mrs. Clerides's class, she'd rather not put pen to paper because of the risk that someone else would master the pen and write gibberish in her exercise book. "Gibberish" was what Mrs. Clerides called it, when she got her up to the front of the class and asked her if she were subnormal.

Mrs. Clerides read out Al's diary in a disgusted tone.

"Slurp, slurp, yum yum," said Harry. "Give us some," said Blighto. "No," said Harry. "Today it is all for me."

"It's a dog writing," Al explained. "It's Serene. She's the witness. She tells how Harry polished his bowl. When he'd done you could see your face in it."

"I don't believe I asked you to keep the diary of your pet," said Mrs. C.

"She's not a pet," Al said. "Bloody hell, Mrs. Clerides, she pays her way, we all have to pay. If you don't work you don't eat." Then she had gone quiet, thinking, the dogs' work is fighting, but what is the men's? They go about in vans. They say, what game am I in? I am in the entertainment game.

Mrs. Clerides slapped her legs. She made her write out something or other, fifty times, maybe a hundred. She couldn't remember what it was. Even when she was writing it she couldn't remember. She had to keep on reminding herself by looking back at the line before.

After that, if she'd got a few words down safely, she preferred to go over them with her blue ballpoint, branding the letters well into the paper: then drawing daisy petals around the "o"s and giving the "g"s little fishy faces. This was dull but it was better to be bored than to risk letting the gibberish in by an unguarded stroke, branching out into white space. It made her look occupied, and as long as she looked occupied she got left alone at the back with the mongols, the dummies, and the spastics.

The men said, the bloody little bitch. Is she sorry for what she's done? Because she don't look sorry, stuffing her face wiv sweets like that!

I am, I am, she said; but she couldn't remember what she ought to be sorry for. It had gone woolly in her mind, the way things do when they happen in the night.

The men said, she don't look sorry, Em! It's a wonder nobody's dead. We're going to take her down the back, and teach her a lesson she won't forget.

They didn't say what the lesson was. So after that she always wondered, have I had it? Or is it still to come?

By the time Al was ten, she had begun sleepwalking. She walked in on her mum, rolling on the sofa with a squaddie. The soldier raised his shaven head and roared. Her mother roared too, and her thin legs, blotched with fake tan, stood straight up into the air.

Next day her mum got the squaddie to fix a bolt on the outside of Al's bedroom door. He did it gladly, humming as he worked. You're the first man was ever handy around here, her mum said, is that right, Gloria?

Alison stood behind her bedroom door. She heard the bolt shunt into its bracket, with a small tight thud. The squaddie hummed, happy in his work. "I wish I was in Dixie, hooray, hooray"—*tap-tap*—"In Dixie Land I'll take my stand. . . ." Mum, she said, let us out. I can't breave. She ran to the window. They were walking down the road, laughing, the soldier swigging from a can of lager.

A few nights later she woke suddenly. It was very dark outside, as if they had been able to shut off the streetlamp. A number of ill-formed greasy faces were looking down on her. One of them seemed to be in Dixie, but she couldn't be sure. She closed her eyes. She felt herself lifted up. Then there was nothing, nothing that she remembers.

ALISON: So what puzzles me, and the only thing that makes me think it might have been a dream, was that darkness—because how did they switch the streetlamp off?

COLETTE: You slept in the front, did you?

ALISON: Initially in the back, because the front was the bigger bedroom so Mum had it, but then she swapped me, must have been after the dog bite, probably after Keef, I get the impression she didn't want me getting up in the night and looking out over the waste ground, which is possible because—

COLETTE: Al, face up to it. You didn't dream it. She had you molested. Probably sold tickets. God knows.

ALISON: I think I'd already been—that. What you say. Molested.

COLETTE: Do you?

ALISON: Just not in a group situation.

COLETTE: Alison, you ought to go to the police.

ALISON: It's years—

COLETTE: But some of those men could still be at large!

ALISON: It all gets mixed up in my mind. What happened. How old I was. Whether things happened once or whether they just went on happening—so they all rolled into one, you know.

COLETTE: So did you never tell anybody? Here. Blow your nose.

ALISON: No. . . . You see, you don't tell anybody because there's nobody to tell. You try and write it down, you write My Diary, but you get your legs slapped. Honestly. . . . It doesn't matter now, I don't think about it, it's only once in a while I think about it. I might have dreamed it, I used to dream I was flying. You see, you wipe out in the day what happens in the night. You have to. It's not as if it changed my life. I mean I've never gone in for sex much. Look at me, who'd want me, it'd need an army. So it's not as if I feel . . . it's not as if I remember. . . .

COLETTE: Your mother should have protected you. If she were my mum I'd kill her. Don't you sometimes think about it, going over to Aldershot and killing her?

ALISON: She lives in Bracknell now.

COLETTE: Wherever. Why does she live in Bracknell?

ALISON: She went off with a man who had a council house over there, but it never lasted, anyway, he went over into Spirit and somehow or other she ended up with the tenancy. She wasn't so bad. Isn't. I mean, you have to feel sorry for her. She's the size of a sparrow. In her looks, she's more like your mother than mine. I walked past her once in the street and didn't recognize her. She was always dyeing her hair. It was a different colour every week.

COLETTE: That's no excuse.

ALISON: And it never came out what she intended. Champagne Hi-Life, and she'd end up ginger. Chocolate Mousse, and she'd end up ginger. Same with her pills. She used to swap other people's prescriptions. I couldn't help but feel sorry for her. I wondered how she kept going.

COLETTE: These men—could you still identify them, do you think?

ALISON: Some of them. Maybe. If I saw them in a good light. But they can't arrest them after they're passed.

COLETTE: If they're dead I'm not worried. If they're dead they can't do any more damage.

When Al was twelve or so, she got cheeky. She said to her mum, "That one last night, what was *his* name then? Or don't you know?"

Her mum tried to slap her around the head but she overbalanced and fell on the floor. Al helped her up.

"Thank you, you're a good girl, Al," her mum said, and Al's cheeks burned, because she had never heard that before.

"What you on, Mum?" she asked. "What you taking?"

Her mum took a lot of Librium and a lot of Bacardi, which does make you fall over. Every week, though, she gave something else a try; it usually worked out, like the hair dye, to have a result she had not foreseen but should have.

Al had to go to the chemist for her mum's prescriptions. "Are you here again?" said the man behind the counter, and because she was going through her brusque phase she would say, it's me or somebody else, what's your opinion? "My God," he said. "I can't believe she gets through this. Is she selling it on? Come on, you're a bright girl, you must know."

"She swallows it all," she said. "I swear it."

The man sniggered. "Swallows, does she? You don't say."

This remark mocked her; but still, when she left the pharmacy she felt ten feet tall. You're a bright girl, she said to herself. She stared at herself in the next shop window: which was Ash Vale Motor Sport. The window was crammed with all the stuff you need for hacking across country with crappy old cars: sump guards, fog lamps, snow chains, and the latest model in a hi-lift jack. Swimming above this equipment was her own face, the face of a bright girl—a good girl, too—swimming in the oily glass.

By this time she had spent years pretending she was normal. She was never able to judge what other people knew and what they didn't know. Take Gloria: Gloria had been clear enough to her mother, but not to her. Yet her mother hadn't seen Mrs. McGibbet, and she'd almost skated across the attic, putting her foot on one of Brendan's toy cars. And then one day—was it after Keith got mashed, was it after she got her scissors, was it before Harry cleaned his bowl?—one day she'd caught a glimpse of a red-haired lady with false eyelashes, standing at the foot of the stairs. Gloria, she thought, at last; she said, "Hi, are you all right?" but the woman didn't reply. Another day, as she was coming in at the front door, she had glanced down into the bath, and didn't she see the red-haired lady looking up at her, with her eyelashes half pulled off, and no body attached to her neck?

But that was not possible. They wouldn't just leave a head on full view for passersby. You kept things under wraps; wasn't that the rule?

What else was the rule? Was she, Alison, seeing more or less than she ought? Should she mention it, when she heard a woman sobbing in the wall? When should you shout up and when should you shut up? Was she stupid, or was that other people? And what would she do when she left school?

Tahera was going to do social studies. She didn't know what that was. She and Tahera went shopping on Saturdays, if her mother let her out. Tahera shopped while she watched. Tahera was size six. She was four foot ten, brown, and quite spotty. Al herself was not much taller than that, but she was size eighteen. Tahera said, "You would be welcome to my castoffs, but—you know." She looked Alison up and down, and her tiny nostrils flared.

When she asked her mother for money, her mother said, "What you want you got to earn, is that right Gloria? You're not so bad, Al, you've got that lovely complexion, okay you're fleshy but that's what a lot of men like. You're what we call two handfuls of bubbly fun. Now you didn't ought to hang around with that Indian bint, it puts the punters off, they don't like to think some Patel's after 'em with a Stanley knife."

"Her name's not Patel."

"All right, young lady! That's enough from you." Her mother hurtled across the kitchen in a Librium rage. "How long you expect me to keep you fed and housed, how long, eh? Lie on your back and take it, that's what I had to do. And regular! Not just Oh-it's-Thursday-I-don't-feel-like-it. You can forget that caper, miss! That sort of attitude will get you nowhere. Make it regular, and start charging proper. That's what you've got to do. How else you think you're going to make a living?"

COLETTE: So how did you feel, Alison, when you first knew you had psychic powers?

ALISON: I never . . . I mean I never really did. There wasn't a moment. How can I put it? I didn't know what I saw, and what I just imagined. It—you see, it's confusing, when the people you grow up with are always coming and going at night. And always with hats on.

COLETTE: Hats?

ALISON: Or their collars pulled up. Disguises. Changing their names. I remember once, I must have been twelve, thirteen, I came in from school and I thought the house was empty for once; I thought, thank Christ for that; I thought I might make some toast then do a bit of cleaning while they were all gone out. I walked through to the lean-to, and I looked up and this geezer was standing there—not doing anything, just standing there leaning against the sink—and he had a box of matches in his hand. Christ, he was evil-looking! I mean, they all were, but there was something about him, his expression. . . . I can tell you, Colette, he was in a league of his own. He just stared at me and I stared back at him, and I thought I'd seen him before, and you have to make conversation, don't you, even if you suddenly feel as if you're going to throw up? So I said, are you the one they call Nick? He said, no, love, I'm a burglar, and I said, go on, you *are* Nick. He flew into a temper. He rattled the matchbox and it was empty. He threw it down. He went, can't even get a light around here, I'm going to sack the flaming lot of them, they're not worth a bench in hell. He whipped his belt out of his trousers and lashed out at me.

COLETTE: What happened then?

ALISON: I ran out into the street.

COLETTE: Did he follow you?
ALISON: I expect so.

Al was fourteen. Fifteen perhaps. No spots still. She seemed immune to them. She had grown a bit, all ways, up and out. Her tits came around the corner before she did; or that's what one of the men remarked.

She said to her mother, "Who's my dad?"

Her mother said, "What you want to know that for?"

"People ought to know who they are."

Her mother lit another cigarette.

"I bet you don't know," Al said. "Why did you bother to have me? I bet you tried to get rid of me, didn't you?"

Her mother exhaled, blowing the smoke down her nose in two disdainful and separate streams. "We all tried. But you was stuck fast, you silly bitch."

"You should have gone to the doctor."

"Doctor?" Her mother's eyes rolled up. "Listen to her! Doctor! Bloody doctor, they didn't want to know. I was five, six months gone when MacArthur buggered off, and then I'd have shifted you all right, but there wasn't any bloody shifting."

"MacArthur? Is that my dad?"

"How should I know?" her mother said. "What you bloody asking me for? What you want to know for anyway? What you don't know can't hurt you. Mind your own bloody business."

Seeing Gloria's head in the bath was more worrying to her, somehow, than seeing Gloria entire. From the age of eight, nine, ten, she told Colette, she used to see disassembled people lying around, a leg here, an arm there. She couldn't say precisely when it started, or what brought it on. Or whether they were bits of people she knew.

If you could understand what those years were like, she told Colette, you'd think I'm quite a triumph really, the way I keep myself together. When I walk out onstage I love it, when I've got my dress, my hair done, my opals, and my pearls that I wear in the summer. It's for them, for the audience, but it's for me too.

She knew there was this struggle in a woman's life—at least, there had been in her mum's—just to be whole, to be clean, to be tidy, to keep your own teeth in your head; just to have a clean tidy house and not fag ash dropped everywhere and bottle tops underfoot: not to find yourself straying out into the street with no tights on. That's why nowadays she can't bear fluff on the carpet or a chip in her nail polish; that's why she's a fanatic about depilation, why she's always pestering the dentist about cavities he can't see yet; why she takes two baths a day, sometimes a shower as well; why she puts her special scent on every day. Maybe it's an old-fashioned choice, but it was the first grown-up scent she bought for herself, as soon as she could afford one. Mrs. Etchells had remarked at the time, "Oh, that's lovely, it's your signature perfume." The house at Aldershot smelled of male farts, stale sheets, and something else, not quite identifiable. Her mother said the smell had been there ever since they took the floorboards up: "Keith and them, you know, that crowd what used to drink down the Phoenix? What did they want to do that for, Gloria? Why did they want to take the floorboards up? Men, honestly! You never know what they'll be up to next."

Al told Colette, "One day I saw an eye looking at me. A human eye. It used to roll along the street. One day it followed me to school."

"What, like 'Mary Had a Little Lamb'?"

"Yes, but it felt more like a dog." Al shivered. "And then one day, one morning when I was leaving the house. . . ."

One day—she was in her school-leaving year—Al came out in the morning and saw a man watching her from the door of the chemist's shop. His hands were plunged into his trouser pockets and he was jiggling an unlit cigarette between his lips.

COLETTE: It wasn't this Nick character? The one in the kitchen, the one who chased you with the belt?

ALISON: No, it wasn't Nick.

COLETTE: But you had seen him before?

ALISON: Yes, yes, I had. But can we switch the tape off, please? Morris is threatening me. He doesn't like me talking about the early days. He doesn't want it recorded.

That same afternoon, she came out of school with Lee Tooley and Catherine Tattersall. Tahera herself was close behind, linking arms with Nicky Scott and Andrea Wossname. Tahera was still rich, small, and spotty—and now bespectacled, since her dad, she said, had "read me the riot act." Catherine had ginger curls and she was the girl who was most far behind in every subject, even farther behind than Alison. Lee was Catherine's friend.

Morris was on the other side of the road, leaning against the window of the launderette. His eyes travelled over the girls. She went cold.

He was short, a dwarf nearly, like a jockey, and his legs were bowed like a jockey's. She learned later he'd been more like normal height, at least five foot six, till his legs had been broken: in one of his circus feats, he'd said at first, but later he admitted it was in a gang feud.

"Come on," she said. "Come on, Andrea. Hurry up. Come on, Lee."

Then, because she was cold, she zipped up her jacket, her cherry-red jacket that only just covered her chest. "Ooh, spastic!" Lee said, because it was not the style to fasten your jacket. The whole group began its shuffling, swaying sideways procession down the street; there seemed nothing she could do to hurry them. The girls walked with their arms folded, hugging themselves. Lee, in a spirit of mockery, did the same. A radio played somewhere, it was playing an Elton John song. She remembered that. The kids began to sing. She tried, but her mouth was dry.

COLETTE: So was he—I feel I'm a bit in the dark here—this man who was watching you outside the school: are we talking about Morris? And was he the man with the yellow face?

ALISON: Yes.

COLETTE: The man you saw behind you, through the mirror? The low hairline?

ALISON: His tie not on straight.

Next day, when she came out, he was there again. I'll go on the aggressive, she thought. She nudged Tahera. "Look at that pervert."

"Where?"

Alison nodded across the road to where Morris leaned, just as he had the day before. Tahera attracted Nicky Scott's attention by kicking her lightly on the back of her calf. "Gerroff me, you bloody bhaji!" Nicky bellowed.

"Can you see any pervert?" Tahera asked.

They looked around them. They followed where Alison pointed and then they swivelled their heads from side to side in an exaggerated fashion. Then they turned in circles, crying out, "Where, where?"—except for Catherine, who hadn't caught on, and just started singing like yesterday. Then they lolled their tongues out and retched, because they confused a perv with a sicko, then they ran off and left her alone in the street.

Morris lurched away from the wall and came limping towards her. He ignored the traffic, and a van must have missed him by inches. He could limp very fast; he seemed to scuttle like some violent crab, and when he reached her he fastened his crab hand onto her arm above the elbow. She flinched and twisted in his grasp, but he held her firmly. Get off me, she was crying, you horrible pervert, but then, as so often, she realized that words were coming out of her mouth but no one could hear them.

After Al's first meeting with Morris, he waited for her most days. "I'm a gentleman, I am," he would boast, "and I am here to escort you. A growing girl like you, you don't want to be out walking the streets on your own. Anything could happen."

In the early days, he didn't follow her into the house. He seemed nervous about who might be in there. As they turned at the corner of the street he would say, "Nick bin in?"

She would say no, and he'd say, "Just as well, never know where you are wiv Nick, if you see Nick you walk the other way, you hear? You don't try any of your tricks round Nick, or he'll upend you, he'll slap you on the soles of your feet till your teeth drop out." Then he would brighten up: "What about Aitkenside, you seen Aitkenside?"

She'd say, "Dunno, what's his other name? Dunno who you mean."

He'd say, "Much you don't, oh, very likely. Pikey Pete been round?"

"I told you," she said, "I don't know who your friends are or what they're called."

But Morris sneered at this. "Not know Pete? The whole country knows him. Wherever there is dealing in dogs they know Pete."

"I don't deal in dogs." She remembered the grown-up coldness of her voice.

"Oh, pardon me, I'm sure! You don't deal with any of my mates, is it? You don't deal with 'em in any way, shape, or form, is it?" He grumbled under his breath. "You're not your mother's daughter, I suppose. Not know Pete? Wherever there is dealing in horses, they know Pete."

When he got to the front gate, he would say, "Emmie not moved that old bath yet?"

She'd say, "Have you known my mum a long time?"

He'd say, "I'll say I have. Known Emmie Cheetham? I'll say I have. Know everybody, me. I know Donnie. I know Pete. Emmie Cheetham? I'll say I have."

One day she said, "Morris, are you my dad?"

And he said "Dad, me, that's a good one! Did she say so?"

"I think MacArthur's my dad."

"MacArthur!" he said. He stopped. She stopped too, and looked into his face. He had turned grey: greyer than usual. His voice came out wobbly. "You can stand there, and say that name?"

"Why not?"

"Cool as a bloody cucumber," Morris said. He spoke to the air, as if he were talking to an audience. "Butter wouldn't melt in her mouf."

They staggered along the street, a pace or two, Morris's hand clamped on her arm. She saw Lee and Catherine going by on the other side of the road. She waved to them to rescue her but they made vomity faces at her and walked on. She didn't know if they could see Morris or not. Under his breath he was muttering.

"MacArthur, she says! Cool as you like." He stopped and propped himself against the wall with his free hand, his bent fingers spread out. He had a tattoo of a snake running down his arm; now its head, darting across the back of his hand, seemed to gulp, and pulse out its tongue. Morris too made a vomity face and retched.

She was afraid of what might come out of his mouth, so she concentrated on his hand, planted against the brick.

"Speak the name of MacArthur!" He mimicked her voice. "*I think he's my dad.* Suppose he is? Is that how you treat a dad? Is it? Got to hand it to her, she has some cheek, that girl."

"How?" she said. "How did I treat him?"

The head pulsed, the snake's tongue flicked out between his spread fingers. "I'll tell you something about that bugger," he said. "I'll tell you something you don't know. MacArthur owes me money. And so if I ever see MacArthur in this neck of the woods, I'll saw him off at the bloody knees. Let the bloody bastard venture, just let him. I'll poke out his *other* eye."

"Has MacArthur only one eye?"

"Oh, tee-bloody-hee," Morris said. "Still, girl, you got paid out. You got a lesson, eh? They taught you what a blade could do."

"I hope you're not," she said. "I hope you're not my dad. I like you worst of anybody. I don't want you anywhere near me. You stink of fags and beer."

"I bin near you," Morris said. "We all have."

COLETTE: But after that, when Morris came along, you must have known that other people couldn't see him, I mean you must have realized that you had psychic powers.

ALISON: You see, I was ignorant. I didn't know what a spirit guide was. Until I met Mrs. Etchells, I had no idea—

COLETTE: We're going to go into that, aren't we? Mrs. Etchells?

ALISON: When?

COLETTE: Tonight, if you've got the stamina.

ALISON: Can we eat first?

(*click*)

Pity Colette, who had to transcribe all this. "When you're talking about Gloria," she said, "I never know if she's alive or dead."

"No," Al said. "Nor me."

"But it worries me. I need to get it straight—for the book."

"I'm telling you what I know."

Was she? Or was she leaving things out? Sparing Colette's feelings in some way, or testing her memory?

"These awful blokes," Colette said, "all these fiends from Aldershot. I keep losing track of their names. Make me a list."

Alison took a sheet of paper and wrote FIENDS FROM ALDERSHOT. "Let's see . . . Donnie Aitkenside," she said.

"The one who said he'd beat up your teacher?"

"Yes . . . well, and rape her, I think he was going to rape her too. There was MacArthur. Morris reckoned MacArthur was worse than most, but I dunno. There was Keith Capstick, that pulled the dog off me. And I thought he was my dad because he did that. But was he? I dunno."

When she talks about them, Colette thought, she slips away somewhere: to a childhood country, where diction is slipshod. She said, "Al, are you writing this down?"

"You can see I'm not."

"You wander off the point. Just make the list."

Al sucked her pen. "There was this Pikey character, who was a horse dealer. I think he had relatives, cousins, up and down the country, you used to hear him talk about them, they might have come by but I don't really know. And somebody called Bob Fox?"

"Don't ask me! Get it on paper! What did he do, Bob Fox?"

"He tapped on the window. At my mum's house. He did it to make you jump."

"What else? He must have done something else?"

"Dunno. Don't think he did. Then there was Nick, of course. The one with the empty matchbox, in the kitchen. Oh, wait, I remember now. Oh God, yes. I know where I saw him before. We had to go and collect him from the cop shop. They'd picked him up on the street, falling-down drunk. But they didn't want to charge him, they just let him sober up, then they wanted rid of him because he'd put slime on the cell walls."

"Slime?"

"And they didn't want a heavy cleaning job. He was just lying there sliming everything, you see. He didn't want to come out, so my mum had to go down and get him. They said—the police—they'd found her phone number in his wallet, so they sent a car to fetch her in, then she had to go down the cells. The desk sergeant said, a woman's touch, tee-hee. He was being sarcastic. He said, he'll be able to go now, won't he, now he's got his bike? My mum said, watch your lip, Little Boy Blue, or I'll fatten it for you. He said, leave that kid here, you can't take her down the cells. And my mum said, what, leave her here, so you can bloody touch her up? So she took me down to get Nick."

Colette felt faint. "I wish I'd never started this," she said.

"He came out on the street and he shouted, can't I get drunk, same as anybody? My mum was trying to calm him down. She says, come back to our house."

"And did he?"

"I expect. Look, Col, it was a long time ago."

Colette wanted to ask, what *kind* of slime was it, on the cell walls? But then again, she didn't want to ask.

COLETTE: Okay, so it's eleven-thirty.

ALISON: P.M., that is.

COLETTE: —and we're about to resume—

ALISON: —as I've now had a bottle of Crozes-Hermitage and feel able to continue reminiscing about my teenage years—

COLETTE: Al!

ALISON: —whereas Colette has had a Slimline Tonic and on the basis of this feels she has the courage to switch on the machine.

COLETTE: My uncle used to tickle me.

ALISON: You mean, your dad?

COLETTE: Yes, come to think of it. My dad. It wasn't ordinary tickling. . . .

ALISON: It's all right, take your time.

COLETTE: I mean it was aggressive, stabbing at you with a finger—a man's finger, you know, it's as thick as that—and I was little, and he knew it hurt me. Oh, God, and Gav used to do it. His idea of a joke. Maybe that's why I went and married him. It seemed familiar.

ALISON: Sounds classic to me, marrying a man with the same sense of humour as your father. I hear about it all the time.

COLETTE: I didn't laugh when he did it. It was more—you know, convulsing. As if I were having a fit.

ALISON: That must have been a pretty sight.

COLETTE: He stabbed into me with his finger, between my thin little ribs. It was like—it really was—the way he'd come at me, sticking it out. . . . Oh, I don't think I can say it.

ALISON: It's not like you to be coy.

COLETTE: As if he was rehearsing me.

ALISON: Giving you a practice for your later life. (*pause*) I suppose that's what dads are for. Here, do you want a tissue?

COLETTE: Let's get back on track. You need an early night, you've got a client phoning for tarot before her breakfast meeting. Mrs. Etchells, you were going to fill me in about Mrs. Etchells.

ALISON: You see, I got to the point where I wanted money of my own. I thought, if I saved up, I could get on the train at Ash Vale and just go somewhere, I wouldn't have minded where. So, the way it was, Mrs. Etchells got me started. You see, one day I was leaning on her front hedge, bawling my eyes out, because Nicky Scott and Catherine and them—because these girls, my friends, at least they were supposed to be my friends—

COLETTE: Yes?

ALISON: They'd been calling me spastic all afternoon, because in English I'd had this—sort of incident. It was Morris really started it off; he'd come in halfway through English and said, oh, William bloody Shakespeare is it? Bloody Bill Wagstaffe, Bill Crankshaft, I know that cove, *he's* dead, he is, or so he claims, and he owes me a fiver. We were doing *Romeo and Juliet* and he said, I seen that Juliet, she's dead, and she's no better than she should be, a right slapper let me tell you. So then I knew he was lying, because Juliet's a fictional character. But at first, you see, I believed him about things. I didn't know what to believe.

COLETTE: Yes, and?

ALISON: So then he squashed up in the chair next to me, because Nicky Scott and Catherine and all that lot, they weren't bothering with me and they were leaving me to sit on my own. He put his hand on my knee—above my knee, really, squeezing—and I couldn't help it, I squealed out. And he was saying, I'll tell you another thing about that Juliet—her mother was at it before she was out of ankle socks, she was no slouch on the couch. Remind you of home, does it, remind you of home sweet home? And he started pulling my skirt up. And I was trying to pull it down and push his hands away, I was slapping at him but it didn't do any good. And Mr. Naysmith said to me, excuse me for intruding on your private reverie, but I don't think I have your undivided attention, Alison. Just then I couldn't stand it and it all came out in a rush, I was crying and swearing and shouting "piss off, you perv," and "bugger off back where you came from." So Mr. Naysmith looking like thunder came belting down the class towards me, and I shout, keep your filthy pervvy hands to yourself. And he got hold of me by the back of my neck. Well, they did. In those days. At my school, anyway. They weren't allowed to cane you but they used to get hold of you in a painful way. And he dragged me off to the headmaster. . . . So I got suspended. Excluded, they call it now. For making accusations against Mr. Naysmith. You see, I was wailing, he was pulling up my skirt, he was pulling up my skirt. And in those days they didn't have sexual abuse, so nobody believed me, whereas these days nobody would believe him.

COLETTE: So how does this fit in with Mrs. Etchells?

ALISON: What?

COLETTE: You said you were leaning on her hedge crying.

ALISON: Yes, that's it, because they'd been tormenting me you see. I didn't care about getting suspended—it was a relief really—they said they'd be calling my mum in but I knew they wouldn't because the headmaster was too frightened of her. Anyway, Mrs. Etchells spotted me and she came running out, she said leave off, girls, why ever are you tormenting poor Alison like that? And I was surprised that she knew my name.

COLETTE: And who was Mrs. Etchells? I mean I know she taught you all you know—you've said so several times—but, you know, who was she?

ALISON: My gran, or so she said.

COLETTE: What?

(*click*)

COLETTE: This is Colette, resuming the session at twelve-thirty. Alison, you were telling us about your reunion with your grandmother.

ALISON: Yes, but it wasn't like that, good God, it wasn't like *This Is Your Life*, and your gran walks in smiling through her bloody tears. I don't know why you put these questions on the tape, Colette. I've just told you how it was.

COLETTE: Oh, for the fifteenth bloody time, it's to have a record—

ALISON: All right, all right, but let me tell it my way, will you? She took me in and made me beans on toast. And do you know it was the first time I ever—I mean, my mum used to get distracted, so the beans and the toast came separate, you'd have your beans at five o'clock and then she'd look at you about ten past and she'd say, oh, you didn't get your toast yet, did you? You know when you go to a café, like on the motorway, and they have those big laminated menus with pictures of the food on? I used to wonder what for, I mean, why do they do that, the food doesn't look like that when it comes, it's all huge and colored in the menus but in real life it's all shrunken up and sick-coloured. Well, the reason they do that—this is what I think—is to help people like my mum, because they don't know what food goes with what. When she'd got some man staying over, one she liked, she'd say, oh, I'm making a big Sunday, by which she meant a big Sunday lunch, but when it came he'd be, what's this, Emmie? I mean, chicken and cauliflower, with white sauce out of a packet.

COLETTE: And mash?

ALISON: No, that would be later, that would come along at teatime. And she'd go to the corner and get curry—that was her idea of making lunch—she'd say, what you complaining about, I paid for it myself, didn't I?

COLETTE: I really don't want to interrupt your flow . . .

ALISON: So that's why they have the pictures, to stop people like my mum ordering a fried egg with their chicken. And make sure they assemble all the bits of their meal at the same time.

COLETTE: And Mrs. Etchells—

ALISON: Made me beans *on* toast. Which made her a winner in my eyes, I mean I was always hungry then, I think that's why I'm big now.

COLETTE: Just leaving that issue aside for the moment—

ALISON: She said, come in dear; sit down, tell me all about it. So I did. Because I had nobody to confide in. And I cried a lot, and it all came pouring out. Tehera. Lee. Mr. Naysmith. Morris. Everything.

COLETTE: And what did she say?

ALISON: Well, the thing was she seemed to understand. She just sat there nodding. When I'd finished she said, you see, like grandmother like granddaughter. I said, what? It's descended to you, she said, my gift, missing out Derek, probably because he was a man. I said, who's Derek, she said, my son Derek. Your dad, darling; well, he could be anyway."

COLETTE: She only said, could be?

ALISON: All I thought was, thank God, so it wasn't Morris. I said, so, if Derek's my dad, and you're my nan, why isn't my name Etchells? She said, because he ran off before your mam could waltz him down the aisle. Not that I blame him there. I said, it's surprising I wasn't drawn to you. She said, you was, in a manner of speaking, because you was always leaning against my hedge with your young friends. And today, she said, I reckon that today you see, something drew you. You were in trouble, so you came to your nan.

COLETTE: That's quite sad, really. You mean she'd been living down the road all the time?

ALISON: She said she didn't like to interfere. She said, your mam minds her own business, and of course the whole neighbourhood knows what that business is—which was no surprise to me, you know, because I'd understood for quite some time why when a bloke went out he put a tenner on the sideboard.

COLETTE: And so, you and Mrs. Etchells, did you become close at this point?

ALISON: I used to go and do little errands for her. Carrying her shopping, because her knees were bad. Running for fags for her, not that she smoked like my mum. I always called her Mrs. Etchells, I didn't like to start calling her Nan, I wasn't sure if I ought. I asked my mother about Derek, and she just laughed. She said, she's not on that old story again, is she? Bloody cloud-cuckoo land.

COLETTE: So she didn't actually confirm it? Or deny it?

ALISON: No. She threw the salt pot at me. So . . . end of that conversation. The way Mrs. Etchells told it, Derek and my mum were going to get married, but he took off after he found out what she was like (*laughter*). Probably (*laughter*) probably she whizzed him up some of her tandoori prawns with tinned spaghetti. Oh God, she has no idea at all about nutrition, that woman. No idea of what constitutes a balanced meal.

COLETTE: Yes, can we get on to how you came to turn professional?

ALISON: When I got towards school-leaving, Mrs. Etchells said it's time we had a talk, she said, there's advantages and disadvantages to the life—

COLETTE: And did she say what they were, in her opinion?

ALISON: She said, why not use your God-given talent? But then she said, you come in for a great deal of name-calling and disbelief, and I can't pretend that your colleagues in the profession are going to welcome you with open arms—which indeed I did find to be the case, as you know yourself, Colette, to your cost, because you know what they were like when I introduced you as my assistant. She said, of course, you could try to act as if you were normal, and I said I'd give it a try, though it never worked at school. I got a job in a chemist in Farnborough. Temporary sales assistant. It was more temporary than they meant, of course.

COLETTE: What happened?

ALISON: Catherine and Nicky Scott would come in, they hadn't got jobs, they were on the social. When he saw them, Morris would start fiddling around with the contraceptives. Taking them out of their packets and strewing them around. Blowing them up like balloons. Naturally they thought it was me. They thought it was the sort of thing a sixteen-year-old would do—you know, have her mates in and have a laugh. So that was that. Then Mrs. Etchells got me a job at a cake shop.

COLETTE: And what happened there?

ALISON: I started eating the cakes.

When Alison decided to change her name she rang up her mother in Bracknell to ask if she would be offended. Emmie sighed. She sounded frayed and far away. "I can't think what would be a good name in your line of country," she said.

"Where are you?" Alison said. "You're fading away."

"In the kitchen," said Emmie. "It's the cigs, I can't seem to give up no matter what. Do my voice in."

"I'm glad I don't smoke," Alison said. "It wouldn't be very professional."

"Huh. Professional," said Emmie. "You, a professional. That's a laugh."

Alison thought, I may as well change the whole thing while I'm about it. I don't have to stick with any part of my old self. She went to a bookshop and bought one of those books for naming babies.

"Congratulations," said the woman behind the till.

Alison smoothed down the front of her dress. "I'm not, actually," she said. Sonia Hart. Melissa Hart. Susanna Hart. It didn't work. She managed to lose Cheetham, but her baptismal name kept sliding back into her life. It was part of her, like Morris was.

Over the next few years she had to get used to life with Morris. When her mum went off to Bracknell she made it clear she didn't want a daughter trailing after her, so Al got a temporary billet with Mrs. Etchells. Morris no longer stopped at the gate. He came inside and exploded the lightbulbs, and disarranged Mrs. Etchell's china cabinet. "He is a one!" said Mrs. Etchells.

It was only when she got older and moved among a different set of psychics that she realized how vulgar and stupid Morris really was. Other mediums have spirit guides with a bit more about them—dignified impassive medicine men or ancient Persian sages—but she had this grizzled grinning apparition in a bookmaker's checked jacket, and suede shoes with bald toe caps. A typical communication from Sett or Oz or Running Deer would be, "The way to open the heart is to release yourself from expectation." But a typical communication from Morris would be: "Oh, pickled beetroot, I like a nice bit of pickled beetroot. Make a nice sandwich out of pickled beetroot!"

At first she thought that by an effort of will and concentration, she would make him keep his distance. But if she resists Morris, there is a buildup of pressure in her cheekbones and her teeth. There is a crawling feeling inside her spine, which is like slow torture; sooner or later you have to give in, and listen to what he's saying.

On days when she really needs a break she tries to imagine a big lid, banging down on him. It works for a time. His voice booms, hollow and incomprehensible, inside a huge metal tub. For a while she doesn't have to take any notice of him. Then, little by little, an inch at a time, he begins to raise the lid.

five

It was in the week after Diana's death that Colette felt she got to know Alison properly. It seems another era now, another world: before the millennium, before the Queen's Jubilee, before the Twin Towers burned.

Colette had moved into Al's flat in Wexham, which Alison had described to her as "the nice part of Slough," though, she added, "most people don't think Slough has a nice part."

On the day she moved in, she took a taxi from the station. The driver was young, dark, smiling, and spry. He tried to catch her eye through the rearview mirror, from which dangled a string of prayer beads. Her eyes darted away. She was not prejudiced, but. Inside the cab was an eye-watering reek of air freshener.

They drove out of town, always uphill. He seemed to know where he was going. Once Slough was left behind, it seemed to her they were travelling to nowhere. The houses ran out. She saw fields, put to no particular use. They were not farms, she supposed. There were not, for instance, crops in the fields. Here and there, a pony grazed. There were structures for the pony to jump over; there were hedgerows. She saw the sprawl of buildings from a hospital, Wexham Park. Some squat quaint cottages fronted the road. For a moment, she worried; did Al live in the country? She had not said anything about the country. But before she could really get her worrying under way, the driver swerved into the gravel drive of a small neat seventies-built apartment block, set well back from the road. Its shrubberies were clipped and tame; it looked reassuringly suburban. She stepped out. The driver opened the boot and lugged out her two suitcases. She gazed up at the front of the building. Did Al live here, looking out over the road? Or would she face the back? For a moment she struck herself as a figure of pathos. She was a brave young woman on the threshold of a new life. Why is that sad? she wondered. Her eyes fell on the suitcases. That is why; because I can carry all I own. Or the taxi driver can.

She paid him. She asked for a receipt. Her mind was already moving ahead, to Al's accounts, her business expenses. The first thing I shall do, she thought, is bump up her prices. Why should people expect a conversation with the dead for the price of a bottle of wine and a family-size pizza?

The driver ripped a blank off the top of his pad, and offered it to her, bowing. "Could you fill it in?" she said. "Signed and dated."

"Of what amount shall I put?"

"Just the figure on the meter."

"Home sweet home?"

"I'm visiting a friend."

He handed back the slip of paper, with an extra blank receipt beneath. Cabman's flirtation; she handed back the blank.

"These flats, two-bedroom?"

"I think so."

"En suite? How much you've paid for yours?"

Is this what passes for multicultural exchange? she wondered. Not that she was prejudiced. At least it's to the point. "I told you, I don't live here."

He shrugged, smiled. "You have a business card?"

"No." Has Alison got one? Do psychics have cards? She thought, it will be uphill work, dragging her into the business world.

"I can drive you at any time," the man said. "Just call this number."

He passed over his own card. She squinted at it. God, she thought, I'll need glasses soon. Several numbers were crossed out in blue ink and a mobile number written in. "Cell phone," he said. "You can just try me day or night."

He left her at the door, drove away. She glanced up again. I hope there's room for me, she thought. I shall have to be very neat. But then, I am. Was Alison looking down, watching her arrive? No, she wouldn't need to look out of the window. If someone arrived she would just know.

Al's flat was at the back, it turned out. She was ready with the door open. "I thought you'd be waiting," Colette said.

Alison blushed faintly. "I have very sharp earsight. I mean, hearing—well, the whole package." Yet there was nothing sharp about her. Soft and smiling, she seemed to have no edges. She reached out for Colette and pulled her resistant frame against her own. "I hope you'll be happy. Do you think you can be happy? Come in. It's bigger than you'd think."

She glanced around the interior. Everything low, squarish, beige. Everything light, safe. "All the kit's in the hall cupboard," Al said. "The crystals and whatnots."

"Is it okay to keep it in there?"

"It's better in the dark. Tea, coffee?"

Colette asked for herbal tea. No more meat, she thought, or cakes. She wanted to be pure.

While she was unpacking, Al brought in a green soupy beverage in a white china mug. "I didn't know how you liked it," she said, "so I left the bag in." She took the cup carefully, her fingertips touching Al's. Al smiled. She clicked the door shut, left her to herself.

The bed was made up, a double bed. Big bouncy duvet in a plain cream cover. She turned the duvet back. The sheet was crisply ironed. High standards: good. She'd seen enough squalor. She picked up her wash bag. Found herself in Al's bathroom—Al hovering and saying, rather guilty, just push up my things and put yours down—shall I leave you to do that? Another tea?

She stared around. *Floris*, indeed. Is she rich or just in need of a great deal of comfort? It's better than we had, she thinks, me and Gavin. She thought of their second-floor conversion, with the clanking and erratic central heating, the sudden icy draughts.

"Come through. Make yourself at home." There were two sofas, square and tweedy; Al flopped onto one, a stack of glossies beside her, and indicated that Colette should join her. "I thought you might like to look at my advert."

She picked up one of the magazines. "Flick through from the back and you'll see me."

She turned back, past the horoscopes. For once she didn't pause to glance at her own. Why keep a dog and bark yourself? Alison's photograph was a beaming smudge on the page.

Alison, psychic since birth. Private consultations. Professional and caring. Relationships, business, health. Spiritual guidance.

"Are people willing to travel to Slough?"

"Once you explain to them it's the nice part. I do telephone consultations, if need be, though given a choice I like to look the sitter in the eye."

"Videophones," Colette said. "Can't be long now. It will make all the difference."

"I can travel to them, if the price is right. I will if I think it's going to be a long-term arrangement. I rely on my regulars, it's where most of my income is. Do you think it's all right, the ad?"

"No. It should be in colour. And bigger. We have to invest." Above it was a listing for cosmetic surgery, displaying BEFORE and AFTER pictures. There was a woman with a sagging jawline who looked, in the second picture, as if she'd been slapped under the chin by a giant. A woman with skin flaps for breasts had sprouted two vast globules; their nipples stood out like the whistles on a life jacket. Below the pictures—

Alison bounced across the sofa towards her, causing the frame to creak. "Surprisingly sleazy, these journals," Al said. She laid her long painted nail on an advert for Sex Advice, with a number to call after each item. "Lesbian anal fun. Did you know lesbians had anal fun?"

"No," Colette said, in a voice as distant as she could manage. Al's scent washed over her in a great wave of sweetness. "I don't know, I mean, I've never thought. I don't know anything about it."

"Neither do I," Al said. Colette thought, *Spicy lesbo chicks.* Al patted her shoulder; she froze. "That was not fun," Al said. "That was reassurance." She dropped her head and her hair slid forward, hiding her smile. "I just thought we'd get the topic out of the way. So we both know where we stand."

The room had magnolia walls, corded beige carpet, a coffee table that was simply a low featureless expanse of pale wood. But Al kept her tarot cards in a sea-grass basket, wrapped in a yard of scarlet silk, and when she unwrapped and spilled its length onto the table, it looked as if some bloody incident had occurred.

August. She woke: Al stood in the door of her room. The landing light was on. Colette sat up. "What time is it? Al? What's the matter, has something happened?"

The light shone through Al's lawn nightdress, illuminating her huge thighs. "We must get ready," she said: as if they were catching an early flight. She approached and stood by the bed.

Colette reached up and took her sleeve. It was a pinch of nothingness between her fingers.

"It's Diana," Al said. "Dead."

Always, Colette would say later, she would remember the shiver that ran through her: like a cold electric current, like an eel.

Al gave a snort of jeering laughter. "Or as we say, passed."

"Suicide?"

"Or accident. She won't tell me. Teasing to the last," Al said. "Though probably not quite the last. From our point of view."

Colette jumped out of bed. She pulled her T-shirt down over her thighs. Then she stood and stared at Alison; she didn't know what else to do. Al turned and went downstairs, pausing to turn up the central heating. Colette ran after her.

"I'm sure it will be clearer," Al said, "when it actually happens."

"What do you mean? You mean it hasn't happened yet?" Colette ran a hand through her hair, and it stood up, a pale fuzzy halo. "Al, we must do something!"

"Like?"

"Warn somebody! Call the police! Telephone the queen?"

Al raised a hand. "Quiet, please. She's getting in the car. She's putting her seat belt—no, no, she isn't. They're larking about. Not a care in the world. Why are they going that way? Dear, dear, they're all over the road!"

Alison tumbled to the sofa, moaning and holding her chest.

"No use waiting around," she said, breaking off, and speaking in a surprisingly normal voice. "We won't hear from her again for a while."

"What can I do?" Colette said.

"You can make me some hot milk, and give me two paracetamol."

Colette went into the kitchen. The fridge breathed out at her a wet cold breath. She spilled the milk as she poured it in the pan, and the gas ring's flame sputtered and licked. She carried it through to Al. "Oh, the pills, I forgot the pills!"

"Never mind," Al said.

"No, wait, sit still, I'll get them."

Al looked at her, faintly reproachful. "We're now waiting for the emergency services. We're slightly beyond the paracetomol stage."

Things happen fast, in the lawless country between life and death. Colette wandered up the stairs. She felt de trop. Her feet were everywhere: weaving, bony, aimless. What shall I do? Back in her bedroom, she tugged the cover back over her bed, for tidiness. She pulled a sweatshirt on; she sat down on the bed and pinched her thin white legs, looking for cellulite. There was a muffled cry from below, but she didn't think she ought to interfere. I suppose this is where people smoke a cigarette, she thought; but she'd been trying to give up. By and by she stabbed her new PC into life. She had it in mind to prepare a series of invoices that would take advantage of the event. Whatever it was.

Only later, when she thought it over, did she realize that she had never doubted Alison's word. It was true that from Al the news arrived piecemeal, but it was more exciting that way. In time the radio, placed beside her, brought the confirming details. The event, in the real world, had actually taken place; she stopped typing and sat listening: *lights, a tunnel, impact, lights, a tunnel, black, and then something beyond it—a hiatus, and one final, blinding light.* By dawn, her mood was one of shock and unholy exhilaration, combined with a bubbling self-righteousness. What did she expect, a girl like Diana? There was something so right about it, so *meant*. It had turned out so beautifully badly.

She dived downstairs to check on Alison, who was now rocking herself and groaning. She asked if she wanted the radio, but Al shook her head without speaking. She ran back to catch the latest details. The computer was humming and whirring, making from time to time its little sighs, as if deep within its operating system the princess was gurgling out her story. Colette laid her palm on it, anxious; she was afraid it was overheating. I'll do a shutdown, she thought. When she went downstairs Al seemed entranced, her eyes on some unfolding scene Colette could only imagine. Her milk was untouched, standing beside her with a skin on it. It was a mild night, but her bare feet were blue.

"Why don't you go back to bed, Al? It's Sunday. Nobody's going to call yet."

"Where's Morris? Still out from last night? Thank God for that."

You can just imagine the sort of inappropriate joke Morris would be making, at this solemn time. Colette sniggered to herself. She got Alison wrapped up in her dressing gown, and draped over her bulk the raspberry mohair throw. She made a hot-water bottle; she piled a duvet on top of her, but she couldn't stop Al shivering. Over the next hour her face drained of colour. Her eyes seemed to shrink back in her skull. She pitched and tossed and threatened to roll off the sofa. She seemed to be talking, under her breath, to people Colette couldn't see.

Colette's exhilaration turned to fright. She had only known Al a matter of weeks, and now this crisis was thrust upon them. Colette imagined herself trying to heave Al up from the floor, hands under her armpits. It wouldn't work. She'd have to call for an ambulance. What if she had to resuscitate her? Would they get there in time? "You'd be better off in bed," she pleaded.

From cold, Al passed into a fever. She pushed off the duvet. The hot-water bottle fell to the carpet with a fat *plop*. Inside her nightgown, Al shook like a blancmange.

By eight o'clock the phone was ringing. It was the first of Al's regulars, wanting messages. Eyes still half closed, Al levered herself up off the sofa and took the receiver from Colette's hand. Colette hissed at her "special rate, special rate."

No, Al said, no direct communication yet from the princess, not since the event—but I would expect her to make every effort to come through, once she gathers her wits. If you want an appointment next week I can try to squeeze you in. Fine. Will do. She put the phone down, and at once it rang again. "Mandy?" She mouthed at Colette, Mandy Coughlan from Hove. You know: Natasha. Yes, she said, and oh, terrible. Mandy spoke.

Al said, "Well, I think in transition, don't you? I shouldn't think at this stage she does, no. Probably not."

Al paused: Mandy talked. Al talked again, her hand absently smoothing her creased nightdress.

"You know how it is when they go over suddenly, they don't know what's happening till somebody puts them right—yes, don't they, hanging around for days. You think Kensington Palace?" She giggled. "Harvey Nichols, more likely. . . . No. Okay, so if you hear anything about the funeral, whatever. . . . A bit sick, you know. Not actually vomiting. Hot and cold. Quite a shock for Colette, I can tell you. . . . She's my, you know, my whatsit, my new personal assistant. . . . Yes, it is good timing, We'll all have quite a week of it, won't we? Need all the help I can get. Okay, Mand. Take care. Kiss-kiss. Bye for now."

She put the phone down. She was sweating. "Oh, sorry, Colette, I said assistant, I should have said partner. I didn't mean to be—you know—patronizing to you. Mandy reckons she'll be returning to Kensington Palace, wandering around, you know, confused." She tried to laugh, but it emerged as a little snarl. She put her fingers to her forehead, and they came away dripping.

Colette whispered, "Al, you smell terrible."

"I know," she whispered back. "I'll get in the bath."

As Al ran the taps, she heard a whistle through the intercom. It was shrill, like a bird call, like a code. Next thing, Morris crashed in. Usually on a Sunday morning he was tetchy from a hangover, but the news seemed to have bucked him up. He banged on the door, shouting tasteless jokes. "What's the difference between Princess Di and a roll of carpet? Go on, go on, bet you don't know, do you? What's the difference between—"

She slammed the bolt on. She lowered herself into the bath: lavender oil. She wiped away the stench of death, exfoliating herself for good measure. Morris slipped under the door. He stood leering at her. His yellow face mingled with the steam. When she came out of the bathroom she was scored all over with faint pink lines, but the cuts on her thighs flared darkest, as if she had been whipped with wire.

In the following week Colette learned things about sudden death that she'd never suspected. Al said, what you should understand is this: when people go over, they don't always know they've gone. They have a pain, or the memory of one, and there are people in white, and strange faces that loom up and there's a noise in the background, metal things banging together—as if there were a train wreck going on, but in another country.

Colette said, "And what are they? These noises."

"Mrs. Etchells says it's the gates of hell clattering."

"And do you believe that?"

"There ought to be hell. But I don't know."

There are the lights, she said, the noises, the waiting, the loneliness. Everything slips out of focus. They suppose they're in a queue for attention but nobody attends. Sometimes they think they're in a room, sometimes they sense air and space and they think they've been abandoned in a car park. Sometimes they think they're in a corridor, lying on a trolley, and nobody comes. They start to cry, but still nobody comes. You see, she said, they've actually gone over, but they think it's just the National Health.

Sometimes, when famous people pass, their fans-in-spirit are waiting for them—their fans and, in the case of someone like Diana, their ancestors too—and often those ancestors have something to say, about the way estates have been subdivided, money frittered, their portraits sold at auction. Also, when famous people pass they attract spirit imposters, just as on this side you have look-alikes and body doubles. This fact, unless kept constantly in mind by a medium, can ruin an evening on the platform, as the tribute bands and the impersonators break through, claiming to be Elvis, Lennon, Glenn Miller. Occasionally some oddball breaks through saying he's Jesus. But I don't know, Al said, there'll be something in his manner—you just know he's not from ancient Palestine. In Mrs. Etchell's day, she explained, people still thought they were Napoleon. They were better educated then, she said, they knew dates and battles. Surprisingly, Cleopatra is still popular. "And I don't like doing Cleopatra, because—"

"Because you don't do ethnics."

Al had explained it to her, in delicate language. She didn't work the inner city or places like downtown Slough. "I'm not a racist, please don't think that, but it just gets too convoluted." It wasn't just the language barrier, she explained, but these people, those races who think they have more than one life. Which means, of course, more than one family. Often several families, and I don't know, it just gets— She closed her eyes tight, and flapped her fingers at her head, as if trying to beat off mosquitoes. She shivered, at the thought of some bangled wrinkly from the Ganges popping up: and she, flailing in time and space, not able to skewer her to the right millennium.

When Colette looked back, from the end of August 1997 to the early summer, when they had met. . . ."It's what you call a steep learning curve," she said. That the dead can be lonely, that the dead can be confused; all these things were a surprise to Colette, who had only ever spoken to one dead person: who earlier in her life had never given them much thought, except insofar as she had hoped—in some limp sort of way—that the dead were best off where they were. She now understood that Al hadn't been quite straight with her in those first few weeks. There wasn't a necessary tie-up between what she said on the platform and the true state of affairs. Uncomfortable truths were smoothed over before Al let them out to the public; when she conveyed soothing messages, Colette saw, they came not from the medium but from the saleswoman, from the part of her that saw the value in pleasing people. She had to admire it, grudgingly; it was a knack she had never acquired.

Until the princess died, Colette had not seen the seamy side of the work. Take Morris out of the equation, and it was much like any other business. Al needed a more modern communications system, a better through-put and process-flow. She needed a spam filter for her brain, to screen out unwanted messages from the dead; and if Colette could not provide this, she could at least control how Al managed those messages. She tried to view Al as a project and herself as project manager. It was lucky she'd got such sound experience as a conference organizer, because of course Al was something like a conference in herself.

When she moved in with Al, Colette had made a pretty smart exit from her early life—a clean break, she told herself. Nevertheless, she expected old workmates to track her down. She practiced in her mind what she'd tell them. I find my new role diverse, rewarding, and challenging, she would say. Above all, I like the independence. The personal relationships are a bonus; I'd describe my boss as caring and professional. Do I miss going to the office every day? You must appreciate I never exactly did that; travel was always part of the brief. Think what I haven't got: no slander at the water cooler, no interdepartmental tensions, no sexual harassment, no competitive dressing. I have to be smart, of course, because I'm customer-facing, but it's a real perk to be able to express yourself through your own sense of style. And that encapsulates, more or less, what I feel about my new situation; I've a role that I can sculpt to suit my talents, and no two days are the same.

All this rehearsal was wasted, except upon herself. No one, in fact, did track her down, except Gavin, who called one night wanting to boast about his annual bonus. It was as if she'd ceased to exist.

But after that death night at the end of August, she couldn't fool herself that her position with Al was just a logical part of her career development. And exactly what was her position with Al? Next day, she, Colette, tried to sit her down for a talk, and said, Al, I need you to be straight with me.

Al said, "It's okay, Col, I've been thinking about it. You're a godsend to me, and I don't know what I ever did without you. I never thought I'd get someone to agree to live in, and you can see that at a time of crisis, twenty-four-hour care is what I need." Only a half hour before Al had been bringing up a clear ropey liquid; once again, rank sweat filmed her face. "I think we should agree on new terms. I think you should have a profit share."

Colette flushed pink up to the roots of her hair. "I didn't mean money," she said. "I didn't mean, be straight with me in that way. I—thank you Al, I mean it's good to be needed. I know you're not financially dishonest. I wasn't saying that. I only mean I think you're not giving me the full picture about your life. Oh, I know about Morris. *Now* I know, but when I took on the job you didn't tell me I'd be working with some foul-mouthed dwarf spook; you let me find that out. I feel as if I don't want any more nasty shocks. You do see that, surely? I know you mean well. You're sparing my feelings. Like you do with the trade. But you must realize, I'm not the trade, I'm your friend. I'm your partner."

Alison said, "What you're asking me is, how do you do it?"

"Yes, that's exactly right. That's what I'm asking you."

She made Al some ginger tea; and Al talked then about the perfidy of the dead, their partial, penetrative nature, their way of dematerializing and leaving bits of themselves behind, or entangling themselves with your inner organs. She talked about her sharp earsight and voices she heard in the wall.

About the deads' propensity to fib and confabulate. Their selfish, trivial out-look. Their general cluelessness.

Colette was not satisfied. She rubbed her eyes; she rubbed her forehead. She stopped and glared, when she saw Alison smiling at her sympathetically. "Why? Why are you smiling?"

"My friend Cara would say, you're opening your third eye."

Colette pointed to the space between her brows. "There is no eye. It's bone."

"Brain behind it, I hope."

Colette said angrily, "It's not that I don't believe in you. Well I do. I have to believe in what you do, because I see you doing it, I see and hear you, but how *can* I believe it, when it's against the laws of nature?"

"Oh, those," Al said. "Are you sure we have them anymore? I think it's a bit of a free-for-all these days."

They had arranged, on the Saturday of the princess's funeral, to do an evening event in the Midlands, a major fayre in an area where psychic fayres were just es-tablishing themselves. Mandy Coughlan said on the phone to Al, "It would be a shame to cancel, sweetie. You can take a sick bag in the car if you're still feeling queasy. Because you know if you pull out they'll charge you full price for the stall, and some amateur from up the M6 will be straight in there, quicksticks. So if you're feeling up to it? Good girl. Do you think Mrs. Etchells is going?"

"Oh yes. She loved Diana. She'll be expecting a contact."

"Joys of motherhood," Mandy said. "Of course. Perhaps Di will come through and let her know if she was up the duff. But how will Mrs. Etchells get to Nottingham? Will there be trains, or will they be cancelled out of re-spect? You're not far away, maybe you could give her a lift."

Al dropped her voice. "I'm not being professionally divisive, Mandy, but there are certain issues around Mrs. Etchells—undercutting on tarot read-ings, slashing prices without prior consultation, trying to lure other people's clients—Colette heard her doing it."

"Oh yes. This person Colette. Whoever is she, Al? Where did you find her? Is she psychic?"

"God, no. She's a client. And before that she was a client of yours."

"Really? When did we meet?"

"Last year sometime. She came down to Hove with some cuff links. She was trying to find out who her father was."

"And who was he?"

"Her uncle."

"Oh, one of those. I can't put a face to her." Mandy sounded impatient. "So is she mad with me, or something?"

"No. I don't think so. Though she is quite sceptical. In patches."

Al said her polite goodbyes. She put the phone down and stood looking at it. Did I do the right thing, when I took on Colette? Mandy didn't seem keen. Have I been impulsive, and is it an impulse I will regret? She almost called Mandy back, to seek further advice. Mandy knows what's what, she's been through the mill: thrown out a lover at midnight and his whole troop after him, some dead druid who'd moved in after the bloke, and a whole bunch of Celtic spirits more used to life in a cave than life in Hove. Out they go with their bloody cauldrons and their spears, Lug and Trog and Glug; and out goes Psychic Simon with his rotting Y-fronts dropped out of a first-floor window, his Morfesa the Great Teacher statue chucked in the gutter with its wand snapped off, and his last quarter's invoice file tossed like a Frisbee in the direction of the sea: and several unbanked cheques rendered illegible and useless, speared by Mandy's stiletto heel.

That was how it usually went, when you were unguarded enough to get into a relationship with a colleague. It wasn't a question of personal compatibility between the two of you; it was a question of the baggage you trailed, your entourage, whether they'd fight and lay waste to each other, thrashing with their vestigial limbs and snapping with their stumps of teeth. Al's hand moved to the phone and away again; she didn't want Colette to overhear, so she talked to Mandy in her mind.

I know it's bad when you go out with someone in our line, but some people say it's worse to get into a thing with a punter—

A thing?

Not a thing, not a sex thing. But a relationship, you can't deny that. If Colette's going to live with you, it's a relationship. God knows you need somebody to talk to, but—

But how can you talk to the trade?

Yes, that's the trouble, isn't it? How can they understand what you go through? How can they understand anything? You try to explain, but the more you try the less you succeed.

They haven't got the language, have they? Don't tell me, sweetheart. They haven't got the range.

You say something perfectly obvious and they look at you as if you're mad. You tell them again, but by then it sounds mad to you. You lose your confidence, if you have to keep going over and over it.

And yet you're paying the rent, mortgage, whatever. It's fine as long as everything's humming along sweetly, but the first cross word you have, they start casting it up, throwing it in your face—Oh, you're taking advantage of me because you've got all these people I can't see, how do you know this stuff about me, you're opening my mail—I mean, why should you need to open their bloody mail? As if you can't see straight through to what they are. I tell you, Al, I went out with a punter once. I let him move in and it was murder. I saw within the week he was just trying to use me. Fill in my pools coupon. Pick me something at Plumpton.

Yes, I've explained it to Col, I told her straight off, I'm no good for lottery numbers.

And what did she say?

I think she could understand it. I mean, she's a numerate woman. I think she understands the limitations.

Oh, she says that *now*. But honestly, when you let them move in, they're like leeches, they're like—whatever, whatever it is, that's at you twenty-four hours a day. Actually my mum said as much. She warned me, well, she tried to warn me, but you don't take any notice, do you? Did you know I was born the night that Kennedy was shot? Well, that dates me! (Mandy, in Al's mind, laughed shakily.) No point trying to keep secrets from you, Al! The point is, my mum—you know she was like me, Natasha, Psychic to the Stars, and my grandma was Natasha, Psychic to the Tsars—this man she was with then, when I was born, he said, didn't you know anything about it, doll? Couldn't you of— oh, he was ignorant in his speech—couldn't you of prevented it? My mum said, what do you want me to do, ring up the White House, with my feet up in stirrups and this withered old nun shouting in my ear, Push, Mother, push?

Nun? Alison was surprised. Are you a Catholic, Mandy?

No, Russian Orthodox. But you know what I mean, don't you? About a relationship with the laity. They expect too much.

I know they do. But Mandy, I need someone, someone with me. A friend.

Of course you do. Mandy's voice softened. A friend. A live-in friend. I'm not judgemental, God knows. Takes all sorts. Live and let live. Who am I to moralize? Al, you can tell me. We go back, you and me. You want a little love in your life, yes you do, you do.

Mandy, do you know the pleasures of lesbian anal sex? No. Nor me. Nor any other pleasures. With Morris around I really need some sort of fanny guard. You know what they do, don't you—the guides—while you're asleep? Creepy-creepy. Creak at the door, then a hand on the duvet, a hairy paw tugging the sheet. I know you thought Lug and Glug tried it on, though you say you had been taking Nytol so were a bit confused at being woken and you suspect it may well have been Simon, judging by the smell. It's difficult to say, isn't it? What kind of violation, spirit or not spirit. Especially if your boyfriend has a small one. I am fairly confident that Morris, when it comes down to it, he can't—not with me, anyway. But what gets to me is all this back-alley masculinity, all this beer and belching and scratching your belly, billiards and darts and minor acts of criminal damage, I get tired of being exposed to it all the time, and it was fine for you, I know you kicked out the druid and Lug and Glug, but they were Psychic Simon's, and Morris is mine. And somehow I suppose, what it is, with Colette as my partner—with Colette as my *business* partner—I was hoping—oh, let me say it—I was aspiring—I want a way out of Aldershot, out of my childhood, away from my mother, some way to upscale, to move into the affluent world of the Berkshire or Surrey commuter, the world of the businessman, the entrepreneur: to imagine how the rich and clever die. To imagine how it is, if you're senior in IT and your system crashes: or the finance director, when your last shekel is spent: or in charge of Human Resources, when you lose your claim to have any.

When she was packing for their trip to Nottingham, Colette came in. Al was wearing just a T-shirt, bending over the case. For the first time, Colette saw the backs of her thighs. "Christ," she said. "Did you do that?"

"Me?"

"Like Di? Did you cut yourself?"

Alison turned back to her packing. She was perplexed. It had never occurred to her that she might have inflicted the damage herself. Perhaps I did, she thought, and I've just forgotten; there is so much I've forgotten, so much that has slipped away from me. It was a long time since she'd given much thought to the scars. They flared, in a hot bath, and the skin around them itched in hot weather. She avoided seeing them, which was not difficult if she avoided mirrors. But now, she thought, Colette will always be noticing them. I had better have a story because she will want answers.

She fingered her damaged flesh; the skin felt dead and distant. She remembered Morris saying, we showed you what a blade could do! For the first time she thought, oh, I see now, that was what they taught me; that was the lesson I had.

six

As they drove north, Colette said to Alison, "When you were a little girl, did you ever think you were a princess?"

"Me? God, no."

"What did you think then?

"I thought I was a freak."

And now? The question hung in the air. It was the day of Diana's funeral, and the road was almost empty. Al had slept badly. Beyond the bedroom wall of the flat in Wexham, Colette had heard her muttering, and heard the deep groan of her mattress as she turned over and over in bed. She had been downstairs at seven-thirty, standing in the kitchen, bundled into her dressing gown, her hair straggling out of its rollers. "We may as well get on the road," she said. "Get ahead of the coffin."

By ten-thirty, crowds were assembling on the bridges over the M1, waiting for the dead woman to pass by on her way to her ancestral burial ground just off Junction 15A. The police were lining the route as if waiting for disaster, drawn up in phalanxes of motorcycles and cordons of watching vans. It was a bright, cool morning—perfect September weather.

"S'funny," Colette said. "It's only a fortnight ago, those pictures of her in the boat with Dodi, in her bikini. And we were all saying, what a slapper."

Al opened the glove box and ferreted out a chocolate biscuit.

"That's the emergency Kit-Kat," Colette protested.

"This is an emergency. I couldn't eat my breakfast." She ate the chocolate morosely, finger by finger. "If Gavin had been the Prince of Wales," she said, "do you think you'd have tried harder with your marriage?"

"Definitely."

Colette's eyes were on the road; in the passenger seat Alison twisted over her shoulder to look at Morris in the back, kicking his short legs and singing a medley of patriotic songs. As they passed beneath a bridge policemen's faces peered down at them, pink sweating ovals above the sick glow of high-visibility jackets. Stubble-headed boys—the type who, in normal times, heave a concrete block through your windscreen—now jabbed the mild air with bunches of carnations. A ragged bedsheet, grey-white, drifted down into their view. It was scrawled in crimson capitals, as if in virgin's blood: DI-ANA, QUEEN OF OUR HEARTS.

"You'd think they'd show more respect," Alison said. "Not flap about with their old bed linen."

"Dirty linen," Colette said. "She washed her dirty linen. . . . it comes back on you in the end."

They sped a mile or two in silence.

"I mean it's not as if it's exactly a surprise. You didn't expect it to last, did you? Not as if she was exactly stable. If she'd been in real life, she'd have been just the sort of slag who'd end up with her arms and legs in left-luggage lockers and her head in a bin bag in Walthamstow."

"Shh!" Al said. "She might be listening. She's not gone yet, you know, not as far as I—as far as we're concerned."

"Do you think you might get a message from Dodi? No, I forgot, you don't do ethnics, do you?"

At each bridge they glanced up. The crowds thickened. As they crossed the border into Northamptonshire, a leather-jacketed man was waving the Stars and Stripes. The hitchhikers lurking by the slip roads had tied black bands around their sleeves.

Alison hummed along with Morris, who was doing "Land of Our Fathers." She struggled to find loyalty within herself: loyalty, compassion, something other than mere fatigue at the thought of the trouble Diana was going to cause her. "Of course," she said, "she was against land mines."

"That doesn't seem much to be against," Colette said. "Not exactly sticking your neck out, is it? Not like being against . . . dolphins."

Silence within the car: except that Morris, in the back, had progressed to "Roll Out the Barrel." A helicopter whirled overhead, monitoring the near-empty road.

"We're much too early," Colette said. "Our room won't be ready. Do you want to stop for a wee? Or a proper breakfast? Could you manage a fry-up?"

Al thought, when I was awake in the night, I was so cold. Being cold makes you feel sick; or does feeling sick make you cold? Nothing to be hoped for from days like these, except nausea, cramps, shortness of breath, acceleration of the pulse, gooseflesh, and a leaden tinge to the skin.

Colette said, "Five miles, shall I pull in? Make your mind up, yes or no?"

Morris, at once, stopped singing and began agitating for his comfort stop. He showed an unhealthy interest in gents' toilets: when he swarmed back into the car after a break at a service area, you could catch the whiff of piss and floral disinfectant from the crepe soles of his shoes. He liked to creep around the parked cars, pulling off hubcaps and bowling them like hoops among the feet of their returning owners. He would double up with laughter as the punters stood jaw dropped at the sight of the metal discs, spinning of their own volition, clattering to rest amid the overspill of polystyrene from the litter bins. Sometimes he would go into the shop and pull the newspapers from their racks, tossing top-shelf magazines into the wire baskets of respectable dads queuing with their families for giant packs of crisps. He would plunge his paw into the pick 'n' mix sweets and stuff his bulging jaw. He would snatch from the shelves of travellers' supplies a tartan box of choc-chip shortbread or traditional motorway fudge; then munching, spitting, denouncing it as ladies' pap, he would head for the lorry park, for the caff where men's men swigged from mugs of strong tea.

He hoped, always, to see somebody he knew, Aitkenside or Bob Fox or even bloody MacArthur, "though if I see MacArthur," he'd say, "the ruddy swindler'll wish he'd never been born, I'll creep up on his blind side and twist his head off." He would sneak around the parked-up rigs, bouncing himself on the bumper bars to snap off windscreen wipers; through the gaps in frilled curtains, he would peep in at the private interiors where tattooed drivers snored against flowered cushions, where hands rubbed lonely crotches: ooh, sissy-boy, Morris would jeer, and sometimes a man stirred from his doze and jolted awake, thinking for a moment that he had seen a yellow face staring in at him, lips drawn back in a grimace to show yellow fangs, like those of an ape behind toughened glass. I was dreaming, the man would tell himself: I was dreaming, what brought that on?

Truth was, he longed for a friend; it was no life, holed up with a bunch of women, always squawking and making leaflets. "Oh, what shall we have," he mimicked, "shall we have a flower, a rose is nice, a dove of peace is nice, shall we have a dove of peace with a flower in its mouf?" Then would come Colette's higher, flatter voice. "Beak, Alison, a beak's what birds have." Then Alison, "It doesn't sound so nice, bill's nicer, doesn't a dove have a bill?" and Colette's grudging, "You could be right."

Bill's nice, is it, he would jeer, from his perch on the back of the sofa: "bill's nice, you should see the bloody bills I've mounted up, I could tell you about bills, Aitkenside owes me a pony, bloody Bill Wagstaffe, he owes me. I'll give him Swan of bloody Avon, I put him on a florin at Doncaster only to oblige, goo-on, he says, goo-on, I'll give you 'alf Morris he says if she romps home, romp, did she bloody romp, she ran like the clappers out of hell, dropped dead two hours after in her trailer, but san-fairy-ann, what's that to me, and where's my fiver? Then he's explainin, ooh Morris, the trouble is I'm dead, the trouble is there's a steward's enquiry, the trouble is my pocket got frayed, the trouble is it must of fallen out me pocket of me pantaloons and bloody Kyd snapped it up, I say, then you get after Kyd and break his legs or I will, he says the trouble is he's dead he ain't got no legs, I says William old son don't come that wiv me, break him where 'is legs would be."

When he thought of the debts he had incurred, of the injuries done and what was rightfully owed him, he would run after Alison, agitated: after his hostess, his missus. Al would be in the kitchen making a toasted sandwich. He was eager to press on her the weight of his injustices, but she would say to him, get away, Morris, get your fingers out of that lo-fat cheddar. He wanted a man's life, men's company, and he would creep around the lorry park waving, gesturing, looking for his mates, making the secret signal that men make to other men, to say they want a chin-wag and a smoke, to say they're lonely, to say they want company but they're not *like that*. Bloody Wagstaffe were like that, if you ask me, he would tell Alison, but she would say, who? Him in pantaloons, he'd say. Come on, I wasn't born yesterday, anybody showing his legs like that 'as got to be of the fairy persuasion. And again she'd say, who? dabbing up a shaving of cheese with her finger, and he'd say, Wagstaffe, he's bloody famous, you must have heard of him, he's coining it, he's got his name in bloody lights and what do I get? Not even me stake money back. Not even me florin.

So in the caff at the lorry park he would roll between the tables, saying, "'scuse me mate, 'scuse me mate"—because he wanted to be polite—"have you seen Aitkenside around here? Cos Aitkenside he used to drive a forty-two-tonner, and he 'ad this belly dancer tattooed on his back, he got it when he were in Egypt, he were in the forces, he were stationed overseas, Aitkenside. And he's a mermaid on his thigh, not that I seen his thigh, I'm not of that persuasion, don't get me wrong." But much as he tried to engage them, much as he thrust his face into theirs, much as he interposed himself between them and their All Day breakfasts, so much did they ignore him, freeze him, give him the elbow and the old heave-ho. So he would wander out, disconsolate, into the open air, sucking up from between his fingers a sausage he had snatched—call this a sausage, it's not what I call a sausage, bleeding yankee-doodle pap, how can you have a sausage wiv no skin?—and around the tankers and the trucks he would slide on his crepe-soled feet, calling, "Aitkenside, MacArthur, are you there, lads?"

For in truth he intended to cripple them but after he had crippled them he meant to make his peace. For they were dead too and in the halls of the dead they were in different halls. And in the lorry parks of the dead they had not coincided yet. He would rub his chin, contemplating his sins, then slide among the trucks, scrambling up to unhook tarpaulins, dragging up the crinkled covers to see what was stowed beneath. Once eyes looked back at him, and those eyes were alive. Once eyes looked back at him and those eyes were dead, swivelled up in their sockets and hard like yellow marbles. When he saw eyes he hooked back the tarp double-quick. Unless the cable had zinged out of his hand. That could happen.

And them silly tarts who was now in the LADIES titivating, he would think of them with contempt: ooh Colette, do you want a gherkin with your toastie? I'll give you gherkin, gel, he would think. But then if he had dallied too long among the men, if he thought they might drive off without him, his heart would hammer at his dried ribs: wait for me! And he would sprint back to the public area, as far as sprint was in him, his legs being, as they were, multiply fractured and badly set: he would sprint back and swish in—bloody central locking!—through the air vent, roll into the back seat, and collapse there, puffing, panting, wrenching off his shoes, and Colette—the stringy one—would complain, what's that smell? It came to his own nostrils, faintly: petrol and onions and hot dead feet.

If his owners were still in the LADIES, he would not sit alone and wait for them. He would insinuate himself into other cars, loosening the straps of baby seats, wrenching the heads off the furry animals that dangled from the back windows: spinning the furry dice. But then, when he had done all the mischief he could think of, he would sit on the ground, alone, and let people run over him. He would chew his lip, and then he would sing softly to himself:

Hitler has only got one ball,
Hitler has only got one ball,
His mother, bit off the other,
But Capstick has no balls at all.

The missus don't like it when I sing that, he would mutter to himself. She don't like reminding, I suppose. Thinking of the old Aldershot days, he'd sniffle a little. Course she don't like reminding, course she don't. He looked up. The women were approaching, his missus rolling towards him, her pal skipping and yattering and twirling her car keys. Just in time, he slid into the back seat.

Alison's spine tensed as he settled himself, and Colette's nostrils twitched. Morris laughed to himself: she thinks she don't see me, but in time she'll see me, she thinks she don't hear me but she'll come to hear, she don't know if she smells me, she hopes she don't, but she don't want to think it's herself. Morris lifted himself in his seat and discharged a cabbagey blast. Colette swung them through the EXIT sign. A flag flew at half mast over the Travelodge.

At Junction 23 a lorry carrying bales of straw cut in ahead of them. The wisps blew back towards them, back down the empty grey road, back towards the south. The morning clouded up, the sky assumed a glacial shimmer. The sun skulked behind a cloud, smirking. As they turned off the M1 onto the A52, the bells peeled out to mark the end of the National Silence. Curtains were drawn in the Nottingham suburbs.

"That's nice," Alison said. "It's respectful. It's old-fashioned."

"Don't be stupid," Colette said. "It's to keep the sun out, so they can see the TV."

They pulled into the hotel car park, and Colette jumped out. A spirit woman slid into her place in the driver's seat. She was little, old, and poor, and she seemed overwhelmed to find herself behind the wheel of a car, dabbing her hands at the indicators, saying, ee, this is a novelty, do you pedal it, miss? Excuse me, excuse me, she said, do you know Maureen Harrison? Only I'm looking for Maureen Harrison.

No, Al said kindly, but I'll tell you if I bump into her.

Because Maureen Harrison were friends with me, the little woman said, aye, she were an' all. A complaining note entered her voice, faint and nostalgic, like the moon through mist. Maureen Harrison were me friend, you know, and I've been searching this thirty year. Excuse me, excuse me, miss, have you seen Maureen Harrison?

Al climbed out. "That's Mandy's car, she's early too." She looked around. "There's Merlin. And there's Merlyn with a y. Dear God, I see his old van has got another bash." She nodded towards a shiny new minivan. "That's those white witches from Egham."

Colette lugged the bags out of the boot. Alison frowned.

"I've been meaning to say something. I think we should go shopping for you, if you've no objection. I don't feel a nylon holdall gives quite the right message."

"It's designer!" Colette bellowed. "Nylon holdall? I've been all around Europe with this. I've been in Club Class."

"Well, it doesn't look designer. It looks like market stall."

They checked in, squabbling. Their room was a box on the second floor, overlooking the green paladins that received the back-door rubbish. Morris strolled around making himself at home, sticking his fingers with impunity into the electrical sockets.

There was a tapping from beyond the wall, and Alison said, "That'll be Raven, practicing his Celtic Sex Magic."

"What happened to Mrs. Etchells, did she get a lift in the end?"

"Silvana went for her. But she's asked to be dropped off at some bed and breakfast in Beeston."

"Feeling the pinch, is she? Good. Cheating old bat."

"Oh, I think she does all right, she does a lot of postal readings. She's got regulars going back years. No, it's just she finds a hotel impersonal, she says, she prefers a family home. You know what she's like. She reads the tea cups and leaves her flyer. She tries to sign up the landlady. Sometimes they let her stop for nothing."

Colette pulled a sheaf of Al's new leaflets out of their box. They had chosen lavender, and a form of wording that declared her to be *one of the most acclaimed psychics working in Britain today.* Al had objected, modestly, but Colette said, what do you want me to put? Alison Hart, Slightly Famous Along The A4?

The schedule was this: a Fayre this evening, Saturday, to be followed next day by a Grand Fayre, where a group of them would have their forty-minute slots on the platform; meanwhile, whoever was not onstage could carry on with private readings in the side rooms.

The venue was an old primary school, the marks of violence still chipped into its red brick. As Al stepped inside she shuddered. She said, "As you know, my schooldays weren't what you call happy."

She put a smile on her face, and lollopped among the trestles, beaming from side to side as her colleagues set out their stalls. "Hi Angel. Hi Cara, how are you? This is Colette, my new assistant and working partner."

Cara, setting down her Norse Wisdom Sticks, lifted her sunny little face. "Hi, Alison. I see you've not lost any weight."

Mrs. Etchells staggered in, a box of baubles in her arms. "Oh, what a journey! What a day after the night before!"

"You got a toy boy, Mrs. Etchells?" Cara asked, giving Al a wink.

"If you must know, I was up all night with the Princess. Silvana, love, help me dress my table, would you?"

Silvana, raising her pencilled brows and hissing between her teeth, dumped down carrier bags and unfurled Mrs. Etchell's fringed crimson cloth into air laden already with the smell from oil burners. "Personally," she said, "I never heard a squeak from Di. Mrs. Etchells reckons she was with her, talking about the joys of motherhood."

"Imagine that," Mandy said.

"So this is your assistant, Alison?" Silvana ran her eyes over Colette; then ran them over Alison, with insulting slowness, as if they had to feel their way over a large surface area.

They hate it, Al thought, they hate it; because I've got Colette, they think I'm coining it. "I thought—you know," she said. "A bit of help with the—with the secretarial, the bookkeeping, the driving, you know. Lonely on the road."

"Yes, isn't it?" Silvana said. "Mind you, if you wanted company on the motorway you could have run over to Aldershot and collected your granny, instead of leaving it to me. This your new flyer?" She picked it up and held it close to her eyes; psychics don't wear glasses. "Mm," she said. "Did you do this, Colette? Very nice."

"I shall be setting up a Web site for Alison," Colette said.

Silvana tossed the leaflet down on Mrs. Etchells's table and passed her hands around Colette to feel her aura. "Oh dear," she said, and moved away.

Seven o'clock. The scheduled finish was at eight, but tonight they would be lucky to get them out by half-past; the caretaker was already banging about, kicking his vacuum cleaner up and down the corridor. But what could you do with the punters: lever them, sodden and sobbing, into the streets? There was hardly one customer who had not mentioned Di; many broke down and cried, putting their elbows on the trestles, edging up the lucky pisky figurines and the brass finger cymbals so they could sob their hearts out in comfort. I identified with her, she was like a friend to me. Yes, yes, yes, Al would say, like her you are drawn to suffering, oh yes, I am I am, that's me. You like to have a good time, oh yes I have always loved dancing. I think of those two boys, I would have had two boys, except the last one was a girl. Diana was Cancer like me, I was born under Cancer, it means you are like a crab, inside your shell you are squidgy, I think that's where her nickname came from, don't you? I never thought of that, Al said, but you could be right. I think they made her a scrapegoat. I dreamed of her last night, appearing to me in the form of a bird.

There was something gluttonous in their grief, something gloating. Al let them sob, agreeing with them and feeding them their lines, sometimes making little there-there noises; her eyes travelled from side to side, to see who was conspiring against her; Colette stalked between the tables, listening in. I must tell her not to do that, Al thought, or at least not to do it so conspicuously. As she passed, ill will trailed after her; let them not cold-shoulder me, Al prayed.

For it was usual among the psychics to pass clients to each other, to work in little rings and clusters, trading off their specialties, their weaknesses and strengths: well, darling, I'm not a medium personally, but you see Eve there, in the corner, just give her a little wave, tell her I've recommended you. They pass notes to one another, table to table—titbits gleaned, snippets of personal information with which to impress the clients. And if for some reason you're not on the inside track, you can get disrecommended, you can get forced out. It's a cold world when your colleagues turn their backs.

"Yes, yes, yes," she sighed, patting the mottled palms she had just read. "It will all work out for the best. And I'm sure young Harry will look more like his daddy as time goes by." The woman wrote her a cheque for three services—palms, crystal, and general clairvoyance—and as she detached it a final fat tear rolled out of her eye and splashed on her bank sort code.

As the woman rose, a new prospect hesitated in passing. "Do you do Vedic palmistry or ordinary?"

"Just ordinary, I'm afraid," Alison said. The woman sneered and started to move on. Alison began, "You could try Silvana over there—" but she checked herself. Silvana, after all, was a fraud; her mother used to manage a newsagent in Farnborough, a fact at odds with her claim to be a Romany whose family origins were lost in the mists of occult tradition. Sometimes the punters would ask "What's the difference between a clairaudient and an aura reader, a whatsit and a thing?" and Al would say, "No great difference, my dear, it's not the instrument you choose that matters, it's not the method, it's not the technique, it's your attunement to a higher reality." But what she really wanted to do was lean across the table and say, you know what's the difference, the difference between them and me? Most of them can't do it, and I can. And the difference shows, she tells herself, not just in results, but in attitude, in deportment, in some essential seriousness. Her tarot cards, unused so far today, sat at her right hand, burning through their wrap of scarlet satin: priestess, lover, and fool. She had never touched them with a hand that was soiled, or opened them to the air without opening her heart; whereas Silvana will light a fag between customers, and Merlin and Merlyn will send out for cheeseburgers if there's a lull. It isn't right to smoke and eat in front of clients, to blow smoke at them over your crystals.

It's this she must teach Colette, that a casual approach won't do: you don't shove your stuff in a nylon holdall and wrap your rose quartz in your knickers. You don't carry your kit around in a cardboard box that used to contain a dozen bottles of lavatory cleaner, you don't clear up at the end of a fayre by bundling your bits and pieces into a supermarket carrier bag. And you control your face, your expression, every moment you're awake. She had sometimes noticed an unguarded expression on a colleague's face, as the departing client turned away: a compound of deep weariness and boredom, as the lines of professional alertness faded and the face fell into its customary avaricious folds. She had made up her mind, in the early days, that the client would not ike to see this expression, and so she had invented a smile, complicit and wistful, which she kept cemented to her face between readings; it was there now.

Meanwhile Colette moved scornfully on her trajectory, helpfully clearing an ashtray or righting an upturned hobbit: anything to allow herself to lean in close and listen. She evesdropped on Cara, Cara with her cropped head, her pointy ears, her butterfly tattoo: Your aura's like your bar code, think of it that way. So your husband's first wife, could that be the blonde I'm seeing? I sense that you are a person of great hidden drive and force of will.

"Would you like a cuppa from the machine, Mrs. Etchells?" Colette called, but Al's grandmama waved her away.

"Have you known the joys of motherhood, dear? Only I'm seeing a little boy in your palm."

"A girl, actually," said her client.

"It may be a girl I'm seeing. Now, dear, and I don't want you to take this the wrong way, and I don't want to alarm you, but I want you to look out for a little accident that could happen to her, nothing serious, I'm not seeing a hospital bed, it's more as if—as if she might just fall over and cut her knee."

"She's twenty-three," said the woman coldly.

"Oh, I see." Mrs. Etchells tittered. "You must have been very young, dear, when you knew the joys of motherhood. And just the one, is it? No little brothers or sisters? You didn't want, or you couldn't have? Am I seeing a little op, at all?"

"Well, if you call it little."

"Oh, I always call an op little. I never say a big op. It doesn't do to upset people."

You daft old beggar, Colette says to herself. What is this *joy*, what is this word and what does it mean? The psychics say, you're not going to find joy in the external world, you've got to go looking for it inside, dear. Even Alison goes along with the theory, when she's in public mode; privately, back in Wexham, she often looks as if it's a hopeless task. Rummaging in your heart for *joy*? May as well go through the bins for it. Where's God? she had said to Al. Where's God in all this? And Al had said, Morris says he's never seen God, he doesn't get out much. But he says he's seen the devil; he says he's on first-name terms with him; he claims he beat him at darts once.

And you believe that? Colette asked her, and Al said, no, Morris, he drinks too much, his hand shakes, he can barely hit the board.

For Saturday night the hotel had put on a late buffet for the psychic party: crinkled chicken legs stained the colour of old walnut, a wheel-sized quiche with a thick cardboard base. There was a cold pasta salad and a bowl of complicated-looking greenery that Colette turned, without enthusiasm, with the utensils provided. Raven sat with his desert boots on a coffee table, rolling one of his special cigarettes. "The thing is, have you got *The Grimoire of An-*

ciara St. Remy? Only it's got forty spells, with detailed diagrams and conjuring charts."

"You selling it?" Silvana asked.

"No, but—"

"But you're on commission for it, am I right?"

Oh, they're such cynics, Colette thought. She had imagined that when psychics got together they'd talk about—well, things of the psyche; that they would share at least a little of their bemusement and daily fear, the fear that— if she could judge by Alison—was the price of success. But now, a little way into their association, she understood that all they talked about was money. They tried to sell things to each other, they compared their rates, they tried to hear of new stratagems—"Believe me, it's the new aromatherapy," Gemma was saying—and to learn about new tricks and fiddles that they could try out. They came to swap jargon, pick up the latest terms: and *why* do they look so ridiculous? Why all these crystal pendant earrings swinging from withered lobes; why the shrunken busts exposed in daylight, the fringes, the beading, the head scarves, the wraps, the patchwork, and the shawls? In their room— just time, before the buffet, to freshen up—she'd said to Alison, "You criticize my holdall, but have you seen your friends, have you seen the state of them?"

Alison's silk, the length of apricot polyester, lay folded on the bed, ready to be draped next day; in private life she flinches at its touch—oh yes, she has admitted she does—but somehow it's necessary, she will claim, as part of her public persona. With the silk around her studio portrait, she loses the sensation that she is shrinking inside her own skin. It blunts her sensitivity, in a way that is welcome to her; it is an extra synthetic skin she has grown, to compensate for the skins the work strips away.

But now Colette moved around the room, grumbling. "Why does everything have to be so tacky? That fairground stuff. They can't think it impresses anybody. I mean, when you see Silvana, you don't say, ooh look, here comes a gypsy princess, you say, here comes a withered old slapper with a streak of fake tan down the side of her neck."

"It's—I don't know," Al said. "It's to make it, like a game."

Colette stared. "But it's their job. A job's not a game."

"I agree, I agree completely, there's just no need these days to dress up as if you were in a circus. But then again, I don't think mediums should wear sneakers either."

"Who's wearing sneakers?"

"Cara. Under her robes." Al looked perplexed and stood up to take off a layer or two. "I never know what to wear myself, these days." Suit your outfit to the audience, to the town, had always been her watchword. A touch of Jaeger—their clothes don't fit her, but she can have an accessory—feels eternally right in Guildford, whereas down the road in Woking they'd mistrust you if you weren't in some way mismatched and uncoordinated. Each town on her loop had its requirements, and when you head up the country, you mustn't expect sophistication; the farther north you go, the more the psychics' outfits tend to suggest hot Mediterranean blood, or the mysterious East, and today maybe it's she who's got it wrong, because at the fayre she had the feeling of being devalued, marked down in some way . . . that woman who wanted Vedic palmistry. . . .

Colette had told her she wouldn't go wrong with a little cashmere cardigan, preferably black. But of course there was no *little* cardigan that would meet Al's need, only something like a Bedouin tent, something capacious and hot, and as she peeled this garment off, her scent came with it and wafted through the room; the whiff of royal mortification was suppressed now, but she had told Colette, do alert me, I shan't take offence, if you catch a hint of anything from the sepulchre.

"What can I go down in?" she asked. Colette passed her a silk top, which had been carefully pressed and wrapped in tissue for its journey. Her eye fell on the holdall, with her own stuff still rolled up inside it. Maybe Al's right, she thought. Maybe I'm too old for a casual safari look. She caught her own glance in the mirror, as she stood behind Alison to unfasten the clasp of her pearls. As Al's assistant, could she possibly benefit from tax allowances on her appearance? It was an issue she'd not yet thrashed out with the Revenue; I'm working on it, she said to herself.

"You know this book we're doing?" Al was hauling her bosoms into conformity; they were trying to escape from her bra, and she eased them back with little shoves and pinches. "Is it okay to mention it on the platform? Advertise it?"

"It's early days," Colette said.

"How long do you think it will take?"

"How long's a piece of string?" It depended, Colette said, on how much nonsense continued to appear on their tapes. Alison insisted on listening to them all through, at maximum volume; behind the hissing, behind whatever foreign-language garbage she could hear up front, there were sometimes startled wails and whistles, which she said were old souls; I owe it to them to listen, she said, if they're trying so hard to come through. Sometimes they found the tape running when neither of them had switched it on. Colette was inclined to blame Morris; speaking of which, where—

"At the pub."

"Are they open tonight?"

"Morris will find one that is."

"I suppose. Anyway, the men wouldn't stand for it, would they? Shutting the pubs because of Di."

"All he has to do is follow Merlin and Merlyn. They could find a drink in . . ." Al flapped her sleeves. She tried to think of the name of a Muslim country, but a name didn't readily spring to her lips. "Do you know Merlin's done a book called *Master of Thoth?* And Merlyn with a *y*, he's done *Casebook of a Psychic Detective?*"

"That's a point. Have you thought about working for the police?"

Alison didn't answer; she stared through the mirror, her finger tracing the ridge her bra made under the thin silk. In time, she shook her head.

"Only it would give you some sort of—what do you call it?—accreditation."

"Why would I need that?"

"As publicity."

"Yes. I suppose so. But no."

"You mean, no you won't do it?" Silence. "You don't ever want to make yourself useful to society?"

"Come on, let's go down before there's no food left."

At nine-thirty Silvana, complaining and darting venomous looks at Al, was parted from her glass of red and persuaded to take Mrs. Etchells back to her lodgings. Once she had been coaxed to it, she stood jangling her car keys. "Come on," she said. "I want to get back by ten for the funeral highlights."

"They'll repeat them," Gemma said, and Colette muttered, shouldn't wonder if we have reruns all next Christmas. Silvana said "No, it won't be the same, I want to watch them live."

Raven sniggered. Mrs. Etchells levered herself to the vertical and brushed coleslaw from her skirt. "Thank you for your caring spirit," she said, "or I wouldn't have slept in a bed tonight, they'd have locked the front door. Condemned to walk the streets of Beeston. Friendless."

"I don't know why you don't just stop here like everybody else," Cara said. "It can't cost much more than you're paying."

Colette smiled; she had negotiated a group rate for Al, just as if she were a company.

"Thank you, but I couldn't," Mrs. Etchells said. "I value the personal touch."

"What, like locking you out?" Colette said. "And whatever you think," she said to Silvana, "Aldershot is not close to Slough. Whereas you, you're just down the road."

"When I joined this profession," Silvana said, "it would have been unthinkable to refuse aid to someone who'd helped you develop. Let alone your own grandmother."

She swept out; as Mrs. Etchells shambled after her, a chicken bone fell from some fold in her garments and lay on the carpet. Colette turned to Alison, whispering, "What does she mean, help you develop?"

Cara heard. "I see Colette's not one of us," she said.

Mandy Coughlan said, "Training, it's just what we call training. You sit, you see. In a circle."

"Anyone could do that. You don't need to be trained for that."

"No, a—Alison, tell her. A development circle. Then you find out if you've got the knack. You see if anybody comes through. The others help you. It's a tricky time."

"Of course, it's only for the mediums," Gemma said. "For example, if you're just psychometry, palms, crystal healing, general clairvoyance, aura cleansing, feng shui, tarot, I Ching, then you don't need to sit. Not in a circle."

"So how do you know if you can do it?"

Gemma said, "Well, darling, you have a feeling for it," but Mandy flashed her pale blue eyes and said, "General client satisfaction."

"You mean they don't come wanting their money back?"

"I've never had an instance," Mandy said. "Not even you, Colette. Though you don't seem backward at coming forward. If you don't mind my saying so."

Al said, "Look, Colette's new to this, she's only asking, she doesn't mean to upset anybody. I think the thing is, Colette, possibly what you don't quite see is that we're all—we're all worn to a frazzle, we've all lost sleep over this Di business, it's not just me—we're on the end of our nerves."

"Make-or-break time," Raven said. "I mean if any of us could give her the opening, just, you know, be there for her, just let her express anything that's uppermost in her mind, about those final moments. . . ." His voice died away, and he stared at the wall.

"I think they murdered her," Colette said. "The royals. If she'd lived, she'd have only brought them into further disrepute."

"But it was her time," Gemma said, "it was her time, and she was called away."

"She was a bit thick, wasn't she?" Cara said. "She didn't get any exams at school."

"Oh, be fair now," Alison said. "I read she got a cup for being kind to her guinea pig."

"That's not an exam, though, is it? Did you—"

"What," Al said, "me have a guinea pig? Christ, no, my mum would have barbecued it. We didn't have pets. We had dogs. But not pets."

"No," Cara said, her brow crinkling, "I meant, did you get any exams, Al?"

"I tried. They entered me. I turned up. I had a pencil and everything. But there'd always be some sort of disturbance in the hall."

Gemma said, "I was barred from biology for labelling a drawing in obscene terms. But I didn't do it myself. I don't think I even knew half those words."

There was a murmur of fellow feeling. Alison said, "Colette didn't have those problems, she's got exams, I need somebody brighter than me in my life." Her voice rattled on: Colette, my working partner . . . my partner, not assistant: she broke off, and laughed uncertainly.

Raven said, "Do you know that for every person on this side, there's thirty-three on the other?"

"Really?" Gemma said. "Thirty-three airside, for every one earthside?"

Colette thought, in that case, I'm backing the dead.

Merlin and Merlyn came back from the pub: boring on with men's talk. I use Transit Forecaster, I find it invaluable oh yes, I can run it on my old Amstrad, what's the point of pouring money into the pockets of Bill Gates?

Colette leaned over to put him right on the matter, but Merlyn caught her by the arm and said, "Have you read *The Truth About Exodus*? Basically it's how they found this bit of the Bible written on a pyramid, inscribed on the side. And how, contrary to popular belief, the Egyptians actually, they actually paid the Israelis to leave. And they used the money for making the ark of the covenant. Jesus was an Egyptian, they've found scrolls, he was actually of pharaoh descent. And it's why they walk round and round at Mecca. Like they used to walk around the Great Pyramid."

"Oh, did they? I see," Colette said. "Well, you've put me right, there, Merlyn, I always did wonder."

"*Mountain K2, Search for the Gods,* that's another good one. *The Lost Book of Enki*. That's one you've got to get. He's this god from the planet Nibiru. You see, they were from space, and they needed gold from the earth to enrich the dying atmosphere of their planet, so they saw that it was on earth, gold was, so they needed somebody to mine it for them, so they therefore created man. . . ."

Al's eyes were distant; she was back at school, back in the exam hall. Hazel Leigh opposite, working her red ponytail round and round in her fingers till it was like a twist of barley sugar—and peppermints, you were allowed to suck peppermints—you weren't allowed much, not a fag: when Bryan lit up Miss Adshead was down the hall like a laser beam.

All during the maths paper there was a man chattering in her ear. It wasn't Morris, she knew it was not by his accent, and his whole general tone and bearing, by what he was talking about, and by how he was weeping: for Morris could not weep. The man, the spirit, he was talking just below the threshold, retching and sobbing. The questions were algebra; she filled in a few disordered letters, a, b, x, z. When she reached question five the man began to break through. He said, look for my cousin John Joseph, tell our Jo that my hands are bound with wire. In Spirit, even now, he had a terrible pain where the bones of his feet used to be, and that's what he relied on her to pass on to his cousin, the knowledge of this pain: tell our Jo, tell him it was that bastard that drives the Escort with the rusty wing, that cunt that always has a cold, him . . . and when in the end the crushing of the rifle butts and the men's boots seemed to drive her own feet through the scuffed vinyl tiles of the exam room, she had let the letters freely intermingle on the page, so that when Miss Adshead came to flick her paper into the pile there was nothing on it but thin pen scrawls, like the traces and loops of the wire with which the hands of this total stranger had been bound.

"Alison?" She jumped. Mandy had taken her by the wrist; she was shaking her, bringing her back to the present. "You all right, Al?" Over her shoulder she said, "Cara, go get her a stiff drink and a chicken leg. Al? Are you back with us, love? Is she pestering you? The princess?"

"No," Al said. "It's paramilitaries."

"Oh, them," Gemma said. "They can be shocking."

"I get Cossacks," Mandy said. "Apologizing for, you know—what they used to do. Cleaving. Slashing. Scourging peasants to death. Terrible."

"What's Cossacks?" Cara said, and Mandy said, "They are a very unpleasant kind of mounted police."

Raven said, "I never get anything like that. I have led various pacific lives. That's why I'm so karmically adjusted."

Al roused herself. She rubbed the wounds on her wrists. Live in the present moment, she told herself. Nottingham. September. Funeral Night. Ten minutes to ten. "Time for bed, Col," she said.

"We're not watching the highlights?"

"We can watch them upstairs." She pushed herself up from the sofa. Her feet seemed unable to support her. An effort of will saw her limp across the room, but she had wobbled as she took the weight on her feet, and her skirt flicked a wineglass from a low table, sent it spinning away from her, the liquid flying across the room and splashing red down the paintwork. It flew with such force it looked as if someone had flung it, a fact that did not escape the women; though it escaped Raven, who was slumped in his chair, and hardly twitched as the glass smashed.

There was a silence. Into it, Cara said, "Whoops-a-daisy."

Alison turned her head over her shoulder, and looked back, her face blank; did I do that? She stood, her head swivelled, too weary to move back to attend to the accident.

"I'll get it," Mandy said, hopping up, crouching neatly over the shards and splinters. Gemma turned her large cowlike eyes on Al and said, "All in, poor love," and Silvana, walking back in at that moment, tut-tutted at them. "What's this, Alison? Breaking up the happy home?"

"This is the fact," Al said. She was rocking to and fro on the bed—she was trying to rub her feet but finding the rest of her body got in the way. "I feel used. All the time I feel used. I'm put up onstage for them to see me. I have to experience for them the things they don't dare." With a little moan, she gripped her ankle, and lolled backwards. "I'm like—I'm like some form of muckraker. No, I don't mean that. I mean I'm in there, in the pockets of their dirty minds. I'm up to my elbows, I'm like—"

"A sewage worker?" Colette suggested.

"Yes! Because the clients won't do their own dirty work. They want it contracted out. They write me a check for thirty quid and expect me to clean their drains. You say help the police. I'll tell you why I don't help the police. First 'cos I hate the police. Then because—do you know where it gets you?"

"Al, I take it back. You don't have to help the police."

"That's not the point. I have to tell you why not. You have to know."

"I don't have to."

"You do. Or you'll keep coming back to it again and again. Make yourself useful, Alison. Make yourself socially useful."

"I won't. I'll never mention it."

"You will. You're that type, Colette, you can't help mentioning and mentioning things. I'm not getting at you. I'm not criticizing. But you do mention, you are—Colette, you are, one of the world's great mentioners." Al uncurled herself with a whimper, and fell back on the bed. "Can you find my brandy?"

"You've had too much already." Alison moaned. Colette added generously, "It's not your fault. We should have stopped for an early lunch. Or I could easily have brought you in a sandwich. I did offer."

"I can't eat when I'm sitting. The cards won't work if you smudge them."

"No, you've said that before."

"Not cheeseburgers. I don't agree with it."

"Nor me. It's disgusting."

"You get fingerprints on your crystals."

"It's hard to see how you could help it."

"Don't you ever drink too much, Col?"

"No, I hardly ever do."

"Don't you ever, ever? Didn't you ever, ever make a mistake?"

"Yes. Not that kind, though."

Then Al's wrath seemed to deflate. Her body collapsed too, back onto the hotel bed, as if hot air were leaking from a balloon. "I do want that brandy," she said, quietly and humbly.

She stretched out her legs. Over her own rolling contours she saw a distant view of feet. They lolled outwards as she watched: dead man's joints. "Christ," she said: and screwed up her face. The cousin of John Joseph was back, and talking in her ear: I don't want the hospital to take my legs off; I'd rather be dead out there in the field and buried, than alive with no legs.

She lay whimpering up at the dim ceiling, until Colette sighed and rose. "Okay. I'll get you a drink. But you'd do better with an aspirin and some peppermint foot lotion." She tripped into the bathroom and took from the shelf above the washbasin a plastic tumbler in a polythene shroud. Her nails punctured it; like a human membrane, it adhered, it had to be drawn away, and when she rubbed her fingertips together to discard it, and held up the tumbler, she felt against her face a bottled breath, something secondhand and not entirely clean, something breathing up at her from the interior of the glass.

She screwed open the brandy bottle and poured two fingers. Al had rolled herself up in the duvet. Her plump pink feet stuck out of the end. They did look hot, swollen. Mischievously, Colette took hold of a toe and waggled it. "This little piggy went to market—"

Alison bellowed, in someone else's voice, "In the name of Bloody Christ!"

"Sorr-ee!" Colette sang.

Alison's arm fought its way out of her wrappings, and her fingers took a grip on the tumbler, buckling its sides. She wriggled so that her shoulders were propped against the headboard, and swallowed half her drink in the first gulp. "Listen, Colette. Shall I tell you about the police? Shall I tell you? Why I won't have anything to do with them?"

"You're clearly going to," Colette said. "Look, wait a minute. Just hold on."

Al began, "You know Merlyn?"

"Wait," Colette said. "We should get it on tape."

"Okay. But hurry up."

Alison swallowed the rest of her drink. At once her face flushed. Her head was tipped back, her shiny dark hair spilling over the pillows. "So are you fixing it?"

"Yes, just a minute—okay."

COLETTE: So, it's sixth September 1997, ten thirty-three P.M., Alison is telling me—

ALISON: You know Merlyn, Merlyn with a *y*? He says he's a psychic detective. He says he's helped police forces all over the southeast. He says they call him in regularly. And you know where Merlyn lives? He lives in a trailer home.

COLETTE: So?

ALISON: So that's where it gets you, helping the police. He doesn't even have a proper lavatory.

COLETTE: How tragic.

ALISON: You say that, Miss Sneery, but you wouldn't like it. He lives outside Aylesbury. And do you know what it's like, when you help the police?

Al's eyes closed. She thought of reliving—over and over—the last few seconds of a strangled child. She thought of drowning in a car under the waters of the canal, she thought of waking in a shallow grave. She slept for a moment and woke in her duvet, wrapped in it like a sausage in its roll; she pushed up and out, fighting for space and air, and she remembered why she couldn't breathe—it was because she was dead, because she was buried. She thought, I can't think about it anymore, I'm at the end of—the end of my—and she released her breath with a great gasp: she heard *click*.

Colette was at her side, her voice nervous, oh God, Al, bending over her now. Colette's breath was against her face, polythene breath, not unpleasant but not either quite natural. "Al, is it your heart?"

She felt Colette's tiny bony hand sliding under her head, lifting it. As Colette's wrist and forearm took the weight, she felt a sudden sense of release. She gasped, sighed, as if she were newborn. Her eyes snapped open: "Switch on the tape again."

Breakfast time. Colette was down early. Listening to Alison while the tape ran—Alison crying like a child, talking in a child's voice, replying to spirit questions Colette could not hear—she had found her own hand creeping towards the brandy bottle. A shot had stiffened her spine, but the effect didn't last. She felt cold and pale now, colder and paler than ever, and she nearly threw up when she came into the breakfast room and saw Merlyn and Merlin stirring a ladle around in a vat of baked beans.

"You look as if you've been up all night," Gemma said, picking at the horns of a croissant.

"I'm fine," Colette snapped. She looked around; she couldn't very well take a table by herself, and she didn't want to sit with the boys. She pointed imperiously to the coffeepot on its hotplate, and the waitress hurried across with it. "Black is fine."

"Are you lactose intolerant?" Gemma asked her. "Soya milk is very good."

"I prefer black."

"Where's Alison?"

"Doing her hair."

"I'd have thought that would have been your job."

"I'm her business partner, not her maid."

Gemma turned the corners of her mouth down. She nudged Cara conspiratorially, but Cara was unfolding the papers to see the funeral pictures.

deceptive; it really was a tie because we put *five* of their players out of action.

Hershey wasn't the only one of my old "home towns" where I suffered grief on my return. Barrie, Ontario, was another. That, you may recall, was where I played my junior hockey with the Barrie Flyers. I always felt a special affection for the town and decided one year that it would be nice to return there and play an exhibition game against the local senior team now being coached by my old pal, Darryl Sly.

This game was a good lesson in how quickly the fans forget. I returned to Barrie not as a home town-hero-made-good but as coach of the enemy team, an *American* enemy team at that. It didn't matter to them that we had come to Barrie to help raise money for the local club. We gave them about $1,400 worth of equipment and it cost us $2,000 just to get there. Well, anyhow, the game began and, as always, we started hitting and the fans immediately got upset. The tension grew more intense as the game got more violent. As it happened, I was in an unfortunate position. Because we were carrying a surplus of players there was no room for me on or in front of the bench so I was cramped into a two-by-three foot space behind our bench, right in front of the regular seats.

Midway through the third period a big fight broke out on the ice and the fans were really going crazy. Two of them walked down from the upper reaches of the arena and sat down directly behind my position at the bench. Their feet were just about at the level of my head. These guys started abusing the players, trainers and me and kept telling us how rotten America was. Granted, with Watergate going on at the time they had a good target, but they finally went beyond the bounds of acceptable fan abuse. The language was awful so I politely asked them to let up. Well, all that did was encourage them into even more profanity. As I walked back and forth in my tiny coaching space they began harassing me in particular and even started to touch me.

I had invited a few friends from Rochester to come over and watch the game that night and I was particularly embarrassed for them. Once more, I tried to quiet the abusing fans but, this time, they turned on me and offered the challenge, "Why don't you come over here and make us shut up?"

Before I could make a move, I felt a sharp whack on the top of the head. Since there were no police or ushers around to maintain decorum, I decided that I had to take matters into my own hands. I dashed from my cramped position, over the boards, and toward my two antagonists. One of them fled, screaming, but I nabbed the other guy and after a bit of a tussle threw him back into the crowd. More fans invaded our bench area and pandemonium reigned. I was knocked down and landed on my back, breaking a bench in the process. At that moment I was stunned, and didn't know what was happening although I was later told that fans were trying to hit me and players, who by now were themselves being attacked, were stepping on me.

In the next moment the wife of one of the two guys who had originally been bugging us, jumped on my chest and began kicking me in the face. (Fortunately, the sharp-pointed women's shoes were not in vogue at the time.) That woke me up. After taking a few more blows, I decided that I would invoke an amendment to the Men's Liberation Act, so I kicked her where the sun don't shine until she retreated, shouting "I wish I had killed you, ya bum!"

The police arrived after the fight had ended but that was just the start of my troubles. I was arrested and charged with assault causing bodily harm. Me, a guy who had never even had a speeding ticket in his life, never been in jail, never been in court. Next thing I knew I was in the police station being fingerprinted and having my picture taken, like a common criminal. I hired a lawyer and he laid the cards on the table.

"One of the guys claims you damaged his suit and it's worth eighty-two bucks. If you pay for the suit and apologize to him and his wife, he'll drop the charges."

To begin with, his clothes weren't worth eighty-two bucks. For another thing, what was I supposed to apologize for? My clothes had been ripped, my adopted country had been insulted, and I had to stay in Barrie for an extra two days while Rose was in a Rochester hospital being treated for a kidney stone. No way was I going to apologize. Which meant only one thing—we would have to go to trial.

Maybe if I had had an idea of the torture I would have to endure at the trial I would have been more restrained to begin with, although I doubt it; the provocation was too severe. In any event, I had to make five trips to Barrie before the actual trial got underway.

The trial opened with my enemy—the guy who started it in the first place—telling the court that I was the rottenest, worst guy in the world. Listening to him, you would have thought snakes looked good by comparison. For the whole day I had to listen to him give it to me. How I had beaten him up and kicked his wife, the whole bit. I couldn't say a word of rebuttal.

My turn came the next day. I stood before the judge and began answering his questions. The more I talked, the more my opponent would chuckle and generally make disparaging asides about me. The more he turned and laughed with his friends the more I became exasperated. I thought to myself, "If I'm going to jail, I'm going out on my shield, because this weasel is not going to laugh at everything I say."

I finally said: "Your Honour, I sat here all day yesterday with my mouth shut, listening to the charges and the answers to your questions. Now that I'm up here, he's making a mockery out of everything I say. Do I have to take this?"

The judge looked down at me and I thought, "Uh oh, he looks mad. I'll bet he says 'control your temper, Mr. Cherry, because that's what got you here in the first place.'" But, the judge cleared his throat. "No, you don't, Mr. Cherry." Then he turned to my accuser and snapped: "One more word or action from you and you'll be put out of this court room."

The questions came fast and furious and I did my best to answer them as did my players, who sought to defend me. Some of my players went wild trying to defend me. For instance, my goalie, Bob Sneddon, said he saw the whole thing and that I never laid a finger on the man. Well, how in the world could Bob have seen it; he was in the net, one hundred feet away, wearing his goalie mask, I found out later.

I tried to be as truthful as possible in answering the questions, but I had no idea how the judge was leaning. Finally, after hearing me for several hours, he said, "Mr. Cherry, you remind me of a person who momentarily lost his cool."

"You're absolutely right, Your Honour." With that, he ended the trial and invited us back for the verdict the next day. I wasn't convinced that I would be handed a "not guilty" verdict, but I wasn't feeling too depressed either because a lot of people had rallied behind me, including Darryl Sly and Bep Guidolin, the former NHL player who preceded me as coach of the Bruins. Somebody asked Bep why he had come and he joked, "If Don is going to get sixty days I wanted to assure him I'd be sending fresh macaroni and chicken to the jailhouse."

Now it was time for the verdict. Preceding me on the stand was the fellow who had originally preceded me at the station house when I had been brought in. This fellow had thrown hot water at his wife in a dispute and the judge sentenced him to ninety days in jail. He was up for assault causing bodily harm, the same charge I had. Was I going to get hit for ninety days, too? I had started to visualize myself in prison stripes behind bars when the judge began addressing me:

"Mr. Cherry, I don't believe a word of what your players said here on the stand. Your players would lie their way to hell for you, so I don't believe them and I'm going to have to convict you!"

My head began to spin and my knees got weak, but the judge went on, turning to my enemy: "On the other hand, I find the actions of the plaintiff disgusting." He then ripped into the guy for defaming the United States and instigating the riot. Finally, "I find Mr. Cherry an honourable gentleman who just happened to lose his cool in the moment of battle. Sentence suspended!"

Instead of keeping my big mouth shut, I immediately got to my feet. My lawyer was afraid I was going to louse up the whole thing and grabbed my arm, but it was too late. "Your Honour," I proclaimed. "Someday I'm going to be coaching in the National Hockey League and I want you to know that I will never allow myself to become involved with people like this again. That is a promise."

"That's all I want to hear, Mr. Cherry," said the judge who then cleared the courtroom.

The question was, could I keep my word? The test came during a game in Richmond, Virginia. We had gotten into an extremely physical match-up with the local club, the Robins, and I was in rare form, standing on the bench, yapping away at the referee. As I stepped down to my normal position, an older man leaned over and corked me dead center and stunned me momentarily, shouting, "How do you like that—you no good sonofabitch!"

Instinctively, I reached up and grabbed him by the collar, pulled my arm back and began the inevitable follow-through to his jaw (which probably would have killed the old guy) when a vision of the judge in Barrie came to mind and activated my arm emergency brake. I merely pushed the guy out of the way and resumed coaching.

That act of contrition probably saved my career, because I would have been drawn and quartered in Richmond for hitting one of their Southern "gentlemen."

The notoriety of the Rochester Americans did not hurt us at home or on the road. During the 1972-73 season our leader was Battleship Kelly. He played in 70 games, scored 27 goals and 35 assists for 62 points and wound up with 206 minutes in penalties. I loved Battleship like a son and I would have liked to have him remain in Rochester as long as I was the coach and general manager, but I also had an obligation to the kid; he belonged in the NHL and I made it my business to try to arrange that he move into the bigs. I made a deal with the St. Louis Blues for $50,000, which was a big profit, because we had originally obtained Battleship for a song.

A week after the deal had been completed a huge box arrived at the house. I opened it up and there was a colour television set with a note from Battleship Kelly (and his agent Charles Abrahams), thanking me for what I had done for his career. That says something for Kelly's class.

With Battleship gone, I needed another enforcer for the 1973-74 campaign. There was only one thing to do; scrounge around the training camps in September, 1973 to see what the big-league clubs had at the bottom of their barrels. Since I had had success in finding Kelly, I figured I might come up with another diamond-in-the-rough. And I did, at the training base of the St. Louis Blues.

The player in question didn't look like a hockey player when I first cast eyes on him. Standing six feet tall and weighing 200 pounds, John Wensink was wearing a hairdo that looked like a willow tree, embellished by a frightening Fu Manchu mustache.

His skating was so atrocious I had half a mind to buy him a pair of double-runners. Yet there was something about him that I liked; call it an animal instinct, a ferocity that went far beyond anything that Battleship had betrayed. The Blues had him ticketed for Port Huron, a team in the International League, which was below the AHL. I made a deal with the Blues and within four days, Wensink was a Rochester American. In my heart I knew that the fans would like him as much as they had enjoyed Kelly.

The Blues g.m., Chuck Catto, and their chief scout came down to see John play his first game. They came to me after the game and said, "Don, we're sorry. We didn't mean to stick you with a player as bad as Wensink. You can let him go." I said, "I thought he played great." They looked at me as if I was nuts, because John had played terribly, but I could tell there was something there.

Besides beef, I needed some scoring punch. Buffalo had a winger called Murray Kuntz. I bought him for the Americans and he made me look like a genius, scoring a league-leading 51 goals that year. Then again, there were some guys who made me look like a bum. The classic example was a moon-faced defenseman, Jean Gauthier, who played for the Montreal Canadiens and about a dozen other teams both in the minors and the NHL. When I spotted him, Gauthier was still Canadiens' property, so I approached Sammy Pollock, general manager of the Montreal club and a fellow regarded as a genius for knowing and manipulating players. "Sam," I said, "I'd like to sign Gauthier."

Pollock agreed, but offered me a bit of advice. "You can have him; but if you're smart you'll only sign him until Christmas." That seemed ridiculous and I told Pollock so. "Sam, I'm gonna sign him the whole way."

So, what happened? Half way through the season Gauthier came up with a sore back *and didn't play a game after Christmas.* I learned then and there that I wasn't so smart after all.

Much as I was personally embarrassed by the Gauthier episode, I really couldn't complain about the season. Wensink became my pet project and he proved to be a winner. We had another big, tough team of mean hard workers who wanted to show everyone that they belonged in professional hockey, and the result was crowds like they never had before in Rochester.

The rink's capacity was about 7,000 but one night we had 8,200 jammed into the place. We even had the fire marshall on our side and I had given him a special spot to stand and view the game near rinkside. (One night a club owner, not realizing who the fire marshall was, ordered him to move from his spot. That cost us a thousand customers a game.)

Although we had a number of quality players, the essence of our club was Wensink. He intimidated the opposition and was loved by his teammates. He didn't have the same offensive skills of Kelly but I worked with him all the time, even after all the other players had finished practice.

One day when we were practising at an out-of-town rink—just Wensink and I—everybody else had left the arena and it was dark. I was trying to teach him how to stand, keeping his position in front of the net while the enemy defensemen try to clear him away. I took the part of the enemy defenseman and John was to try and keep me from upsetting him. So, there were the pair of us high sticking, punching and generally knocking each other all over the place. We were so intent on this personal battle that we did not even notice that the home team had arrived at the sidelines and were watching us intently, completely incredulous. You see, by this time Wensink was punching me and I was counterpunching him until, finally, I looked over to the sidelines and there was this collection of players, all standing there with their mouths agape. Needless to say, that team was a little bit more afraid of us the next night. The special relationship I had enjoyed with Wensink endured throughout his stay in Rochester, but don't imagine that I enjoyed all my players on the Americans or that the vice was versa.

We had a goalie named Gaye Cooley who shared the goaltending chores with Lynn Zimmerman. Although Zimmy was our property, Cooley belonged to the Boston Bruins and was "on loan" to us.

Superficially, you might get the impression that Cooley was a reasonable guy. He attended Michigan State University and had been a star in the National Collegiate Athletic Association tournament in 1966. But college doesn't always guarantee knowledge nor does it invariably produce level-headed hockey players.

Once, we were enroute to Jacksonville, Florida (which then had an AHL franchise, believe it or not,) and had to make a special stop at the airport in Atlanta. While we were waiting, Cooley had a few drinks, and then a few drinks too many. By the time we got back on the plane he was feeling no pain, which I wouldn't mind except that there were a few dozen passengers on the plane who took a dim view of him. As we moved to the back of the plane, Cooley patted one of the stewardesses. I quickly moved in on him and thrust him into a back seat, then I took the seat immediately ahead of him.

I had had my fill of Cooley from other incidents and I was hoping that we could settle down for a peaceful ride on to Jacksonville when I heard the goalie grunt, "You son of a bitch."

He had grated the nerve. I flew out of my chair, grabbed him by the throat and sunk my fingernails into his Adam's apple. Cooley tried to get up but I had him well-pinned and my fingernails were now digging his flesh. Some of the guys got scared and started to get up. "Don't anybody move!" I insisted. "This guy has had it coming to him for a long time." Cooley's eyeballs were tilting up to his head.

I slammed his head against the tray that was hanging from the chair in front and then let him go. Cooley knew, instinctively, that he should not attempt an act of retaliation. I knew that the lesson had been well-administered. I returned to my seat secure in the knowledge that my goalie would no longer be a problem to me.

Wensink, on the other hand, *was* a problem although for different reasons. He had taken his enforcer role very seriously; maybe too seriously and for that I have only Don Cherry to blame. On the other hand, you have to remember that this was the 1973-74 season when the Philadelphia Flyers were rampaging through the National Hockey League making goonism the key to victory. Wensink, whom everyone called Wire, because of his hair, desperately wanted to make it to the NHL and he figured that the shortest route was via the upper cut.

Well, he very nearly got thrown out following a game against the Nova Scotia Voyageurs at our rink in Rochester. Wensink's opponent on this night was a big winger named Len Cunning. He and John weighed about the same but Cunning had three inches on John. That hardly mattered once the punches began to fly. Wensink flattened him and once Cunning was down, wouldn't let him up. By the time the officials separated them, Cunning was in such bad shape that he had to be taken to the hospital.

Normally, I don't get unnerved over a hockey fight, but this one put the fear of God in me. Meanwhile, the police had been summoned and they questioned Wensink who really didn't seem very bothered.

After talking to reporters, I made my way to my office, where eight owners had gathered. They didn't look happy but I was pleased with the 2-2 tie so I couldn't figure out their problem. Finally, one owner said "I have a high reputation in this city and I'm not going to see it go down the drain connected with a player like Wensink. That animal goes!"

I knew John and I were in trouble. John was only doing what I had encouraged him to do, although he had gone too far this time, but I couldn't let him down. I said, "If he goes, so do I."

I won my point and, ironically enough, a month later, when Wensink had been sidelined with a knee injury, our attendance dropped about a thousand per game, and the same owner who had wanted to can Wensink kept bugging me about him coming back because our gate was slipping. Strange people in this world we live in, yes?

The sudden peace-in-our-time bleats of a few of the media made absolutely no impression on me or my players. Wensink knew that I wanted him to play rough and we continued on our merry way. Mind you, we did not barrel through the AHL with impunity. There were some teams who gave us a hard time and some who could be almost as tough. We learned that lesson one evening in Providence during a game against the Reds. Their version of Wensink was a husky left wing named Bertwin Hillard Wilson, Bert for short. On this night Wilson began doing a number on Doug Ferguson, a little guy out of Cornell University who was playing center for us. You could hear the drumbeat on Ferguson's head all over the Providence rink.

One of Wensink's jobs — and any "policeman's" for that matter — was to protect the little men from being stomped on by the bullies. As soon as I saw what was happening to little Ferguson I leaned over Wensink's shoulder and calmly intoned: "John, would you like to go out on the ice for a spin?"

John tilted his head upward and replied: "I'd love to go out on the ice for a spin, Grapes."

"Well," I suggested, "be my guest."

You would have thought World War III had just begun. François Ouimet, one of our defensemen, and Andy Peloffy of the Reds went at it and then there was a wild battle between our goalie, Lynn Zimmerman, and Ron Fogal, a huge Providence defenseman. (Zimmy ultimately received a $200 fine as well as other automatic fines totalling $150 "for malicious use of a stick in an attempt to injure an opponent." Fogal's fines totalled $500. Zimmerman also was suspended for three games for his stick attack. Fogal was sidelined two months with torn knee ligaments suffered in the fracas.) Meanwhile, Wensink was out there getting Wilson off Ferguson and bodies were flying in all directions. John Muckler, coach of the Reds, left his bench with a stick in his hand, trying to attack me. By now the melee had gotten so out of hand that the State Troopers had been summoned, but they couldn't get there soon enough. Blood was being spilled all over the place (including on the glass partitions) and the Reds were still trying to destroy Wensink. But he kept knocking them down as fast as they came at him. For once, I used my head and stayed cool. I would not be suckered out there and I'm glad I stayed put. I knew I was in enough trouble already.

For being such a nice guy I was hit with a $500 fine. Naturally, it bugged me but I still maintained my cool. When a reporter asked me about it I said, "If that's the penalty I'll take my punishment — I only wish I hadn't bought my wife a fur coat for Christmas. Maybe I'll have to take it back now."

The fellow I was worried about was Wensink. He received a ten-game suspension because *I* had sent him out on the ice. I was tormented by my action and by the thought that I might have ruined the kid's career. Only time would tell. Meanwhile, Wensink, under suspension, returned to his home in Maxville, Ontario, and we went on with our business of playing hockey, and trying to duck criticism. The worst of it emanated from Providence where John Muckler and the Reds' owners tried to play saints while portraying me as the devil incarnate. (I liked it.)

The schedule called for us to return to Providence eleven games later, which was precisely when Wensink's suspension was to end. Needless to say, all those Providence hypocrites who had been criticizing us weeks earlier now were trumpeting the return engagement as the greatest game of all time: Wensink returns to the scene of his crime. Unknown to the Providence promoters, Wensink had been called up to the National Hockey League for a three-game trial with the St. Louis Blues. (He wound up with no goals, no assists, no points, no penalties.) I decided to rub it in a little, and phoned the Providence papers: "Seeing that you and your city figure John Wensink for an animal, I'm not going to bring him to Providence!"

Of course, the owner of the Reds went berserk because Wensink's absence figured to cost him 5,000 fans at the gate—and it did. But we still managed to have some fun. You see there was a little Italian guy in Providence who was a wild hockey nut.

More than anything in the world, this guy wanted to get on the ice in uniform and skate with a professional hockey team. Naturally, he wanted to do it with the home team, so he asked Muckler about it and Muckler said nothing doing. That's when he got in touch with me. "If you let me skate in the warm-up with the Americans," he said, "I'll give you 500 bucks."

I thought to myself: 500 bucks isn't bad. With that money we could throw a team party. Why the heck not? Besides, the guy looked like a hockey player. He was 26, and solidly built. I said, okay, he was on. So, the guy got dressed with us, put on the skates and walked out on to the ice with the rest of the Rochester Americans.

As soon as he stepped on the ice a group of about 300 fans went crazy. You see, the guy had made a $500 bet with his friends that he would skate with the Americans and there he was!

Of course, I use the term "skate" loosely in this case. He could hardly stand on his pins and as he laboured around the rink I could hardly look. But he was undaunted; he waved to his friends like a conquering hero and also waved to the crowd. Unfortunately, one of the spectators happened to be Jack Butterfield, the president of the American Hockey League.

My Italian hockey player completed the warm-up without mishap and returned to the dressing room where, as promised, he peeled off five one hundred dollar bills and shook my hand. (I also received a stern letter from Butterfield cautioning me against further indiscretions, and saying that I was ridiculing the game, etc. He was right—what a dumb thing to do.) I gave the money to the team captain, Rod Graham, and what a party we had.

The departure of Wensink to the St. Louis Blues gave me cause for concern because I feared they would use him exclusively for goon purposes when, actually, he was developing into an efficient, if not high-scoring, forward. The Blues, somehow, managed to mis-use Battleship Kelly and ultimately traded him to the Pittsburgh Penguins. As luck would have it, the Penguins and the Blues were scheduled to meet on the night that Wensink was to make his NHL debut.

This bothered me a great deal. I had babied John along and I realized that there were still some fighters around it would not be good for him to meet, at least not just yet. Kelly was among them. The prospect of Wensink fighting Kelly disturbed me because it would be like two of my sons going at each other. I had to do something about it, so I took Rose, Cindy, and Timothy to Pittsburgh and checked into the same hotel as the Blues. I phoned Battleship and invited him over for lunch after his morning skate.

Wensink was already at the table. I introduced them and the three of us chatted and ate and then John excused himself. He had to attend a team meeting. Once Wensink was out of earshot, I leaned over the table and levelled with Battleship. "You know, Bob, I've never asked you for anything but today I'm going to ask you a favour. I know why St. Louis brought John up. They're going to throw him out there near the end of the game to fight with you but John isn't ready to fight you. I'm asking you as a favour not to fight with John tonight." I said good-bye to Battleship and wondered what would happen.

Sure enough, Wensink was kept on the Blues' bench until the final five minutes of the game. At last, out he came and he plied his wing as best he could. Not surprisingly, he was matched up with Battleship. Once, twice, three times, Wensink checked Kelly. (In those days if anyone hit Bob that hard his gloves would fly off and he would start swinging while the Pittsburgh organist played *Anchors Aweigh*.) But this time Battleship minded his business. He didn't fight; he didn't even *look* at John. I'll always respect Battleship for his class that night.

After his three-game trial with the Blues, Wensink returned to the Americans and continued to play his robust game. Then, he injured his knee and was out for a few games, so we let him go home and rest up until he was ready. Meanwhile, we had taken off for Jacksonville where we were to play a game that would determine first place. Suddenly, I got a brainstorm. Wensink has been such a great help to the club, why not bring him down so that he could enjoy some sun and relaxation.

We got the message through to him and he said, fine, he would love to meet us in Jacksonville. Our game was scheduled for the next night but Wensink had not yet arrived. About an hour before game time I began making up our lineup which had to be turned in to the referee prior to the opening face-off. As I scrawled in the names I realized that we were two men short so just for the sake of filling up space I wrote Wensink's name on the roster. I just liked to see John's name on our lineup even though I knew that he wasn't going to play, let alone show up in Jacksonville. Who knows, maybe I figured that the sight of John Wensink on our card would scare the other coach. In any event the game began and Jacksonville really took it to us. Knowing that John wasn't on the ice, they began pushing our club around.

With about five minutes remaining in the first period, I casually looked over my shoulder at someone standing about ten feet from the bench. It was John! He had quietly arrived during the first period and was minding his own business, watching the game. I walked over to him, shook his hand and said, "John, go get your equipment on."

He thought I was kidding. "John," I insisted, "go get your equipment on." Now he knew I wasn't kidding.

When the second period began the Rochester Americans had one more player in the lineup than they had had when the game began. Once the Jacksonville players saw him they went bananas. The coach yelled, "You can't do that. You can't put him in the game. He's not in the lineup."

I called the referee over and requested that he produce the lineup. There it was, John Wensink's name in the lineup. I had no intention of playing him; all John did was stand at the end of the bench, growling at every Jacksonville player who skated by. From that point on the home team became infinitely tamer and, from our viewpoint, more manageable. We won the game and clinched first place over-all. After that we went out and partied well into the night, almost forgetting that we had chartered a fishing boat to take us out in the Atlantic the next day. We made it to the boat a half hour late on a beautiful, sunny morning. But we were so hung over from the partying that not one single guy from the team had the energy to drop a fishing line into the water. The captain just cruised around while we slept in the sun, getting a burn. Eventually, one of the fellows dropped a line into the water but all he caught was a turtle!

For all intents and purposes I could have remained in Rochester for the rest of my life. As general manager, I could do exactly what I wanted with the team. I was given a free car. I was making $25,000 a year. I was doing commercials and banquets. I had my own players. If I didn't like a player, I could get rid of him without a hassle. There was no pressure.

But, there also was no big-time. The entertainer in me demanded that I make it to the top. Rochester was beautiful but, no matter how you say it, it wasn't *numero uno*. When the Boston Bruins called I had to answer.

CHAPTER FOURTEEN

Remembering Bobby Orr, Phil Esposito, Brad Park, And Other Friends

Looking back, the second best thing about being hired by the Boston Bruins was the fact that, at long last, I had made it as a coach in the National Hockey League.

The first best thing was that I was coach of the team for which Bobby Orr was a player. Mind you, I didn't say that I *coached* Bobby Orr because that would be the most presumptuous thing any coach could ever say. *Nobody* coached Bobby Orr. He was the greatest hockey player I have ever seen, Gordie Howe and Wayne Gretzky included. I felt that there was very little I could do to improve on Orr's perfection. From time to time, though, I would drop little hints here and there.

Actually, it was not easy to deal with Bobby on any level—player or friend—because he was such an unusual person; and I don't mean that in a negative way. It was simply that with all the pressures on him, socially, physically, and otherwise, he became a significantly detached individual; one who was conspicuously wary of others.

A case in point: I was brand new at the job in Boston and really hadn't had a chance to sit down with Bobby. One day I noticed him sitting alone in a hotel coffee shop in Chicago. I walked over, sat next to him and tried to make conversation. At first, he seemed friendly so I began thinking about what subjects might interest him. I knew he was from Parry Sound, Ontario, a town on Georgian Bay, so I figured it would be a good idea to talk fishing. "Whaddya catch?" I asked him and immediately we swung into a chat about hooks, lines, and sinkers.

At first he seemed very enthused about the chat but then, like a smart defenseman divining an attacking play, he quite obviously sensed that the only reason I was talking about fishing was to make conversation with him—and he clammed up. I didn't lose him forever with that incident, but it did take me a while to get to know him.

Unfortunately, Orr didn't have a press agent who could trumpet the good works he did very quietly. Bobby would visit a Boston-area hospital three times a week just to cheer up the sick kids. He didn't tell anybody, not even his close friends on the team and certainly not me. But one day I had to take my son, Timothy, to the childrens' division of Massachusetts General Hospital and I began chatting with some of the nurses. They told me that my all-star defenseman was a regular visitor.

Orr wouldn't tell anyone because, despite his widespread appeal, he loathed the limelight. Game after game, win or lose, whether he was the hero or insignificant, the reporters would chase after him. If we won a game, 3-0, the newspaper guys wouldn't seek out the goalie who got the shutout or the guy who scored the hat trick, they'd want to see Bobby. This bothered him to the extent that he began to hide in the trainer's room just so that some of his teammates could get some of the limelight.

Demands upon him were relentless wherever he played. Once, we had an exhibition game in Moncton, New Brunswick, and we left Bobby home to rest. The fans were furious when they learned that Orr had not come. They even threw cans and pop bottles at us when we took to the ice. Another time we were in Springfield, Massachusetts, and the arena was packed in anticipation of Orr. Bobby played that night, but he got into a fight early in the game and referee Dave Newell threw him out.

As Orr trooped off to the dressing room the owner of the Springfield hockey club realized that he'd have a riot on his hands if Orr only played a couple of minutes and then was finished for the night. He grabbed Newell. "Are you crazy? Do you want a riot? You gotta get Orr back in the game!"

I give Newell credit. Instead of going through the red tape rigamarole that some others might have, he simply sized up the situation and ordered Orr back on to the bench. And Bobby obliged.

It was but another example of Bobby's unselfishness; a trait I got to know and respect as I coached the Bruins. There was one time when Orr and Phil Esposito were running neck-and-neck for the scoring championship. Time and again Bobby would find himself in excellent scoring position, but instead of firing the puck he would look around for someone to pass to and often it was Phil. So, finally, I asked my defenseman Carol Vadnais what was going on with Bobby and why he was squandering potential points. "Don't you know?" he said. "He's trying not to get too far ahead of Phil for the scoring title." He risked the Art Ross Trophy in order to make the team play better.

Orr was so intense about winning that he would react in curious ways to success; like the time we were playing the Canadiens in an exhibition game and Bobby let one of the Montreal forwards walk right around him. He felt a sense of personal insult about being beaten and on the very next play he grabbed the puck and went through the entire Canadiens team to score. When he returned to the bench, I leaned over and said, "Nice goal, Bobby!" But he was still hot under the collar over being beaten. In a very derogatory tone, he shot back at me: "Oh, thanks, coach. Thanks a lot." What he was really telling me was, "Are you kidding—just shut up and coach." I learned early just to let him play his game; you don't pull the reins on Secretariat.

Those who had the good fortune to watch Orr in action have special manoeuvers they treasure, I have fond recollections of a trick he pulled one day while all alone after a practice. I was there having a relaxed skate with Vadnais while Orr was standing alone with a puck at the far corner of the rink parallel to the net. Bobby hit the puck so that it flew about four feet in the air, then he took the stick and batted the puck again high in the air about ten feet over his head. As the rubber came down, and without even looking at it, he batted the puck forty feet into the top corner of the net—on a backhander no less.

Well, I couldn't believe what I had seen and, privately, Vadnais couldn't believe it either. After about a minute Vad and I looked at each other and, finally, Vad said: "Did you see what I just saw?"

I said, "Yes, and I'm glad you mentioned it because I thought my eyes had failed me."

Of course that wasn't the only time I felt that Orr had caused me to see strange things. Another time we were playing the Flames and I had Bobby out on the ice killing a penalty. He had a habit of going behind the net, coming out to the east and then doing figure-eights back behind his net again. On this occasion Bobby got the puck behind our net and slowly moved up along the right boards. None of the Atlanta players dared run at him at the time because they knew they would be deked and caught out of position, so they all sat back as he moved up the side. He crossed our blue line, the center red line, the Flames' blue line and then moved into the corner near the Atlanta net. Now the Flames figured that they had him trapped—literally in a corner, so the whole team ran at him, including the goaltender. Suddenly, Bobby accelerated, went behind the net, came out the other side and put the puck into the twine on his backhand while the entire Atlanta team was flat on the ice!

Most players would jump around or hot-dog it after scoring a goal like that, but not Bobby. As soon as the red light flashed he put his head down because he knew he had embarrassed the entire Flames team; he hated embarrassing people.

While all these amazing accomplishments were taking place Bobby was suffering constant pain in his ailing knees, especially his left knee. If it had been up to me I would have spotted him as a regular rather than subject him to all the pain he was enduring, but there was no way he'd allow me to bench him. He *had* to play. From time to time I would pretend to ignore him and select other players to take the ice when it would have been Orr's turn but he made sure that I knew he was there, reminding me that he *expected* to take the next shift. I simply could not ignore him.

One of Bobby's idiosyncracies was the manner in which he laced his skates. He would lace them so loosely that they were almost falling off his feet. Interestingly, the only other guy I ever saw lace his skates like that was Eddie Shore who, with Orr, was one of the two greatest defensemen of all time, and one of the two greatest skaters.

Another strange thing about Orr was that he disdained new equipment. He liked to wear beat-up old shin pads that weren't fit for a neighbourhood rink. Once Bobby had the shin pads in place he would insert a thick layer of cotton to build up the cushion between his knee and the pads. That five inches of cotton meant a lot to Orr. Once, our trainer, Frosty Forristall, thought he had lost the cotton and you would have thought, judging by Bobby's reaction, that the plans for the atomic bomb had been lost. Fortunately, Frosty found the cotton.

Unlike most players, Orr didn't wear socks when he played; just skated in his bare feet. He felt it gave him a better feel for the skates. Then, there were his gloves, which were really unusual. Instead of thick padding, he had a thin lining sewn in that gave him a special *rapport* with his stick.

To Bobby, his stick was a finely-tuned instrument. In between periods, no matter how tired he was, he'd get up and shave his stick. I once asked him why he didn't have one of the equipment men or trainers do it for him, but he just shrugged and kept on shaving.

It was pretty clear to Orr that I made it a practice not to tell him how to play his game but one day he approached me and said, "Grapes, give me a little crap, too, won't you please? Include me in when you're givin' it to the rest of the guys."

I decided to take him up on his generous offer and began looking for an aspect of his play to criticize. I finally hit on something. In one-on-one situations, where an opposing forward would skate in on Orr, Bobby had a habit of training his eye on the puck rather than on the man. I told him I thought he could improve on his defensive work if he concentrated on the man and not the rubber. Right after that we had a game against the Los Angeles Kings. In the second period one of the Kings bore down on Orr and Bobby made a textbook play, right in front of our bench, taking the man out as perfectly as a coach could expect. But while he was doing it, Bobby looked over at me and laughed, waving and pointing to be sure I saw what he was doing. The players broke up.

Another time we were playing the Washington Caps and Bobby was out for a face-off. The Caps center was lining up his players around the face-off circle and motioned to a young rookie defenseman to stand over to the right. At that moment the rookie looked at Bobby and Bobby shook his head and told him to go back over to his left—and the guy did it. I couldn't believe it: the kid thought so much of Bobby that he knew Bobby wouldn't lie to him. (P.S. The puck went to the kid.)

Considering his knees, Orr probably absorbed more abuse than any other hockey player. Once he was playing in an All-Star game when Bobby Hull was playing left wing for the Chicago Black Hawks. When Hull was in form he could fire the puck at a speed of 120 m.p.h.

On this occasion Hull wound up for his big slapshot and the puck rammed Bobby right in the groin. Orr crawled off the ice in frightful pain and crawled down the hallway. Five minutes later he was right back on the ice again—in an All-Star Game!

Another time he was crosschecked in the back of the neck by a Washington player and suffered whiplash. The blow was so severe that Orr couldn't hold his head up and when he came off the ice at the end of the second period, he had to lie down. When the buzzer signalled the players back onto the ice, a couple of guys had to lift up Bobby's head and body at the same time. He insisted on taking the ice for the next period. "Bobby," I said, "we've got the game won. Take it easy; there's no problem at all with these guys." But he wouldn't take it easy. He went out and played; how, I don't know. But to this day, if you see Bobby Orr in the street and you're behind him and call his name, he won't just twist his neck around, he'll have to turn his whole body—all because of the whiplash suffered that night against the Caps. (I know, by now you are thinking, "Can this guy really be this great? And is this guy Cherry in love with Orr?" My answer to the former question is yes and my answer to the latter question is . . . yes.)

As difficult as the physical aspect of Orr's life had been, the social part left him little pleasure, simply because the fans were always after him. Solitude was virtually impossible, what with the demands of the media and fans. I remember once after we had played an afternoon game at Boston Garden, we then had to catch a plane for an out-of-town game. Rose, Timothy, Bobby, Phil Esposito, Carol Vadnais and I were all driving out to the airport together from Boston Garden. The car was parked in the Garden and from there we would drive down a ramp and out the Garden's back exit. The problem, as it usually was in Orr's case, was that the fans always seemed to figure out where the players were and how they were making their exit.

Sure enough there were a hundred kids waiting for us as we headed out of the building. It was frightening and Bobby, who had had enough trouble with fans already, sensed that there would be trouble if we stopped. "Grapes," he implored me, "don't stop! We'll never get to the plane."

But Phil wanted me to stop. "Hey," he said, "we'll sign a few autographs. What's the difference?" And with that, Rose rolled down the window.

Well, I'd never seen anything like it. The kids, seeing Bobby, began storming the car, climbing through the window, ripping his tie, his clothes, throwing books at him to autograph; it was unbelievable. We finally escaped with our lives, but there never was peace for Bobby. I remember when he and his wife, Peg, went shopping for a toy to give to their baby son. It was the first time he had ever bought anything for the baby and was in a toy shop when somebody recognized him. The people pushed him against a wall and he couldn't escape for an hour.

Even his own players would bug him. Before a game other players would send him sticks to be autographed for their fans or their uncles or cousins. Bobby would take all the sticks into the showers and sit down and autograph them just so the other guys wouldn't see him. He felt embarrassed about the whole business.

Working with Orr, for me, was like being a museum curator watching an extremely valuable piece of art disintegrate before your eyes. It was evident to me—as, I'm sure, it was to Bobby—that the relentless pressure he applied to his body would ultimately take its toll on his ailing knees. Doctors had made it clear that there was a limit to the abuse he could absorb and, likewise, a limit to the number of times they could employ surgical techniques to repair the damage.

I would try to find ways and means to lessen the punishment doled out to Bobby, but it was virtually impossible to curb his reckless—and great—play. He would not take it easy during a game when we had it won, no matter whether the foe was a humpty-dumpty team or champions like the Montreal Canadiens. It all was rooted in Orr's pride in his workmanship. He felt that he had to play to the hilt, even in an exhibition game. When we lost Bobby felt it was his fault.

I'm glad he never went into coaching, because he had the curious notion that everyone on the team thought and would act the way he did and thus would expend as much energy. As a result he was ruthless with teammates he felt did not try as hard as he did.

Opponents had so much respect for Orr that few would ever deliver a cheap shot at him. There was one exception and that was Hilliard Graves, a journeyman forward who had bounced around the league and was playing for Atlanta at the time. Graves had one thing going for him; a somewhat sly method of skating up low against an opponent from the side, and nailing him around knee level. The element of surprise combined with Graves' lower center of gravity enabled him to disable a few players around the league. We knew he was after Bobby and did our best to ensure that he didn't hurt him.

One time in Atlanta Graves took a run at Bobby. He missed, and Orr just laughed. But it drove me nuts! I grabbed a player named Hank

Nowak and threw him on the ice, yelling, "Get him¦ Hank!" Hank skated into the play, but then came back to the bench almost immediately. "Get who?" he asked seriously. The bench broke up. (Hank once told me he only needed six games for a full pension, but couldn't find anyone who'd give him a break. Life is cruel . . .)

I'll never forget the very last game Bobby Orr played for the Boston Bruins. We were at Madison Square Garden and big John Davidson was in the nets for the Rangers. Playing great at the time, Davidson had the biggest, heaviest catching glove I had ever seen in my life.

On this night John was really hot, and he robbed Bobby twice of sure goals. The score was tied in the second period when Orr glided over the red line, moved up to the Ranger blue line, and uncorked a real beauty of a slapshot. As he wound up, I could almost hear Bobby saying to himself: "Davidson, this puck's goin' by you . . . or it's goin' through you!" Bobby's shot was so hard it knocked the glove off Davidson's hand, and actually drove Davidson back into the net—no mean feat.

An hour after the game I noticed Bobby limping onto the bus. Asking him what happened, he replied, "Geez, Grapes, I don't know. I was standing and talking to Rod Gilbert at the top of the tunnel, and when I turned to go, something popped. My knee seems to be locking." Little did I know at that moment that he was saying to me, "Goodbye, Stanley Cup."

The Jacobs brothers had bought the team. Since they were from Buffalo, I don't think they really knew what Bobby Orr meant to the people of Boston. The Jacobs seemed like nice enough guys; but I could see that the team was going to be run like a business and nothing else. They left the hockey to Harry Sinden, including signing Orr. Meanwhile, Alan Eagleson was Orr's agent and I could see fireworks ahead.

When the Jacobs folks realized how troubled Bobby's wheels were, their attitude toward Bobby turned negative, just as he was up for a new contract. Naturally Orr wanted a multi-year deal, but he also wanted the deal guaranteed.

The Jacobs weren't interested in any of that and the rumours immediately began to swirl that Bobby Orr, a Boston institution, would soon become a Chicago Black Hawk. Although the contract was none of my business, I asked Bobby about it. "Grapes," he said, "they're treating me like I'm a horse ready to be shot."

Cripes! he was still the best in the league—even on one leg!

The kid who once was in love with life and hockey was now turned off and bitter about the game he still was playing. In a sense he was still naive. He couldn't quite understand the all-business attitude of the Jacobs family, nor could he fathom why Harry Sinden wasn't helping him; especially in view of the fact that Bobby had done so much to help put Harry on the hockey map.

Once the negotiations between Orr, his attorney, Al Eagleson, and the Bruins began to make print, the stilettos came out and it seemed that everyone was at everyone else's throat. I must admit that I acted like a dummy. I kept telling the press that, oh, yeah, Bobby will be back with the Bruins and, the fact of the matter is, he almost *was* going to return to the team rather than move on to Chicago.

The turning point occurred—and nobody really knew this until now—over an article Bobby read in the local paper. Orr had become disgusted with all the bickering. He finally decided—based on what he told me—to hell with the negotiations, to hell with the contract guarantee; he wanted to stay with the Bruins, no matter what.

Bobby had become a Boston institution just like Bunker Hill. It was unthinkable, even to him, to go elsewhere to finish out his playing career.

He was returning to Boston and had just flown into Logan Airport. In his mind, he was prepared to wear the Bruins' black-and-gold until they told him he couldn't lace on the skates anymore. As he left the airport he picked up a paper and turned to the sports pages. When he got into a cab he began reading a hockey story. He was appalled by what he read.

There in black and white was Sinden's mouthpiece, Tom Johnson, saying that he thought Bobby Orr had had it. Orr told the cab driver to turn the taxi around and take him right back to the airport. He booked himself a flight and flew home. He was through as a Bruin because he didn't want to play with these people anymore.

Management played it cagey and even as we approached the June draft meetings there was some hope held out that Orr would remain a Bruin. But when I met with Harry and Tom at the Montreal meetings, I knew it was game over for Bobby. I was absolutely heartbroken because not only was I losing the greatest hockey player who ever lived, but I was losing a good friend. After a while, though, I began thinking as a coach, mulling over the compensation—in terms of players—we would receive if Orr wound up in a Chicago Black Hawks uniform.

I already had about four solid Chicago players picked out and from my standpoint, it looked like we'd have a Stanley Cup contender just based on the compensation alone. What I didn't realize was that there would be *no* compensation for the Bruins in this particular deal. The greatest hockey player who ever lived would simply go from the Bruins to the Black Hawks, and all Boston would get in return were newspaper stories about the deal. That was it.

Then, of course, there was Phil Esposito. Esposito, to me, was one of the most colourful persons ever in the NHL. I have to laugh when people would say he scored "garbage goals." Phil would laugh, too, and say, "Who cares what they call them—they all look like slap shots in next morning's papers. Who cares how they go in, as long as they count?"

The thing I will always remember most about Phil was the 1972 Canada Cup. He had the courage to go on TV between periods and say that the team and players didn't deserve the abuse Vancouver fans and fans across Canada were heaping on them. He said that the players were truly doing their best and that, instead of booing and ridiculing, they should all get behind the team. It's the first time a hockey player rallied a country. Phil Esposito turned around the fans, the media—and most of all, he turned around the players. I think Phil Esposito won the Canada Cup that hot night in Vancouver.

There were some who charged that Phil was more interested in his own point total than the welfare of the team. I never felt this way. I honestly think that Phil figured he was doing the best for the club by playing three and four-minute shifts instead of coming off the ice sooner. Maybe he was right. He won a lot of scoring championships and he also played on two Stanley Cup winners.

Unfortunately, Phil's demand for ice time did have an adverse effect on others, particularly Andre Savard, a young French-Canadian center for whom the Bruins had high hopes. Andy's line would generally follow Phil's onto the ice, except that Phil always stayed on extra long. I can still see poor Andy's face as Phil would go through two or three extra shifts. Andy would sit astride the boards waiting and waiting and waiting for Phil to get off. We all said that Andy sat astride the boards so long waiting to get ice that by the time he got married he'd be sterile!

Among Phil's high priority sensitivities, his hair ranked right at the top. He loved his hair and would treat it accordingly. After a game he would sit in his brown-and-white kimono, apply a white solution to his hair and then sit with the conditioner settling in to make it even more beautiful. I remember one night, we were playing a crucial game at Boston Garden and as I patrolled the area behind the bench I noticed the back of Phil's neck. A dark substance was running down his neck. "Phil," I said, "you look like you're oozing dark blood." He felt the back of his neck, looked at his palm and said: "Grapes, I'm gonna kill that hair-dresser!"

Phil was superstitious, but not nearly as much as some people thought. The one thing he insisted upon was that his sticks and gloves be laid out in front of him in the dressing room before each game. Heaven help the trainer or player who would accidentally kick those sticks or move those gloves.

Esposito's natural talent for scoring once prompted me to ask him how he had learned to become such an efficient goal machine. "Grapes," he said, "when I'm goin' good I just get the puck and fire it at the net and I just figure the net hasn't moved in fifty years so I'm bound to be on target. The rest will take care of itself. It's like being a baseball pitcher; he should never aim the ball, just rear back and throw it. I never aim the puck because I know that when I aim it I'm not goin' good."

Phil could score from any angle. I once saw him split the enemy defense, fall to his knees and, while still on his knees sliding toward the net, put the puck in the top corner of the cage.

We had gotten off to a terrible start. We had been hammered badly in Philadelphia by the Flyers and then in Buffalo by the Sabres. After the Buffalo disaster Harry huddled with me. "What do you think of us sending Phil and Vadnais to the Rangers for Brad Park and Jean Ratelle?"

It was a dynamite package but I had to think for a moment. We had lost in the first round of the playoffs the previous year. Now we were playing terribly. One of two things was about to happen—either we changed players or we changed coaches. Needless to say, I preferred the former option.

Harry insisted to me that, yes, the deal was very much alive and that he was heading for Buffalo to discuss it with Emile Francis, his counterpart with the Rangers. I had mixed feelings about the deal even though my survival instinct told me that I had to choose between me and Phil. Still, there were signs that Phil was trying to adapt to my grinding style of hockey and that he was at least willing to make adjustments in his own offensive behaviour. While Sinden and Francis were conferring at the Buffalo airport Phil approached me and revealed that he had been thinking about his playing and was willing to listen to me. "Grapes," he said, "I'm gonna try it your way from now on."

I thought to myself, how ironic. The wheels of the trade were turning and, even if I had wanted to stop them, there was nothing I could do about the Sinden-Francis negotiations. As I headed with the team to Vancouver, I couldn't help thinking about what would happen if the deal did take place. I wondered about Phil and how he'd take it and also Vadnais, who was one of my best friends. Vad sat next to me on the jet heading west. It was one of the most uncomfortable flights of my life; I felt as if I was going to a guy's execution but I couldn't say a word about it. I kept thinking how cruel this business of sport can be.

When we arrived at our hotel in Vancouver I did something I rarely do when on the road, I stayed in my own room glued to the telephone. Sooner or later, Harry *had* to call, either to tell me that the deal had fallen through (then maybe it meant that *my* goose had been cooked) or to give me the final details of the trade. Finally, at 11:30 p.m. the phone rang.

Harry: "Don, they went for it."

Me: "I can't believe it."

Harry: "Believe it. And now the crap's gonna hit the fan. You watch, tomorrow."

Me: "Whaddya mean?"

Harry: "You're out there with them; I'm here. You're gonna have to tell 'em. It's Phil and Vad to the Rangers for Jean Ratelle, Brad Park and Joe Zanussi."

Me: "I still can't believe it."

Harry: "Don't tell 'em tonight. Wait til tomorrow morning. There's no sense telling them tonight. They might as well get a good night's sleep since they're going to Oakland tomorrow. Besides, you never know what they're gonna do when they hear this. I'll be in touch."

Harry hung up and I sat there for a moment, numb from the neck up. Finally, I picked myself up and went down to the hotel bar where I had a few beers by myself and thought about what was going on. I had mixed emotions. On one hand, I was losing two friends. On the other hand, I had to think of the club and I also had to think about *my* future. Besides, I was elated to be getting two quality hockey players like Park and Ratelle.

Bobby Orr was still with the team at the time and the prospect of having *both* Orr and Park on the points for the power play was just too good to be true. Then, I realized that *I* had to deliver the news to Phil and Vad the next morning. How to do it? I went back up to the room to catch a few winks because I knew that I'd have to phone them first thing in the morning. I placed a wake-up call for 7 a.m. and then hit the sack.

As soon as I got the wake-up call I washed my face, went back to the phone and called Phil.

Me: "This is Grapes. Phil, I want to talk to you, I'm comin' right down."

Phil: "Don, don't tell me."

Me: "I can't talk about it here, I'm comin' down."

Phil: "Grapes, tell me it didn't happen!"

(Years later Phil told me he thought *I* had been fired and wanted to come down to his room to talk about it; to get some anger off my chest.)

I dressed and, fifteen minutes later, I knocked on his door. Phil opened it and I walked over to a chair near the window and sat down. Phil sat on the bed.

Me: "Phil, I might as well give it to you straight; there's no use beating around the bush. Phil, you've been traded."

His body contorted. He was in physical and mental agony. He got up, sat down; got up again, sat down again. At least five minutes went by before he even said a word; then the words came blurting out.

Phil: "Grapes, please tell me, they traded me to *any team but the New York Rangers.*" (Funny how things work out. Much later Phil told me that the Rangers were the best team he could have gone to. He was made for New York.)

I looked out of the window and watched the raindrops course down to the window sill. Then, I looked at Phil and saw the tears filtering down his face. I couldn't hold it back any longer.

Me: "Yes, it is the Rangers."

Phil: "But, Grapes, when I signed my last contract with Harry I said I wouldn't ask for a 'no-trade' contract. All I asked was that Harry give me his word that I would go to any team *except* the New York Rangers. And we shook on that."

Me: (To myself) "You should have known that old Yogi Berra saying that verbal agreements aren't worth the paper they're written on."

Now I had to go down the hall and tell Vad. I knocked on his door and his roommate, Gary Doak, answered. I asked Gary to leave, then sat down and gave it right to Vad. He just sat at the edge of the bed and stared into space for what seemed like an eternity. Finally, he turned to me and said: "You know what, Grapes? I *can't* be traded during the season."

I asked why, and he said that it was written right in his contract. Sitting there in Vad's room, I got a little queasy so I phoned Harry to tell him what Vad had told me. Harry said that Vad was wrong and that he was at his desk and would pull out his contract just to be sure.

Sure enough, Harry pulled out the contract and began assuring me that there was no clause saying that Vad couldn't be traded. Suddenly, Harry fell silent and I could hear nothing but pages being flipped frantically but still no sounds from Harry. Finally, the flipping stopped but still no Harry. I was getting worried. All I could hear was heavy breathing. Vad asked what was going on so I hollered for Harry a few more times and still got no response so I hung up.

"Vad," I said, "I don't know what to tell you but sit tight and as soon as I find out, I'll tell you."

I went right back to my room and as soon as I turned the key in the keyhole the phone rang. It was Harry. As it turned out Vad *did* have a no trade during the season clause in his contract, but there was no way Harry—or the Rangers, for that matter—would let the deal fall through. New York wanted Phil and Vad. So the Rangers, who had lots of money to unload, came up with a bundle for Vad and that persuaded him to drop his objections.

Now that all the dirty work had been done, I finally had a moment to relax. I stretched out on the bed and turned on the radio just as the sports report was coming over the air. The first thing they mentioned was that Phil and Vad had been traded.

Apparently someone in the East had leaked the news. Can you imagine the position I would have been in if Phil and Vad had heard about it on the radio before I had had a chance to tell them?

Whatever, life had to go on and I had a team to coach. At least I *thought* I had a team. When the guys finally convened on the bus heading for the Vancouver Coliseum there was a deathly silence that carried over to the practice. As the guys glided around the ice, Bobby Orr, who had been side-lined with one of his injuries, sidled up to me and asked whether I had played a part in the deal. I admitted that I had. "Look," he said, "I don't want to sound as if I'm bragging or anything but why couldn't you guys have waited til I came back to see how the team would have played with me back in the lineup. Maybe we would have been all right." I told him that Harry and I felt that there was no time to waste otherwise the Rangers might have nixed the deal.

I left Orr and got ready to launch into the accelerated part of the skate. I blew the whistle, which meant the guys were supposed to move into high gear, but nothing happened. There was no reaction; as if I hadn't even blown the whistle. I blew it a second time and, again, it was as if my whistle were mute. Exasperated, I called them over to the corner of the rink. "Listen, you guys," I snapped. "Espo and Vad are gone and we all feel bad about it. I know how you feel. But if you guys don't smarten up, you'll be gone, too—and that means everybody! Now, when I blow the whistle, you guys had better get goin'."

I knew I was on the spot. If they didn't respond this time, it meant that I had lost the team. The whistle cut through the quiet of the Coliseum and they reluctantly sped up. They were a sullen bunch and I knew there would be trouble for a while because Phil and Vad had meant a lot to them. But we went on with the practice until there was a *real* downer: Phil and Vad came by the rink to pick up their sticks and skates and to make their goodbyes.

(I must add a postscript here about Vad. In 1967, the Rochester Americans had been given rings for winning the Calder Cup three years in a row. Anyway, the little glass chips in the rings were so cheap that they turned green.

One night, while we were with Team Canada in 1976, and remember, we had just traded Vad, he and I were in a jewelry store buying some stuff for our wives. I turned to Vad and I told him that now would be a good time to fix those glass chips. Vad took the ring from me, said something to the jeweler in French, and told me that the ring would be ready in a week.

A week later I went to pick up my ring, and when the jeweler gave it back to me I was stunned. There was an enormous diamond in the middle and two big diamond chips around it. I said to the guy, "Oh my gosh! How come you did this? I can't afford this!" He said that the job would cost me nothing. I said, "What do you mean nothing?" He told me that it was all taken care of by Carol Vadnais.

Vad, it seems, never wore diamonds, so he had had the gems removed from his two Stanley Cup rings and put into storage. He told the jeweler to put the big diamond and the two chips on my ring and to send him the bill. That's the kind of person Vad is.)

Needless to say there wasn't a dry eye in the place as the two veterans moved around the dressing room, shaking hands with everyone. My heart was with them, but my mind said the deal had to be made if the team was to be straightened out. That night we went out and were beaten by Vancouver. Right after the game I phoned Harry to give him the result. "I know you won't believe this," I added, "but I see some good things on the horizon. We're going to start winning soon and everything's gonna' be all right." As it worked out, we went from the basement to first place and stayed in first place for the next four years.

Harry said he would be on the next flight West and when we met the following day, he looked like he had just come out of the grave. He told me that the Boston papers had crucified him over the deal. Emile Francis was depicted as a burglar stealing Esposito and Vadnais from Boston while

Park was said to have a couple of bad legs and Ratelle was considered over the hill.

"Don't worry," I comforted him. "Wait til you see Park and Orr working the points together."

When all was said and done, the big deal saved my career. I give Harry full marks for a lot of guts on the deal. He knew we were in trouble and went out and did something, even though he knew it would be unpopular with the players, the fans and the media. Park, who was supposed to be out of shape and possibly at the end of his career because of his knee problems, played sensationally for me, as did Ratelle. Of course, at the time we had no way of knowing that it would work out so well, and a number of players on the Bruins suffered grave doubts. Phil and Vad were popular with their teammates and Park was high on the Bruins' hate list. He had written a book as a Ranger, called *Play the Man* in which he was severely critical of some of the Boston players, inspiring intense resentment among the guys. Nobody had feelings either way about Ratelle who was always considered a quiet and classy guy.

One particular player took the trade harder than most. The night the trade was announced, he was drinking quite heavily. Then he returned to his room, where the guys had a lot of beer and shrimp on the table. I joined them for awhile.

He had been very close to Phil and after a while he began ranting and raving about what a lousy deal we had made. I listened and listened and, after about an hour, I could take no more, so I got up and left. But I told some of the other guys to keep an eye on him, because I could tell he was going to get himself into trouble. They didn't heed my warning and a short time later he proceeded to demolish the room—literally. Had you seen the place, you would have guessed that a large bomb had been planted there, because there wasn't a single piece of furniture that wasn't in splinters.

It wasn't difficult for the hotel detectives to get wind of the ruckus but, the funny thing was, they wouldn't allow anything to be put back into place until photos were taken of the damage. The next morning, when we were about to leave, I phoned the player involved. He thought I was calling to bawl him out, or even to fine or suspend him for what he had done to the place. Instead, I said, "I left a red tie at your place last night. Can you check to see if it's still there?"

He asked me to wait a minute. I could hear furniture being moved, glasses falling. Then he returned to the phone and said, yes, he had found the tie. I said, "Good, bring it to the bus." Was he ever happy that I had only called about the tie!

Some people have criticized me for not disciplining him severely for his outburst, but I wouldn't think of it. For one thing, he wrote a cheque for a couple of thousand dollars in damages as he left the hotel. For another, over the years he had given his heart and soul to the Bruins.

When the going got rough, he was there. You couldn't ask for a better ally to be in the trenches with you in time of war.

In time, Park would make a similar contribution to the team although, at first, his teammates were extremely wary of the defenseman. Park was as unhappy leaving New York as Esposito was sad about leaving Boston. My first impression of Park was not good. He had a reputation in the NHL of being "The Pillsbury Doughboy" on skates and upon first look, it was well-earned. He was significantly overweight and I told him he would have to lose some pounds if he wanted to be in my good graces. He took my advice and became a one hundred percent Bruin. About two months afterwards I met him at Boston Airport and he said to me, "Grapes, look what you did to me!" He had lost fifteen pounds and his suit was two sizes too big for him (I like 'em lean and mean.). Fans who had booed him as a Ranger immediately took him to their collective hearts. One leather-lunged spectator in the balcony echoed the sentiments of the others when he chanted one night: "Hey, Pahk, welcome to the Gahden!" From that point on Brad knew that he was a genuine Bruin.

What most people haven't realized about Brad was that he was as quick-witted off the ice as he was patrolling the blue line. And he was especially good at feeding me lines to tell the reporters in the post-game press conferences. For example, one night we played the Minnesota North Stars and completely dominated them in every way. After the game Brad stuck his head through the door opening in my office and said: "All right, here's what you tell them: 'It was an up-and-down game. They got up and we knocked them down!'"

Much as I grew to admire Park, I can't say that I always was especially fair to him. One night we were playing the Washington Capitals when they were the doormats of the league. Late in the third period we were leading, 5-4, when Park coughed up the puck, a Caps player grabbed it and rifled it home to give them a 5-5 tie. What I should mention up front is that the incident took place just two days after Brad had returned to the lineup following knee surgery.

Of course the only thing on my mind was the blown lead and the culprit. I was so worked up at that time that I threw a water bottle and three towels at him.

Why did I do it? I imagine that I had reached a point in my coaching career where I expected almost the impossible from my players and most of them responded accordingly. Brad tried, but his knees wouldn't let him. Needless to say, Brad was hurt by my behaviour.

A day after the episode Park phoned me and said he wanted to meet right away at a bar. I agreed and we sat down over several beers, whereupon he proceeded to tell me how hurt he had been and how he didn't deserve the treatment he received the previous night.

"Grapes," he said. "Your throwing that bottle and towels at me hurt worse than any knife could have. I think a lot of you, but this has me thinking of quitting. I think I deserve an apology."

I laughed. He couldn't be serious—me apologize? Me, whose father had always said, "Never apologize; it's a sign of weakness." I looked closer; he was serious.

For some perverse reason—I don't know why—I was still in an obnoxious mood and instead of talking quietly with Park, I proceeded to lambaste him again. I told him that if he ever repeated the mistake again, I'd give him the same kind of crap, and if he didn't like it, he knew what he could do. I kept blasting at him until I suddenly looked up and realized there were tears in his eyes. This was a first all-star defenseman, tough as nails, one of the nicest guys you'd ever want to meet, who had returned to the team in seven weeks where most others would take six months, and here I was berating him. Here was a player who had likely saved my career and risked his own by returning prematurely to the lineup and I threw a water bottle at him, embarrassing him in front of his teammates.

I was close to destroying him; close to making him quit. When I left him at the bar, I began thinking about what I had done. I started questioning my desire to win at all costs and I began to move back closer to reality.

The next day I called a team meeting. I walked up and down the dressing room trying to get up my nerve and apologize—the hardest thing I ever had to do. I had almost made up my mind *not* to after all, when I saw Brad looking at me. Ah, well, here goes . . .

My players sat there in stunned silence. I tried to explain that, sometimes, in the heat of battle I did things that I later came to regret and that this episode had been an example of that. At first they couldn't believe what they were hearing, but I think that moment brought me closer to the team than at any time during my entire stay in Boston.

In retrospect, I wonder whether I did it for Brad or rather to approach the team in a different direction. I looked at the guys' faces as I talked, and I said to myself, "These guys are really eating this up: Grapes in the humble role."

Shortly after I finished the talk, Park approached me, his eyes a little moist again and a look of gratitude across his mug. "Thanks!" he said warmly and walked away. I knew I had done the right thing.

Brad had two traits I didn't like: he would fight at the drop of a hat and he would continually lead rushes up the ice when he should have been spending more time in the defensive zone. Two of my major projects were trying to cure Park of these traits. I realized that neither would be easily treated, but I tried nevertheless. Now let me say right here: deep down, I loved it when Brad fought, but I had my designated fighters, and he wasn't one of them.

The fighting syndrome was particularly difficult because opponents understood how valuable Brad was to the Bruins and consistently tried to goad him into a fight, thereby getting him off the ice and making it easier to beat us. I finally got fed up during a game with the Detroit Red Wings. They had a pesky little forward named Dennis Polonich, who was always stirring up some kind of brouhaha or other. This time he needled Park until Brad finally went after him and, naturally, got thrown out of the game.

That did it. Instead of directly bawling out Park, I took another route. I contacted the newspaper guys and told them I was going to prevent Brad from getting into any fights in the future. Then, I told the same thing to the television people and, finally, I went to my own players. Furthermore, I added, that if Brad *did* get into a fight he would have to answer to me and he would be fined, to boot. What I *really* wanted to do was take the onus off Brad. I told the entire league, in effect, that Park was no longer permitted to fight so he, therefore, no longer felt obliged to display his toughness and we were all the better for it.

Next, I tried to contain his rushing tendencies. Perhaps it was selfish on my part, but I felt that if Brad did less rushing and concentrated more on defense, he would expend less energy and I would be able to play him up to forty minutes a game instead of twenty or twenty-five minutes. I also felt that the rushing would, ultimately, shorten his career. Eventually, I sat down and had a heart-to-heart with him. "Look, Brad," I said, "for the good of the team I'd like you to hold back more, stay in our half of the ice, don't rush so much. It'll cost you the Norris (best defenseman) Trophy, but you'll be helping the team a lot more than you think." He didn't hesitate. "No problem," he said, and that was that.

What made me feel bad was the fact that Park was, technically, good enough to win the Norris Trophy, but the writers who vote on the award always look at the scoring statistics of the defensemen and fail to take into account the players defensive strongpoints. To win the Norris Trophy, a defenseman has to *score* 25 to 30 goals in a season and there was no way Park could do that under my new instructions. But he accepted them and we all were better for it—except for his trophy case. He never has won the Norris which I think is a crime.

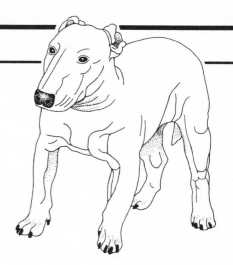

CHAPTER FIFTEEN

The Lunch Pail Gang And Some Good Referees

The Bruins were known as "The Lunch Pail Gang," courtesy of a column written by Boston writer Fran Rosa. He wrote, "They punch the time clock at 7:30 p.m. and never stop working." Somehow Harry took offense at this name because he thought it was demeaning. He thought it meant we had no talent.

I, of course, was proud of the name. To me it meant that we were proud but honest, and that we gave one hundred percent all the time. We did have the talent, as our first place finishes certified. Besides, who says being a "hard worker" isn't a talent?

In my estimation we had the toughest team ever in the league. Guys like Cashman, Schmautz, O'Reilly, Wensink, Jonathan and Secord would do anything to win.

In his book, *The Hammer, Confessions of a Hockey Enforcer*, Dave Schultz wrote that he couldn't sleep the night before playing the Bruins, out of fear of the consequences. We intimidated, to be sure, but we were "tough fair." That is, we never picked on a star—not a Marcel Dionne or a Guy Lafleur. We'd go after the opposition's biggest gunfighter and get him, not the star.

We expected this unwritten rule to be honoured by the enemy, and if it was disregarded, the foe had hell to pay.

Here's an example: our classiest—and most non-violent—player was

Jean Ratelle. Ratty was so clean-living that, to him, a terrible curse word was "damn!" When I went into one of my obscene tirades in the dressing room, I'd always do a double-take and feel like cringing when my eyes fell upon Jean. He sat there calm and unruffled and I felt as if I were confronting the parish priest. Just the sight of Ratelle made me stop the outburst.

As a rule, Ratty was treated with the same respect by the opposition, but there was one exception. His name was Gerry Hart and he was playing defense for the New York Islanders at the time. On this occasion Hart, who was relatively small for a defenseman, really messed up Ratty with a cheap shot. When Ratty got hit, everybody on the team felt it.

John Wensink, who was one of my main enforcers at the time, remedied the situation. He immediately grabbed Hart, took him by the scruff of his neck and rammed his head into the boards. As he held him there, he quietly whispered in his ear, "Next time you touch Mr. Ratelle, your head will go *through* the boards." Naturally we won the game, and Hart never laid a hand, glove or stick on Ratelle again as long as I was with the Bruins.

The ingredient that made our club especially fearsome was that we were tough from the goal out. They talk about Billy Smith of the Islanders being tough among today's goalies, but he's nothing more than an unoriginal facsimile of my number one goalie, Gerry Cheevers.

As Cheevers saw it, the goal crease was his eminent domain. Stray too close to that crease and you were apt to have your toes, ankles or knees chopped up by his big goalie stick. Although he carried up to forty pounds of equipment, Cheesie, as we called him, thought nothing of engaging the enemy with his stick. As goalies go, he was the original "puck's bad boy."

But he was also a good guy to have around the dressing room, and I speak from experience because Cheesie and I played together in Rochester under coach Joe Crozier. He was in his early twenties then, but he had the savvy of a veteran.

One of the things that impressed me about him was that he had the knack of losing more than twenty pounds *on a weekend*. Gerry would drink only beer—and eat nothing—from Friday night to Monday morning. Sure enough, at the Monday scrimmage he would be the shell of the man I had seen Friday afternoon.

Cheevers' midsection always had been a problem, going back to his early days as a pro in Rochester. And even though he had the ability to trim off large amounts of weight in a very short time, there were occasions when Cheesie simply did not want to take off any pounds. I shared that sentiment with him and, as a result, Gerry and I frequently would get into trouble with Crozier.

I should note at this point that there are two methods for losing weight; the first being the traditional method of cutting down on beer and the second being tampering with the dressing room scale.

Cheesie and I specialized in this department, employing an assortment of very practical techniques. We discovered that by putting pennies *underneath* the scales the poundage would be reduced by two. Another effective method was affixing a well-chewed piece of gum to the inside arm of the scale. That would subtract up to four pounds. Unfortunately, Crozier eventually caught on to each of those tricks. But one that always eluded him was the "grab-the-post" method. Whenever we were weighed on a Toledo scale, Cheesie and I would grab hold of the post as we were being clocked, and push down. That saved us five pounds, easily, many, many times.

Like so many goalies, Cheevers was eccentric. Put him in the nets and he was utterly fearless. He would stand in front of shots travelling 115 miles per hour without flinching, but if you asked him to room alone on the road he would quake in his boots. At first I found this hard to believe. Once, when we were neck-and-neck in a race for first place with the Buffalo Sabres, we had two critical games, back-to-back. The first was in Toronto against the Maple Leafs followed by the second in Buffalo against the Sabres. Instead of having Cheesie stay over in Toronto, I sent him ahead of the team to Buffalo so he could get some extra rest and relaxation. Little did I know.

Against the Sabres, he was just awful and it was only then that I learned that he was so afraid of rooming alone that he hadn't slept all that night and was a wreck by game time.

In time, I began rooming Cheesie with one of my favourite defensemen, Gary Doak. It was the perfect marriage of hockey player-roommates. Gerry said that Gary was the only guy he could room with and Doak said Gerry was the only guy *he* could room with; now Cheesie is coaching the Bruins and Doakie is his assistant.

Gerry had no fears when it came to partying and, in that regard, he can be thankful that his wife, Betty, was so understanding. Here's proof positive: we had lost a tough game at Boston Garden and Cheesie and some of the guys decided to go out and chase their sorrow with a couple of beers. And then a couple more and a couple more after that.

One day went by and then another and, still, Gerry hadn't returned home. On the third day, we had a practice and, sure enough, who trooped into the dressing room but Cheesie, unshaven, looking like a fugitive from Skid Row. I knew that Betty had been worried about him so the first thing I did was insist that he phone her. "Nah," he said, "I'll do it after practice."

"She's concerned," I demanded, "do it now!"

After a bit more cajoling and pushing, I got him into the trainer's office and handed him the phone. I sat there wondering what he could possibly say. After a couple of rings someone at the other end picked it up. "Betty," Cheesie said with great exultation, "it's me, Gerry. DON'T PAY THE RANSOM; I JUST ESCAPED."

Gerry bought a colt named Royal Ski, paying $20,000 for the horse. It turned out to be a big winner and made something like $800,000 for Gerry who, in turn, sold the horse for $1,700,000 to a Japanese horseman, who made a $500,000 down payment on it. Suddenly, Royal Ski took sick and the Japanese horseman decided that he wanted to back out of the deal. That was fine, but Gerry had the right to keep the 500 grand. Instead, he gave the money back and waited and hoped. Sure enough, Royal Ski got better and, this time, he sold him for $1,300,000.

The one time I remember Cheese getting teed off with me, believe it or not, was when I swung into a duet with his father, Joe, an Irishman through and through and one of Canada's best lacrosse players. We had lost to the Maple Leafs that night in Toronto and Gerry was quite upset about the game. His father came into the dressing room and he and I put our arms around each other and began singing "If You Are Irish Come Into The Parlour."

Gerry was upset and didn't want us to sing in the dressing room after a loss because he thought it would make Harry mad.

A week later, I got a phone call from Gerry, telling me he couldn't come to practice. I said, "How come you can't come to practice?" Gerry answered, "Joe died." I said, "You're kidding." Gerry replied, "Nope, and it's his first time, too." Gerry was devastated at Joe's passing and this was his way of covering up.

I had a real problem with Cheevers in practice. He simply would not try to stop shots and this invariably ruined our scrimmages. To remedy that I called a meeting of the players, minus Cheevers, and said, "During the scrimmage, if you can hit Cheevers' goalie pads, we'll count it as a goal." After three practices Cheevers came to me and said "Geez Grapes, have you noticed how great I've been in practice lately?" When some wise guy told him the truth he was absolutely furious, because he thought I had made a fool out of him.

Another winner on the Bruins was Terry O'Reilly, a big right wing from Niagara Falls, Ontario. We nicknamed him Taz, short for Tasmanian devil, a powerful carnivore that seeks its prey at night.

The first time I ever saw him in action, he was skating for the Boston Braves, then the Bruins' farm team in the American Hockey League.

It is safe to say that I had never seen a professional player fall down as much as Terry did. He seemed to be horizontal as often as he was vertical. When I next saw him, a year later, I couldn't believe that he was the same man. He had improved by about 180 percent. He had gone to power skating school and had diligently practised to the point that he had made a more significant improvement in his skills than any professional athlete I've ever known. Terry had only one problem; he played the game too honestly. At the beginning, he was the epitome of what fair play is all about.

If an enemy seriously fouled a player like Bobby Schmautz, that player, more likely than not, would be carved up *without warning*. But if that very opponent fouled Terry in the same way, O'Reilly would go after the guy, tap him on the shoulder, allow him to turn around, invite him to fight and then permit the enemy to strike the first blow. The Marquis of Queensbury would have been terribly proud of him. The problem was that O'Reilly's ritual hurt the team. Invariably, he would wind up with an additional two minute penalty for going after the guy and a five minute major for fighting. The other fellow would get away with just a five minute penalty.

Try as I might, I couldn't convince O'Reilly that he was being too nice, but one of the best fighters in the league cured Terry of his etiquette. We were playing the Los Angeles Kings, when Dan Maloney was the Kings' number one gun fighter. I had been cautioning O'Reilly that he had to stop permitting the enemy to take the first punch at him. I didn't want him to go around sucker punching the opposition but, on the other hand, I didn't want to see him getting hurt by being too nice. Well, on this night Maloney not only hit him first but he did a pretty good number on Terry. It was a painful experience but Maloney had done me a favour because, now, Taz made sure he got the first punch in before the other got started jabbing.

I found Terry to be a very paradoxical character. As tough as he was on the ice, that's how lamb-like he was when he wasn't in uniform. He was an avid antique collector. If he had one flaw it was a vicious temper.

Sometimes Terry pushed his courageousness too far. He and his wife Lourdes were vacationing one spring in Acapulco when Terry decided to go for a swim. As it happened, he misjudged the waves and the undertow and, before he knew it, he had drifted out far beyond the acceptable limit. Strong as he was, he still had a difficult time making headway with all the waves and the undertow. In time it became apparent that he was in trouble—big trouble. Just when it appeared that he might fade out of sight, a couple of lifeguards spotted him, swam like the devil through the waves, and reached him just in time. It took them a half-hour to haul him in, but they did and, thoroughly exhausted by the ordeal, they laid him out on the beach.

Apart from the fact that he had nearly drowned, O'Reilly also had pulled his ankle so badly in the rescue operation that he could hardly walk, but he finally pulled himself together and headed back to his cabana, limping all the way. As he walked along the beach he passed a bunch of guys who had hang gliders, surf boards and other gismos. One of the fellows noticed Terry and began goading him. "Hey, big fella, let's see ya do some surf gliding."

Terry politely shook his head, but the guy persisted. "No, thank you sir," Terry repeated, but the hustler wasn't satisfied. "How come," he snapped. "Are ya' yellow, or too cheap?"

The man who had just come this close to drowning and was hobbled by a bum ankle, looked over at his adversary and replied: "I'll show you who's yellow," and proceeded to grab the guy and bury his head in the sand. You just don't say things like that to Terry O'Reilly.

Of course, I've said a few things to O'Reilly, but sometimes my words went flying past him like a slapshot aimed wide of the net. The classic example took place one day when Terry, Dwight Foster, Mike Milbury, Peter McNab, and I were helping Terry move to his mansion in Georgetown. The address, by the way, is One Cherry Lane. (Terry says he's changing it to One Cheevers Lane.)

When it came time to load the fridge I said, "Terry, we better take all the food out of the fridge before we pick it up." "No Grapes," he laughed. "Remember, you're not my coach in the summer. I don't have to listen to you now. The stuff won't come out." There was not much I could say to that, so I watched as Terry, Mike, Peter, and Dwight lifted it.

A split-second later, the door flew open and everything poured out of the refrigerator. It looked like Fibber McGee's closet. After the last bottle of milk hit the ground, I patted Terry on the shoulder. "Taz old boy," I said, "you should always listen to your coach."

Terry really demonstrated the kind of friend he is during a family crisis. In 1979, our son Timothy had to have a kidney transplant. As you can imagine, we were all absolutely devastated. He was on a dialysis machine, and the whole ordeal was extremely hard to take. Rose and I were tested to see whether or not our kidneys were compatible for a transplant, but as it turned out, our daughter Cindy's kidney was almost identical to Tim's. Cindy was a miracle throughout the whole thing. She just said, "Take mine," without hesitation.

The whole experience was getting to be a little hard for me, so much so that I began to look forward to road trips so I could get out of Boston. I left the whole burden on Rose's shoulders.

Some people might wonder how I could leave my family at a time like this; how could I even function. Well, when you're a professional, you have to work all the time. You separate one aspect of life from another. I didn't realize the seriousness, the importance of the operation, until I saw both Cindy and Tim being wheeled into the operating room. Then, I finally realized the sacrifice Cindy was making.

Throughout all of this, the Bruins won twenty of our first twenty-two games. Someone asked Terry why we had gotten off to such a good start and he said, "Well, we had a meeting and decided that Grapes was having enough trouble, so let's give him one less thing to worry about." That's the kind of guy Terry is and that's the kind of guys they all are. They all went to donate blood so that Tim would have enough blood for the operation. Now you see why I loved them.

Stan Jonathan, a tough Tuscarora Indian from Brantford, Ontario was one of my favourites, too.

Of all my discoveries, Jonathan is the one in which I take the most pride. It happened this way: in 1975 our number one draft pick was Doug Halward, who earlier had been playing junior hockey for the Oshawa Generals. One day Harry Sinden suggested that the two of us take a look at Halward in Oshawa to see how he was shaping up. As bad luck would have it, Halward was injured early in the game so that part of our trip was ruined but, as the game progressed, I couldn't help noticing this rugged little Indian. He didn't play an exceptional game, but there was something about him that made me take notice.

I didn't say much about Jonathan to Harry, but I filed his name in the back of my mind for future reference and at draft time I called Harry aside and said: "Do you think you could get me one hockey player?"

Harry was not as impressed as I was and bypassed Jonathan on the first, second, and third picks. We finally got him the fourth time around and sent him to the Dayton Gems of the International League. A year later he made our team.

In Jonathan's first big fight he so thoroughly destroyed Keith Magnuson, the Chicago Black Hawks defenseman, that he gained notoriety throughout the league and my infinite praise. But beating up on Magnuson was not that big a deal because Keith, for all his tenacity and gutsiness, was a real catcher.

Stanley reminded me of my pet dog, Blue, a bull terrier. They were both relatively small but enormously tough. I liked Stanley so much that I took a beautiful painting of Blue from home and had it hung directly above Jonathan's locker. One day Stanley's father was visiting Boston and was introduced to me in my office. "You've got a great son there, Mr. Jonathan," I said. "He reminds me of my dog, Blue."

Old man Jonathan was aghast. Comparing his son to a dog. Well, this big Indian stared at me and stared at me until I thought I was going to get scalped. I had to do a lot of fast explaining there or I would have gone the way of General Custer.

If I had had the time I would have explained to Mr. Jonathan that Blue was not only my pet, but also my alter-ego. You don't have to take my word for it, just ask Jim Coleman, the noted Canadian sports authority. Coleman, whose column is syndicated across the country by the Southam News Service, once observed that Blue has been the real brains behind my success. "It is a matter of public record," wrote Coleman, "that Don never made an important long-range decision as a coach until he had consulted Blue."

What is Blue like? Superficially, she is a white bull terrier. That says nothing. Here's how Coleman described her: "Blue is a canine aristocrat, a highly cultured and highly intelligent individual who despises vulgarity and pretension." He might have added that Blue was tough, a discovery my Bruins made soon after she visited the dressing room.

One afternoon Wayne Cashman, as hard-bitten as any player I've ever had, went after Blue with a hockey stick. She grabbed the stick from Wayne *and broke it in her mouth.* Cashman hadn't had enough so the next day he grabbed a blowtorch the players use for curving their sticks and stuck it in Blue's face, figuring that she would be afraid of the fire. Blue chased Cashman right into the stickroom!

Rose and I had to take Blue to the veterinarian one day, and while we were sitting in the waiting room a man walked in with a Scottish Terrier. The terrier began barking at Blue, as if it wanted to start a fight. The owner said: "This terrier is so tough he'll take on anything." With that, Blue looked up at me as if to say, "What do you think Dad?" And I looked over at Rose and Rose said to me: "DON, DON'T YOU DARE!!"

Another time we were at the vet because Blue needed some shots. Now I kid you not when I say that Blue is afraid of nothing, not even a needle. Well, this particular doctor—I don't know if he was a sadist or not—just jammed the needle into Blue extra hard and farther than he had to and Blue looked at him as if to say: "Now, you didn't have to do that." Before the vet knew what had happened Blue grabbed his watch band—a rather expensive one at that—with her teeth and pulled it back and finally released it so that it snapped back on his hand with great force. It was Blue's way of saying, "Next time, don't be such a wise guy!"

I used Blue as a role model for my players. I remember telling Stan Jonathan, John Wensink and Al Secord that they should maintain *eye contact* with the enemy the way Blue does. "After you hit somebody," I told them, "don't skate away with your head down. That's like saying, 'Hey, look, guys, I didn't do anything wrong; the coach put me out here and made me hit, so don't get mad at me, it's just hockey.' When you want to hit them, *look them in the eye* and say, 'Yeah, I hit you, what are you gonna' do?'"

Then I brought Blue into play and pointed out that even though I was her master and she loved me, if I had eye contact with her she'd come at me. I then proceeded to stare at her and she stared at me for ten seconds. Then, she started getting angry, glaring at me as though saying, "Hey, what's goin' on here?" Staring at eye level meant a challenge to her. At that moment Blue came at me and I turned away, letting her know I was only kidding around. But Jonathan, Wensink and Secord got the point; and from then on when they hit somebody, they'd stare into the eyes of their foe and, inevitably, the other guy would turn away. That meant they had conquered him.

Blue had a winning *attitude.* When my son, Timothy, was young I would tell him that life is a matter of *attitude.* It all depends on how you view things; if you accentuate the positive, you're likely to come out on top. I'll give you an illustration: Half a mile from our home on Wolfe

Terry O'Reilly scoring the winning goal at 1 a.m. against Philadelphia in overtime. Terry was put on by accident—one of my better moves.

obby Schmautz saying, "Another enius move," after the Boston rowd booed when I put Wensink n for a powerplay and he scored in 8 seconds.

*Boston team photo, 1976-77. This picture appeared in the paper
the next day with the caption: "Bruins going to the dogs."*

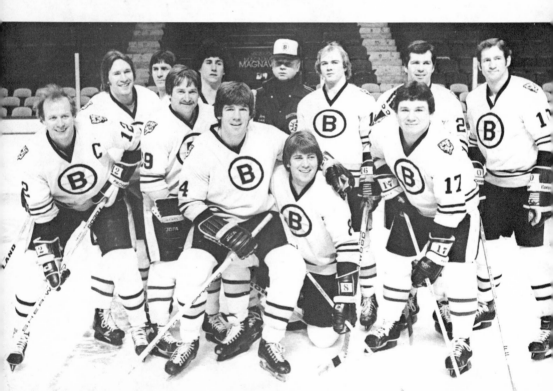

A. ALTMA

*Record-setting group — eleven 20-goal scorers on one team. (left to right)
Wayne Cashman, Al Sims (who shouldn't be there), Bobby Schmautz, Gregg Sheppard, Bobby Millar,
Terry O'Reilly, me, Peter McNab, Rick Middleton, Stan Jonathan, Don Marcotte, and Jean Ratelle.
(Brad Park is missing.)*

Island, near Kingston, some fellows had two enormous Great Danes. Well, one night I was out for a walk and was carrying a bushel basket. For no reason at all these Great Danes attacked me and I suppose I would have been dead if I hadn't been able to protect myself with the basket until the owners came and called the dogs off.

Three days later I was with Blue near our house when the two Great Danes appeared. They looked like the Hounds of the Baskervilles and, to be honest, I figured that one or both of them would devour Blue on the spot. There was no way she could beat these monster Great Danes. But Blue confronted them with the attitude "Hey, you two stiffs, what are you gonna' do now?" Guess what? They were absolutely terrified of her; they didn't do a thing. In fact, she walked right around them and they didn't even so much as snarl. It was Blue's *attitude*.

Jim Coleman claimed that Blue's attitude toward Denver was responsible for my demise with the Rockies. "The dog hated Denver on first sight," said Coleman. "She regarded the citizens of Denver as brash and pushy. Blue went on strike; she simply refused to give Cherry any help in making important decisions."

Even in distant Denver, Blue was in demand. I once received an offer to do a Miller Lite beer commercial with Blue. The advertisers had me come to New York and audition for the commercial with another dog — which, by the way, was a brilliant performer — and then said they were ready to shoot it with me and Blue.

"We'll fly Blue into New York from Denver next week," the advertising guy told me.

That floored me. I had assumed they understood that Blue doesn't fly. They hadn't known so I had to tell them. "I thought you guys were going to come out to Denver." No, nooooooo, they said. If I wanted the fifteen grand for the commercial, I had to bring Blue out by plane. (P.S. I'm the only guy in the world who turned down $15,000 because my dog wouldn't fly!)

It goes without saying that I'm very sensitive about Blue. One day a woman from a charity organization phoned my wife and asked if she would enter Blue in an "Ugliest Dog Contest." Rose told her she was lucky I was out of town. The woman diplomatically suggested that Blue be *the judge*, which is what Blue did. Unfortunately, some papers said that Blue had won the ugly dog contest, which was not the case and I'm setting the record straight right now.

All of which is another way of saying that when I compared one of my players to Blue it was like nominating him for knighthood; and that is precisely how I felt about Stan Jonathan.

Now, don't get the mistaken impression that I coddled Stanley, just because he reminded me of Blue. I never wanted to see any of my players get spoiled and, if I detected signs of that failing, I immediately took action. In Jonathan's case, he had a spell when he scored eight goals in ten games for the Bruins at one point and *I sent him down to our minor league affiliate in Rochester.* He couldn't believe it until I explained to him that I didn't want him to forget what had got him to the NHL in the first place; hard work and hitting, not goal scoring. "Stanley," I said, "you're starting to think you're a Guy Lafleur. Forget it, and be Stan Jonathan. I don't want you to fall into that ego trap." He got the message.

Perhaps such a drastic move on my part was unnecessary. At best, that's debatable. My concern was the welfare of the team which would have been best served by Jonathan hitting and intimidating the opposition. When he concentrated on that, he was virtually invincible and it was a lesson vividly dramatized for Scotty Bowman and the Montreal Canadiens during a Stanley Cup playoff series we had with them.

The Canadiens had a big defenseman named Pierre Bouchard, whose father Emile (Butch) Bouchard had been a great NHL blueliner on the Canadiens when Maurice Richard and Toe Blake were in their prime. Pierre was not as good as his dad. Scotty Bowman, who coached the Canadiens, kept him around as a fifth defenseman and used him occasionally as a regular. He had a reputation as a fairly clean player, but one who could really handle his dukes. He once flattened Teddy Irvine, a pretty big New York Rangers winger, with one punch at Madison Square Garden, and word got around the league that Bouchard was not to be trifled with, although Jonathan never paid much mind to that warning—or any warning for that matter.

Although Scotty has from time to time decried rough hockey, NHL history has clearly shown that when it suits his purposes he will ice as rough a bunch of skaters as any coach. He did it when he coached the St. Louis Blues in the late 1960s (the Plager brothers and Noel Picard were no blushing violets) and even with the Canadiens he had a knack for delivering a "no-nonsense" message from time to time. In this particular case he sent Bouchard, Gilles Lupien, a gigantic defenseman who could do little else but fight, and Rick Chartraw, a utility forward with a reputation for toughness, out on the ice.

Originally, I had the Peter McNab-Terry O'Reilly-John Wensink line out there but I sent Jonathan out to replace McNab. (Peter later told me getting off the ice at that point was one of the happiest moments in his life.) Anybody with half a brain knew that there was going to be trouble, although I was *not* looking for it; after all, I had a game to win. But for some reason Scotty *was* looking for it, else he wouldn't have loaded the ice with those troublemakers.

As soon as the linesman dropped the puck, the sticks came up, there was a flurry of action, a whistle for an offside and Jonathan and Bouchard were side-by-side, elbows at the ready. Stanley gave Pierre a little shot. All of a sudden they dropped their gloves and started swinging. Pierre got in the first good blows, but Stanley was virtually impervious to pain and he took the best shots Bouchard had to offer and kept swinging.

By this time, no matter who would eventually be the winner, I knew that I was watching the best hockey fight of my life. Even though Stanley was considerably shorter than Pierre he traded punches evenly with him. Then, without any warning, Jonathan, who was leading with his right hand, switched to his left and caught Bouchard off guard. He pounded Pierre's face with a series of lefts until Bouchard crumpled to the ice, his nose and cheekbone broken, and his face covered with blood.

Bouchard's reputation as a fighter was destroyed by that bout and, if the truth be known, he was never the same as a big-leaguer after that. As for Jonathan, he instantly became the undisputed middleweight *and* heavyweight champion of the NHL. Yet, in some ways, Stanley wasn't as nasty as one of his teammates, Bobby Schmautz.

Built along approximately the same lines as Jonathan (although somewhat more on the wiry side), Schmautzie was one of the most feared NHL players because of the manner in which he used his stick on the foe. The enemy called him "The Surgeon," and not because he was genteel with his scalpel. Bobby, himself, liked to be known as "Doctor Hook." Whatever the label, Schmautz was so vicious when it came to carving up the opposition that even *I* would caution him. He'd always reply: "Grapes, I'm small and the stick is the old equalizer."

His teammates used to kid him a lot about it. We used to say that at Christmas, instead of using a knife, Schmautzie carved the turkey with his hockey stick. I once phoned him in the off-season at a hunting lodge out west and his daughter answered the phone. "Did your Dad kill anything?" I asked her and she said no, he hadn't. "Well," I suggested, "he should have taken his hockey stick, then he would have killed something!"

While his stick may have been "the great equalizer," Schmautzie got his comeuppance every so often. Once, he got into a row with Larry Robinson, the towering Canadiens defenseman, whose arms were almost as long as Bobby was tall. Robinson got ticked off one night because of Schmautzie's stick work and grabbed him around the neck right in front of our bench and proceeded to pound him in the head with the other hand.

My players wanted to go over the boards to rescue Schmautzie, but I wouldn't let them go because I felt that if they did pour over, Bobby would be embarrassed. He could take on anyone, no matter how big and even though he was getting his lumps this time, he was showing a lot of courage. "Don't worry guys," I told the team, "Schmautzie is all right." What Schmautzie got was a good pasting and later, he took me aside and said, "Grapes, when I heard you tell the guys not to come, I was saying to myself, 'You SOB, Grapes, let them come!'" Well, you learn something new everyday.

True, Schmautzie was ruthless with his stick against others, but he was also ruthless with himself when it came to playing hurt. His knees were so beat up that he actually skated with a brace on each one. There was a time when he was suffering through an awful scoring slump and we were approaching the playoffs. He suggested that I bench him for the good of the team. I said, "No, sir, I don't care how badly you play, Schmautzie, you and I will go to the end together."

I kept him in the lineup for the series against the Los Angeles Kings and he scored eight goals on eight shots. Another time he went down to block a shot and the puck smashed into his nose, breaking it in five places. My only comment to Schmautzie about his broken nose was, "It hit you in the face, how could it miss your nose?" He also took ribbing from his daughter. She asked her mother if Daddy's nose was going to look like Rick Smith's. (Whose nose was like a winding road. Sorry, Rick!) Against Toronto, Schmautz tried to split the Maple Leafs' defense and was hit so hard by their defenseman, the late Scott Garland, that the metal brace on his leg was bent. Three months later, we played them again, he tried the same play and this time he split the defense and scored.

Schmautzie was trouble for the opposition but he also was trouble for me. We were in Minnesota for a game with the North Stars and Bobby was out one night drinking. He later walked into the hotel's coffee shop and broke the crêpe machine. Just like that. The hotel socked him with a bill for $1,000, so I took up a collection for him. But Schmautzie refused and wrote out a cheque for the damages.

I was still furious with him because I could not tolerate that kind of behaviour from my players in the hotel, even though he had gotten carried away that night. My revenge was to play him to death against the North Stars. I played him on a regular shift, on the power play, killing penalties and even on other shifts. I wanted him to look bad in front of everybody, although I knew he was dying from a hangover. I didn't relent and when we got a penalty with five minutes left in the game I threw Bobby out as a penalty-killer. The score was tied 2-2 at the time and, wouldn't you know it, he got a breakaway, scored the winning goal and then collapsed in a heap in the corner of the rink.

We had another toughie, Al Secord, who was terrific with his fists. For some reason, though, he never was a favourite of Harry Sinden's. That proved to be his ruination with the Bruins. While I was there, though, I tried to use him as much as possible. Although Al was born in Sudbury, Ontario, and had played his junior hockey in Hamilton, like so many Canadian kids, he looked upon Maple Leaf Gardens in Toronto as the cathedral of the sport.

We were headed for Toronto one night when Secord asked me, as a special favour, if I would let him start the game at left wing. I realized that this would be a special thrill for him but I asked for a favour as well. I told him that I would start him if he took off his helmet.

I didn't like Secord in his helmet and I thought he would be more intimidating without it on. So I said to Al, "If you take off your helmet, I will not only start you in Toronto, I will play you on every power play." So Al took off his helmet and started the game. On his first shift he picked a toughie, Dave Hutchison, to get into a fight with. I said to myself, "Oh no, please help him, Lord, to not get his clock cleaned." But he did a sweet number on Hutchison.

There are players who fight because they must to stay in the league and there are players who fight because of personal pride. But there are few players who fight because they like to. Al was one of them. I came into my office at 8:30 in the morning once and there was Al showing his family the tapes of his best fights.

Sinden always liked fighters, which is why I couldn't understand why Secord didn't make a hit with him. After I left the Bruins, I ran into Al one day in Boston and he was really depressed. "I don't understand what the Bruins are doing to me," he said.

"I'm on the bench. I asked why I wasn't playing and they told me, 'Because you're not playing your game, you're not aggressive and not hitting.' So naturally I go out and be aggressive and start hitting and naturally I get a few penalties. Then they bench me again. I say, 'Why aren't I playing?' They say, 'Because you're getting too many penalties.' My head is all screwed up."

I could see the kid was falling apart, so I grabbed him by the lapels and looked straight in his eyes. "DON'T CHANGE, AL." He looked at me. "There are twenty teams in this league that will take you. Just don't change your game."

Sure enough, the Black Hawks got him in 1981 and he became a big scorer—though still fighting—overnight. Besides, he made Chicago stronger and braver, as a team, just with his presence. He finished the season with 47 goals, tops on the Black Hawks, and 303 penalty minutes.

One player who listened to me was Mike Milbury. Like Terry O'Reilly, Mike seemed to have minimal talents at first, but he developed rapidly because he was simply determined to make good. He was a Boston boy who originally had been a football player at Colgate University, but had then tried his hand at hockey. I first met him at my hockey school in Rochester.

By this time he had his heart set on a professional career as a defenseman, but I was very skeptical about his chances. I told him straight out that one of the first things he would have to learn was how to turn into the corners to get the puck. For some reason, all young American defensemen seem to have the same problem, turning and going into the corners.

He took my word and, I remember, one morning I showed up at the rink before seven and there was Mike, with his pregnant wife, Debbie, out on the rink. She was standing at center ice, in the cold, damp arena, dumping pucks from the red line into the corners. And there was Mike, chasing down those pucks, turning in the corners, working his tail off, practising his turning and picking the puck up, making himself a better hockey player, and eventually a big-leaguer with the Bruins.

Mike and I had a curious relationship in that, while I loved him like a son, we disagreed on many topics. (Sort of an Archie Bunker/Meathead relationship.) And we had plenty of time to disagree, because we lived only five doors away from each other in North Andover and drove back and forth to practice.

We were talking about our favourite people one day and I mentioned that I was very fond of John Wayne. When Milbury told me that he didn't particularly care for John Wayne, I nearly went through the roof. "How could anyone not like John Wayne?" I demanded. "Not like the Duke? You gotta' be crazy." Then I asked him who his favourite actor was and he told me Woody Allen. As soon as I heard that name I called him a college freak and a hippy. Then, we moved on to the next topic.

Mike was sent down to Rochester after a great camp, as I told you earlier. I knew his heart was broken and sometimes when a young player has his heart broken like that he never recovers. I heard that he was playing poorly, not hitting, without enthusiasm. This was a sure sign of a broken spirit. Well, I talked Harry into bringing him up for a couple of games, near the end of the season. We had first place locked up, so I figured, let's see what this guy will do in the playoffs. He came up and he was a complete pacifist. During the game, in between every shift, I screamed in his ear, "You hippy, liberal pacifist, you'll never make the big time." Harry was going to send him back to Rochester.

I talked Harry into keeping him for one more game, against Toronto. Bobby Schmautz spelled it out for him, "You want to stay here, hit, be aggressive, and a fight wouldn't hurt."

The night before a game in Toronto I wandered by a bar (The Stable) and who should I find standing outside the bar a few minutes after curfew but "Muldoon" Milbury. I politely asked him what he was doing there and he answered that he couldn't sleep. When I answered him the paint started to peel off the walls of the bar. "You big stiff! You're hanging by a string! I'll kick your ass all the way back to Rochester if you don't play well tomorrow night. Let's go!"

He walked five paces in front of me like a little school boy. I cursed at him all the way back to the hotel. Needless to say, he played an aggressive, tough game the next night and has never looked back since.

Mike and I got so close that he asked me if I would be the godfather to his child, Luke, and naturally I accepted. Not long after that, Mike was interviewed on television and was unusually nervous. The questioner asked him if he was fond of me and Mike, said yes, he was.

"I think so much of Don Cherry," Mike added, "that I made him *father of my child!*" Thus ended one of Boston's most embarrassing sports interviews.

Only Mike and I could fall in love with a lowly weed, but this actually happened during our drives to and from Boston Garden. As we were motoring along the highway one day, I noticed a single weed, about two feet high, growing through a crack in the concrete at the side of the road. Suddenly it dawned on me that this weed had great symbolic value. Although it was ignored by everyone and maligned as a mere weed, it had managed to survive storms, salt, spraying, blizzards and whatever else might have been dumped on it. Still it managed to stand tall and I offered this bit of insight to Mike.

He immediately understood how I felt about this weed and I instantly knew that he, too, felt for the little shaft of green. "Mike," I said one day, "that weed shows character. Any plant that can grow out of a crack in concrete and survive all the climactic indignities has to be something special. Our team has to have character like that." Milbury agreed and, each day, we would acknowledge the weed as we headed for Boston.

But one day a terrible thing happened. As we were driving to the Garden we noticed that a highway clean-up truck was grooming the side of the road *and was heading straight for our favourite weed*. "Mike," I shouted, as if a human life was in danger, "they're going to get our weed!"

He slammed on the brakes, jumped out of the car and ran—dodging the rush-hour traffic—back in the direction of the weed. Several times I thought he was going to get killed as he raced to beat the cleaning truck to the weed. Sure enough, he got to it just in time, plucked it from the concrete crack and then zigzagged back through the traffic again until he safely reached the car. As he slammed the door, he said, "Grapes, they aren't gonna get *our* weed. No way!" When I got home I took some fertilizer and planted the heroic weed in my backyard.

Two days later, Rose was weeding the garden and came to our weed. She looked at it and thought, "What's this old weed doing here?" She uprooted it and threw it in the garbage. I suppose there is a moral here, but I haven't figured it out yet.

There are some people I wouldn't treat as nicely as I treated that weed. People like referees.

Major league baseball umpire Ron Luciano once said that managers argue with umpires for three reasons. "One, they believe the umpire has made an error in judgment and should be so informed. Two, they are trying to prevent a player or players from being dismissed from the game. Three, temporary insanity."

As a hockey coach, I would say that temporary insanity was the primary reason for arguing with the referees. Start with the fact that officiating a hockey game flawlessly is an impossible task. There is only one man who is trying to keep an eye on ten skaters going up to 25 miles per hour with half of them behind the referee's back. There's no way one person can detect all the infractions. When a ref missed one—or two, or three—I would get insane. It was part of the business of coaching.

I did learn *something* about handling referees from all my experience as a player and a coach. The important thing was not to embarrass the official. Referees don't even mind if you swear at them, but you have to do it the right way. The best way to do it is skate over to the official and look as if you're adjusting your stick, or taking a piece of tape off the blade, then hand it to the ref while speaking your mind about his lousy call.

My problem was that the moment I became a coach I started embarrassing referees. I would stand on the boards and rant and rave, making the ref feel like two cents. Once, when Andy van Hellemond made a particularly (in my eyes) awful call, I screamed bloody murder at him. But Van Hellemond very wisely stayed so far from the bench he couldn't hear me. He finally sent Brad Park over to the bench and Brad said that if I had a message for the ref to give it to him and he, in turn, would transmit it back to Van Hellemond. "Tell him," I said, "to go f--- himself."

I meant it as a joke, but damned if Park doesn't skate right back to Van Hellemond and deliver the message exactly as I had said it!

Some referees could accept a situation like that with a sense of humour. John McCauley was one of them, and that's why he was my favourite.

McCauley was handling one of our games when a fan tossed an egg from about 200 feet up in the stands and it hit him right in the middle of his forehead; dead-center. I have never seen a shot like that before or since and I wondered how McCauley would handle it. He skated over to the bench and was handed a towel. As he wiped the yolk off his face, he turned to me and said: "Nice shot, wasn't it, Grapes?" You've got to like a man for that.

Another good one is Dave Newell. He was handling a Bruins-Maple Leafs game in Toronto. I let him have it almost from the opening face-off and how I escaped without a bench penalty I'll never know. Finally Newell reached what I thought was his breaking point. He called time for a moment and skated over to our bench. I figured I really was going to catch hell. It was Saturday night, the game was on network television; there were 16,000 fans in Maple Leaf Gardens and everybody was watching me and Newell as he headed for the bench.

Before he actually got to me, I tried to anticipate his diatribe. "Yeah, okay, Newell," I snapped as he arrived at the sideboards. Dave took his forefinger and pounded me on the chest with it and then said: "Grapes, this is the sharpest suit I have ever seen!"

As I live and breathe, this was the first time in my career that anyone pulled so perfect a squelch on me that I was actually speechless. Then, to cap the great line, Newell slowly skated back to center ice and added: "And don't you forget it."

The fans thought he was really giving me the going over, and they were hollering, "That's the way Dave, don't let that stiff get away with that." Even the TV commentators said, "Cherry has been severely reprimanded by Newell." But the players loved it because they finally saw me at a loss for words.

For some reason a ref we had a great deal of trouble with was Ron

Wicks. I once chased him down the rink after a game in Washington, not meaning to do anything but yell, but I couldn't put on the brakes in time and banged right into him. I was called on the carpet by NHL President Clarence Campbell for that one.

Another time we were playing a big game against the Islanders and Wicks was (in our estimation) calling an atrocious game. At the end of the second period, the ref headed for his dressing room and Harry was there waiting for him to step off the ice. Instead of actually lunging at him, Harry calmly stood next to the wall and as Wicks headed for his room, he said: "Nice game, Wicksie." When we arrived back on the ice for the start of the third period the public address announcer was reading off a penalty against us for unsportsmanlike conduct. It was the one and only time I ever heard of a team being penalized because a g.m. told the ref he was calling a nice game.

My hassles with the refs did not wear well with Clarence Campbell. Clarence was a Rhodes Scholar, a lawyer and as distinguished an individual as ever graced the NHL. He was a man of few words, but I had the misfortune of hearing those words quite often. Shortly after I would be involved in an incident with a referee I would get a message that Mr. Campbell wanted me to call him. Our conversations went something like this:

Mr. Campbell: "Campbell here!"

Me: "This is Don Cherry, Mr. Campbell!"

Mr. Campbell: "Explain your actions in Washington."

Me: "I didn't think the referee was calling a very good game and I got carried away etc. etc."

Mr. Campbell: "Unacceptable." (Click of telephone.)

A few days later I would receive a letter from NHL headquarters informing me that I had been fined $500. In five years of dealing with the NHL President the only words I remember are "Explain your actions . . ." and "Unacceptable."

On one of the other "Unacceptables" that cost me $500, Mr. Campbell followed up the fine with a visit to Boston Garden. Rose and Timothy were at the game. Rose said to Tim, "Mr. Campbell is up there in the crowd." Tim said, "Gee, I'd like to meet Mr. Campbell." Rose said, never thinking that he would go, "Well, why don't you go up and introduce yourself?" So Tim went up to Mr. Campbell and said, "Hello, Mr. Campbell, I'm Tim Cherry." Clarence didn't make the connection to Cherry, coach of the Bruins, so Tim said, "Mr. Campbell, my Dad just wanted to know if you got his cheque." Mr. Campbell, who almost never lets his hair down said, "Oh, you're *that* Cherry." Then he burst out laughing and told Tim, "tell your Dad I got the cheque, and tell him thanks a lot!"

CHAPTER SIXTEEN

Triumph And Disaster

The Boston Bruins club had become a formidable force in the NHL, though still not the champions, and I had been named the league's Coach of the Year. Such recognition was a balm for my ego which was further enriched when I was invited to be one of the coaches involved in the Team Canada 1976 organization. This was quite a feather in my cap because the members of Team Canada would be selected from among the best professionals in the dominion. I was highly elated.

The tournament would be played in September 1976 and earlier in the year, the key men behind Team Canada—Al Eagleson, Sammy Pollock and Scotty Bowman—officially gave me their blessing to help run the club. Now I was really in select company.

As head of the players' union, an attorney and an agent as well, Eagleson was the most powerful man in hockey; more powerful, even, than the President of the league or even the Chairman of the Board of Governors or even some of the power brokers among the club owners.

The Eagle runs the Team Canada operation. The Canada Cup was basically his idea, and he is the guy who makes all the arrangements, from choosing the coaches, right down to selecting the sites and making it all go.

Sammy Pollock, architect of the Montreal Canadiens dynasty, was a logical choice to oversee the operation. He was a no-nonsense guy who seemed to have an intuitive knack for doing the right thing at the right time. His record as general manager of the Canadiens proved that. Pollock always favoured the gung-ho "firewagon" style of hockey practiced by his Flying Frenchmen, so it was no surprise that Sammy put the accent on players who were the best skaters, the best shooters and, of course, the best scorers. There was no argument about that—he simply wanted the best offensive hockey players in the league and wanted to blow the opposition out.

Scotty, who had had a successful run as coach with the St. Louis Blues, had gone to work for Sam and the Canadiens. He was a stern, opinionated individual whose sense of humour was not very apparent. Although there were other coaches aboard—Al MacNeil, Bobby Kromm and myself—it was evident to us that Scotty would be the number one man behind the bench, as it should be.

Kromm had been an effective coach of Canadian amateur teams in international competition and MacNeil had coached the Canadiens to the Stanley Cup in 1971. I didn't suffer any illusions about my role. Scotty would be *the* coach of Team Canada and the rest of us were there to share the blame if anything went wrong—and maybe to help, a little.

If there had been any doubt about who was dictator of the operation, that was removed at our very first meeting at the Queen Elizabeth Hotel in Montreal.

One of the fellows who was feeling a little stronger than he should have been was Bobby Kromm. While we were sitting around, Bobby announced "I'm gonna tell the reporters a few things about the team ... " Before he could finish, Eagleson laid him out cold: "NO YOU WON'T!!" There was never any doubt in my mind about The Eagle's power after that. Bobby just sat there stunned. Like everyone else in the troupe, he was awed by Eagleson. The man was a bundle of energy. When he entered a room he absolutely annexed the place. He made everyone, no matter how many people happened to be there, feel as if they were his most personal friends. And the weird thing about him was his knack of being able to handle his enemies almost as easily as he does his friends. He would joke with them and act almost as if they weren't his foes at all, even though everyone—especially The Eagle—knew that they were.

Our high command was a curious mixture of the young and old. I was still a little wet behind my ears in terms of NHL experience and there I was sitting with Toe Blake, who had once coached the Canadiens to five straight Stanley Cups, and Keith Allen, who had managed the Philadelphia Flyers to Cup wins in 1974 and 1975. Keith and Toe were there to help Sammy, and the bunch of us convened for our first formal dinner in the very posh Beaver Room of the Queen Elizabeth Hotel. The scene was right out of a movie. Violinists played in the background as the waiters—each table had its own special waiter—presented one of the most lavish menus I had ever seen.

Al MacNeil, who is a native of Sydney, Nova Scotia, ordered some exotic fish. When the dish arrived at our table, the maitre d' instantly appeared with a magnificent sauce that could only be obtained at a high class restaurant such as the Beaver Room. "Would you like some sauce?" the maitre d' asked MacNeil.

With that, Al replied very matter of factly, "Nah, just bring me some ketchup." It was as if a bomb had just been dropped. The maitre d' was consummately embarrassed yet he was obliged to pass along the order. He leaned over and whispered Al's request to the waiter who immediately turned red. The poor waiter had to go to the kitchen for the ketchup and when the chef learned what Al wanted to put on his coveted item he almost ran out and chopped Al with a cleaver. What did Al care? He was a Maritimer who happened to like ketchup on his fish.

Now that we were getting ready for the start of camp, there was a lot of talk about whether or not the National Leaguers could keep up with the highly-trained Russians and Czechs. I had no fears, but there were some in our group who felt that conditioning would be in the Soviets' favour. With that in mind the Canadian government spent a lot of money to send some physiotherapists and physical instructors to work with our professionals. The minute I got word of that I cringed. I remembered an experience when instructors from the Royal Military College had come to our Toronto training camp to help whip the players into shape. They had been more interested in doing scientific experiments than producing a winning hockey club. I didn't like the idea of the government people coming in at all, and my worst fears were soon realized. The minute I saw these instructors I confronted them. "What are you doing?" I asked. They said they were running tests.

"Running tests for what?"

"For everything."

I walked into the training rooms and found out out what "everything" meant. They had players doing marathon sit-ups and, already, the guys were pulling their stomach muscles. Another instructor had players riding a stationary bike. He would increase the pressure to see how long the players could continue without collapsing. The problem was that three guys had already suffered groin pulls.

What these instructors didn't comprehend was that they were dealing with superstars who were so proud that they would not quit any challenge and, as a result, they kept going and going until their muscles couldn't cope with the demands and, consequently they were injuring themselves.

The real topper was an order that the players should run up to the top of Mount Royal, the mountain that sits in the middle of the city of Montreal, just off the downtown area. Once again, the players tried to meet the challenge and some of them fell by the wayside. Literally. Gerry Cheevers, one of our goalies, hurt his knee trying to run up the mountain and the knee was never the same after that. Bobby Hull, physical nut that he was, tried to outrun everybody, hurt his back and wound up in the hospital. These physical education experts were doing more damage to Team Canada than the Russians and Czechs could ever do.

Not that all of the players were as gung-ho as Hull. Cheevers was a problem when it came to working out, especially on the ice. He never liked practice to begin with and he certainly wasn't crazy about the idea of having the NHL's best shooters taking aim at him every day. The way things turned out, Gerry was probably the only goalie in the history of hockey to be yanked from an intra-squad game for indifferent play, and *I* was the guy who did the yanking.

Steve Shutt of the Montreal Canadiens, one of the hardest shots in the business, let one go and Cheevers just stepped aside and let it into the top corner of the net. I skated over to him and said, "Cheesie, you better get out of there; that puck almost hit you." Sure enough, he skated straight to the bench and was tickled not to have to practice anymore. This, naturally, ticked off a lot of people in the camp. Toe Blake was going crazy about him and so were some of the other players, but it really didn't matter that much in terms of our goaltending quality because we also had Rogie Vachon and Dan Bouchard, two pretty good goalies, who were more willing to take practice seriously.

Some of the upset players were irreplaceable. Picture this. Guy Lapointe of the Canadiens, who was the best defenseman in camp, was about to be cut from the squad because he refused to run up to the top of Mount Royal. I pleaded with the high command, but they still wanted him to go up Mount Royal. I finally swung a compromise solution; I got the high command to call off the Mount Royal run at the end of the week and then persuaded Guy to dash up the mountain during the couple of days we had left before the end of the week.

To the average hockey fan, the sacrifice being made by these superstars may not seem to have been much, but I can assure you that it hurt them a lot more than one might think. For example, they already had a full 80-game schedule to contend with, not to mention a playoff season that extended to the end of May. So, if you have a guy like Lapointe, whose team would make it all the way to the Stanley Cup finals, you have a man who was playing ten months of hockey without a break. Unfortunately, there were some opinion-moulders who failed to understand the sacrifice they were making. One of then was Christie Blatchford of the Toronto *Globe and Mail*.

Ms. Blatchford, who now writes for *The Toronto Star*, was then one of the few women sportswriters in Canada. Her column in the *The Globe and Mail* was widely read.

According to Blatchford, the "sacrifice" being made by the players really didn't amount to much. She called it a "crock," pointing out that Team Canada stayed at the best hotels, ate the best food, and was generally treated like royalty. When the players read the column, they were furious and bitter, especially since the criticism came from a Canadian. The players felt that they were in a no-win situation. If they won the tournament, well, they were expected to come out on top. And if they lost they were nothing but a bunch of choke artists.

My gripe was that journalists like Blatchford didn't bother to get all the facts because, if she did, I think her viewpoint would have been rearranged by about 180 degrees. I don't think she was tuned into people like Dan Maloney of the Toronto Maple Leafs. Dan was a big left wing who was not exactly twinkletoes, but an asset to the club anyway. He was in his prime at the time of the Canada Cup. About five days after the start of training camp we put a call in to Maloney, asking him to come to our camp. I'm not sure what the powers-that-be had in mind by inviting Maloney, because he certainly wasn't in the same class as Bobby Hull, Bobby Orr, or Denis Potvin. But I imagine that they wanted a lot of players there to make the auditions as competitive as possible. There was only one problem; at the time they decided they wanted Maloney, Dan was off with his family somewhere in Alaska.

Somehow they tracked him down and extended the invitation. Dan must have realized that there was no way he would make the team, yet he said, no problem—I'll be there. He grabbed the first available flight and was in camp a day later. Watching him practise that first day, I knew that he didn't have a chance to make the team—and he knew it as well. But he busted his gut every time he got on the ice, as if this was the most important challenge of his entire professional life. He worked and he worked, until that most difficult of all times came along; the day when the roster cuts had to be made. And Dan, when told he was cut, replied, "Thank you for inviting me, it was an honour." Of all the things I remember about Team Canada, I think Dan Maloney's class stands out.

Ever since I became a coach I've always been puzzled over the "best" method for telling a player that he's not good enough to make the team. It always reminds me of the "Kowalski" story. There was a tough Marine sergeant who got word that the father of one of his men had passed away. At roll call he snapped: "Hey, Smith, your father died!" The Marine fainted on the spot. A week later the sister of another Marine died, and the sergeant once again called his men together. "Jones," he yelled out, "your sister died last night!" The Marine burst into tears. Finally, word got back to the general about the sergeant's insensitivity, and he was called on the carpet and told to be less direct and gruff when one of his troops suffered a tragedy. Sure enough, a week later the sergeant was notified that one Private Kowalski had just lost his mother. Remembering what the general had said, he lined up his troop and demanded: "Everyone whose mother is alive, please take one step forward—NOT SO FAST, KOWALSKI!" In retrospect, some coaches cut their players in the same manner.

I suggested that the guys be taken aside and told quietly—nice and easy. Spare them the humiliation. But these street-smart hockey players were away ahead of us, anyway.

The players found out that the cuts were to be made on Tuesday. So early Tuesday morning they went down and asked the hotel clerk for the Wednesday and Thursday room lists. The lists, obviously, would only include those fellows still with the team, so it was easy enough to deduce who the losers were. Of course the high command didn't realize this, and that afternoon the entire group was summoned for lunch, and after lunch we read the names of those who *made* the club. To this day I'm not sure whether the guys who were cut were more angry because of the method employed, or simply because they weren't considered good enough to make Team Canada.

One such individual was Jean Pronovost, a damn good goal scorer who figured he was good enough to stick with the team. I ran into him in the hotel lobby an hour after the public cut had been made and told him I was sorry he was out. "Nice try, Jean," I said.

He murmured something about not understanding how players who had scored 20 goals less than he had were still on the roster and yet he was a goner. I extended my hand for the token goodbye handshake and he stunned me. My hand was relatively limp. He grabbed it and squeezed, harder and harder, almost crushing my hand in his anger. Then he let go, turned and walked away. The more I thought about it afterwards, the angrier I got. So I waited for him in the lobby the next morning. When I spied him, I made a bee line for him and shook his hand again. I was going to put him to the floor, but this time *his* hand was limp. So I said, "Jean, you almost crushed my hand yesterday. I hope it was nothing personal, because if it was, we'll settle it right here."

By the time the words had come out, I knew he had acted out of despair the day before. Now he had cooled down, and sure enough, he apologized. This time we shook like normal pepole and each went his own way.

It would be nice to say that that was the last of the bruised egos, but we had a few more. Invariably, there were personality clashes. Scotty Bowman and Phil Esposito, among others, couldn't get along for some reason. Phil's high scoring didn't impress Scotty as much as it did others.

One of the things that bothered Phil was that Scotty had him wearing black sweaters during the workouts. Phil didn't like black because, from time immemorial, a black jersey connoted players who were fourth-stringers; otherwise known in hockey circles as the Black Aces. There are few lower insults in the business than to label a hockey player a Black Ace. Funny thing was, I asked Scotty about the black sweaters, and he said he didn't know a thing about them—the trainer just happened to have passed them out that way!

I was pleased with the team, particularly Bobby Orr. If Orr had been a selfish person, he wouldn't have even tried out for Team Canada; he would have remained at home, taken it easy and conserved his damaged limbs for the upcoming NHL schedule. But, as those of us who knew him realized, Orr had an unquenchable thirst for combat and, once again, he proved that he ranked among the most glorious warriors in hockey history (I know, I know; I'm getting carried away again!).

With Orr leading the way, we breezed over Finland, 11-2, in the opener and then took the measure of Team USA and Sweden. To our surprise, the Soviet club was not as overpowering as had been expected, and we beat them too. Naturally, there was a media alibi for why we beat them—it was never that we were simply good, or, God forbid, even great. No, it was always that the Russians were breaking in new players, or weren't taking the series seriously. No matter what, it was a no-win situation, even if we won!

But the Czechs were just dynamite. Before we were up against them, I was chatting with Red Fisher, columnist for *The Montreal Gazette*, about the upcoming matches.

"I'm not all that worried about who we dress or don't dress," I mused. "Goaltending's what bugs me."

"Goaltending?" asked Red, somewhat baffled. "You mean you're down on Rogie Vachon?"

"No, no, no!" (I didn't want this misquoted) "not *our* goaltending. *Their* goaltending. I've been saying since the first day we came to camp, the only thing that can beat us, is if somebody else's goalie gets unconscious."

I still carried around in the back of my head the nightmare of the 1975 playoffs, when my Bruins had hammered the Chicago Black Hawks, 8-2, in the opening game of the best-of-three preliminary round. But the Hawks had rebounded to beat us, 4-3, in overtime of the second game. In the decisive third game we should have clobbered Chicago, but it didn't happen.

We threw everything at their goalie, Tony Esposito—something like 63 shots—but he was having one of those games. When the game was over it was the Hawks, not us, who went on to the next round.

Now we were ready to play the Czechs at The Forum in Montreal. Our record was three wins and no losses; their record was two wins, no losses and a tie. By the time the night was over the Czechs were the only undefeated team in the tournament; a chubby goalie named Vladimir Dzurilla saw to that. He drove us crazy with a miraculous performance that was so good, the partisan Canadian fans at The Forum gave him no less than three standing ovations.

Needless to say it wasn't Dzurilla alone who stopped us. As our players grew increasingly frustrated in the Czech zone, we became lax in our end of the rink and Rogie Vachon produced a number of sensational saves to keep us in the contest. Unfortunately, Dzurilla was playing as if he had the entire four-by-six-foot cage boarded up and the final was 1-0 for the Czechs.

I didn't mind the fans cheering Dzurilla for his fine play, but what did bug me was another occasion in Toronto when we faced the Swedes. Prior to the match players from each team were introduced. Lanny McDonald and Darryl Sittler, both regulars on Team Canada, were then with the Toronto Maple Leafs and each drew applause from the Maple Leaf Gardens audience. But when the Swedes were introduced and the public address announcer mentioned the name of Borje Salming, the crowd went wild. A standing ovation. I was in the press box at the time and there were journalists there who got up and began cheering. I couldn't figure that one out; I mean here they were, Toronto writers, cheering a guy who was going to be skating against their own team and country and not even giving the same applause to Sittler and McDonald.

I stood up in the press box (where Al MacNeil and I worked, phoning down observations to Bobby Kromm who was behind the bench) and bellowed that anyone who dared to cheer on a Swede against Canada once the game was on, purely and simply, sucked. In fact I carried on so much along this theme that my companion in the next seat became terribly upset. He happened to be "Gentleman" Joe Primeau, a Hall of Famer who centered the great Maple Leafs' "Kid Line" of Busher Jackson and Charlie Conacher. One of the nicest guys of all time, Primeau kept soothing me: "Don, you'd better sit down. Don't get so carried away—it's only a game."

Apparently the Canadian players got carried away as well. They didn't care that much for Salming (nor some of the other Swedes, for that matter) and were running at them all night, with Bobby Hull leading the hitting (now figure that one out!).

Bobby Orr's knee was still bothering him, but he never let on and you'd never have known it—he was simply sensational (Scotty told me off the record that of all the guys on the team, we could least afford to lose Orr). Bobby had told me that the one thing he wanted to do before he retired was play the Russians and, boy, was he turning it on. Game after game he was selected as the best player of the game, and it was a popular decision with the players—only they knew the pain he was going through just to skate.

The only player who disagreed with the decision was Denis Potvin. Denis always resented the fact that people always called him a "Second Bobby Orr" when he was young. Actually I could never really understand the resentment: would a baseball player resent being called another Babe Ruth? He said he did not like being constantly measured against Orr and I guess I can't blame him for that. But they measured him against Orr nonetheless, and when Bobby ultimately was named the Most Valuable Player in the tournament, Potvin burned. He could not understand why he had been picked and even went public with his thoughts in the *Toronto Star Weekly*. Needless to say, he was not too popular with a lot of people when that piece hit the newsstands. Truthfully, I always thought Rogie Vachon was second to Bobby in the "Most Valuable" category.

The individual stars of one game were given hand-carved seals, sculpted by the Canadian Eskimos. Denis beefed about not getting one of the seals and the players picked up on the complaint. One day the players called a meeting on the ice and naturally everyone figured something terribly serious was about to happen. Just then a couple of players skated on to the ice carrying a huge stuffed toy seal and presented it to Denis!

Bobby Clarke, the Philadelphia Flyers center, was injured quite a bit during the series, but still gave 100 percent. Clarke's reward for his efforts was delivered on his birthday after a scrimmage. His teammate and old pal, Reggie Leach, made the presentation and, quite frankly, I had never seen anything like it before.

Another meeting was called on the ice whereupon Leach skated out with an enormous white cake with the inscription, HAPPY BIRTHDAY, BOBBY, on top. Before the presentation was actually made the boys swung into a chorus of "Happy Birthday" and Clarke seemed truly touched by the gesture; so much so that once the singing subsided he began to utter a few words of gratitude. Leach wound up and hurled the entire hunk of pastry in Clarke's face. Reggie threw it so hard—remember, Bobby's mouth was open at the moment of impact—that the cake was driven right down his throat and into his eyes and damn near knocked him right off his feet. Imagine, a guy nearly choking to death on his own birthday cake!

Clarke took it graciously, accepting the humour of the situation and, for me, it was a pleasure to be associated with players of such high calibre. Their classiness was detectable in a lot of different ways. Orr, Clarke and Guy Lafleur, for example, displayed their devotion by coming to the rink extra early. For an eight o'clock game, Orr would be in the dressing room at two in the afternoon, puttering around with his sticks, chatting with the trainers and just plain getting himself "up" for the game. Clarke would arrive an hour or so later and Lafleur might be in the room by four, pacing back and forth like a caged tiger, chainsmoking cigarettes with half of his equipment on.

By contrast, Peter Mahovlich, Frank's kid brother and potentially one of the best players in the business, would drive Scotty Bowman nuts.

Peter, essentially, is a loosey-goosey guy who likes a good time as much as he cares about good hockey. Which is fine and dandy, until the priorities collide. Mahovlich would drive Bowman crazy with his nonsensical yelling in the dressing room. (Scotty would be standing outside in the hallway saying, "Just listen to that jerk. He's doing that just to bug me.") Another time, we were having a team dinner the night before a big game and, according to protocol, the players were to sit at their tables and the high command was to eat at their own table. Now, I don't know why Peter did this, but instead of sitting with his teammates, he plunked

After we won the Canada Cup in The Montreal Forum. (left to right) Al Eagleson, Bobby Kromm, Toe Blake, me, Keith Allen, Al McNeil, and Sam Pollock. (Imagine me with no tie!)

Team Canada, 1981.   JAMES LIPA

Lanny McDonald, Timothy, and me.

Larry Robinson, Guy Lafleur, and me, after Guy had been injured.

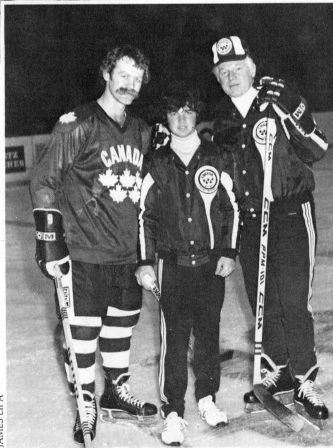

himself down at management's table. I knew that he hadn't been drinking that much, but he pretended that he had for some reason and that just made Sammy Pollock and Scotty Bowman furious. But that was Peter and maybe that little scene helps explain in capsule form why a fellow with immense ability never was able to harness it and, in effect, threw away what could have been a great career.

Team Canada prevailed to the final game, neck-and-neck with Czechoslovakia for the championship. The Russians had already been disposed of and, on paper at least, it appeared that we should romp to the title.

But the Czechs had shown us in the 1-0 upset that they were not only capable of playing tight hockey, but that they had a great goaltender in Dzurilla. I figured that if we could solve that guy between the pipes we'd be able to top them.

Conservatively speaking, I would say that the final match between Team Canada and the Czechs was one of the finest I have ever seen or played in, anywhere, anytime. Rogie Vachon was magnificent in the nets for us, but that sonofagun Dzurilla was proving that his shutout in the earlier game was far from a fluke.

The score was tied with about a minute left in regulation time when one of the Czechs broke through our defense and it looked like curtains. But Vachon came up with one of the greatest saves I've ever seen and we went into sudden-death overtime. The Czechs were playing almost flawless hockey except for one thing. Dzurilla seemed to betray one weakness that I thought our guys ought to know about so I sent a message down to the dressing room from my private spotter's box: "He's moving further and further out of his net. I think you can fool him if you get a chance. Anybody who breaks in on him should delay his shot a bit. Dzurilla will keep coming. You might wind up with a lot of room to shoot at."

Sammy Pollock ordered me downstairs to give the message directly to the guys. So, I went down and talked it over with Cheevers and Bowman. "Whether they're coming down the left or right side," I explained, "have them fake the slapshot, then keep going wide and slide the puck along the ice."

It seemed like a good idea, but as I made my way back to the booth, I wondered whether the guys would ever get the chance to use the ploy and if they did, what would come of it. Fortunately, it didn't take very long for me to find out. The sudden-death period began and not too far into the period Marcel Dionne, the Los Angeles Kings center, got control of the puck and gave a pass to Darryl Sittler who was moving down the left wing. Sittler couldn't have made a better move if I had been manipulating him with strings from above. He faked the slapshot, took an extra stride or two and then pulled the trigger. By this time Dzurilla had obliged by sliding way out of position and Sittler finished the play by sliding the puck into the net. While the capacity crowd was screaming, I sat there, more dumbfounded than anybody.

When I finally made my way down to the dressing room, I expected to find the kind of jubilation normally associated with winning the Stanley Cup. There was, of course, an aura of happiness, but not nearly the intensity I had anticipated. Instead there was more a feeling of relief that, at last, the pressure was off. Then someone mentioned that now the guys had to get ready for the NHL training camp. We had just played a season against the Russians, Czechs, Swedes, Americans and Finns, and now we had to start the NHL trek from September to, with luck, May.

Personally, I felt great. I was one-for-one as an international hockey coach and had actually come out of it without getting into trouble once! As I left for the Bruins training camp, I assumed that I would never experience anything like international hockey again. Little did I realize that just five years later I would be leading a club featuring Guy Lafleur into the world championships at Stockholm, Sweden; only this time I would be hellbent for disaster.

As an international hockey coach, I was batting a thousand. Of course, the record was a mere one-for-one but, what the hell, serving on the staff of the Canadian entry in the 1976 Canada Cup victory had been a feather in my cap. A lot of people remembered my Dzurilla strategy (my mother and Blue) so it really wasn't all that surprising when my name came up as a coaching candidate for Team Canada in the 1981 World Championships in Sweden. Do you really want to know the reason I was chosen? I was the best unemployed coach still being paid by an NHL club. The NHL liked that because they wouldn't have to pay me. I was supposed to be doing this for the "glory." (I told you my brother had all the brains in the family.)

The Eagle was running the show again. He called me and asked me if I wanted the coaching job. At first, I was hesitant. Instead of giving him a yes-or-no answer, I countered, "O.K., but my son Timothy comes along as assistant trainer." (Somebody in the Cherry family was going to enjoy themselves over there!) The Eagle said it was okay, so I agreed to take the job although I still suffered some doubts.

My brother, for one, told me that I was dumb to accept. He, too, pointed out that I'd be in a no-win situation. If the club did all right, so what? And if they lost—which was what figured to happen—I'd come out looking like a chump.

Another thing that worried me was the effect it might have on my television career, such as it was. I had spent a successful year as a commentator with *Hockey Night in Canada* and now the Stanley Cup playoffs were about to begin, the best part of the season. On top of that, I'd have to forego banquets which, surprisingly, bring in a lot of money.

I realized that I'd be at a disadvantage, because there would be so little time to prepare. That didn't bother me half as much as the ridicule being heaped on our club by our own people. We hadn't even assembled the squad and already we had been dubbed Team Terrible and Team

Losers. I was quietly encouraged. I loved to take a bunch of players and tell them that nobody believed in them—but me. From a motivational point of view, it was ideal. I figured that with their pride at stake the pros would come through.

I also figured that, no matter who was beaten in the first playoff round, I'd wind up with a star or two. The best bet was that the Canadiens would knock off the Oilers meaning that Wayne Gretzky could join our club and give us terrific power at center.

My superior in this venture was John Ferguson, who had been the "policeman" on some of the great Montreal Stanley Cup-winning teams and later was coach and general manager of the Rangers. Now Fergie was general manager of the Winnipeg Jets and co-manager of Team Canada 1981. Before I left for Europe my brother once again provided me with the deathless message: Get along with the boss.

"You can't afford to fight with Fergie," he said, "or get him mad. For Heaven's sake, get along with him." Richard's voice kept ringing in my ear as we jetted across the Atlantic. Meanwhile, I was getting excited about the tournament and mulled over a number of strategies. A factor I had to keep in mind was the rink size. European rinks are considerably larger than the ones we are accustomed to in the NHL so I decided it was imperative that we work out on a big rink as soon as we could arrange a scrimmage. When we finally regrouped in Stockholm and headed for our first workout, the Swedish hockey authorities gave us a small rink. Obviously, they had every angle figured.

I did get a few good hockey players. Lo and behold, the Oilers upset the Canadiens in three straight games of the first Stanley Cup round which meant that some very good talent would be headed my way. Larry Robinson, the big, rangy defenseman, and Guy Lafleur, were both enroute to Sweden. Frankly, I didn't believe Lafleur would show up. He had suffered through one of the most miserable seasons any athlete could endure. First of all, he had been hurt for a large part of the hockey season; then he had fallen asleep at the wheel of his Cadillac only a month earlier and had almost been killed. Finally, his club had been humiliated by the upstart Oilers.

The day Guy arrived in Stockholm, I could see that he was fatigued beyond belief. I told him I only wanted him to play when he was ready. He replied that he would play whether he was tired or not. Our next game was against the West German team which had a few German Canadian players who would have liked nothing better than to cork Lafleur. In fact, before the game I mentioned to my assistant coach Andre Boudrias "This game bothers me, some of these Junior B Canadians would love to get their names in the paper back in Canada by hurting Guy." (Robinson was too big, they would never come near him.) I hesitated using Guy because I saw no point in getting him unnecessarily banged up just after arriving; but he insisted on lacing up the skates so, like a fool, I relented. On the very first shift Lafleur was fed a sucker pass at center. A German-Canadian player—from Toronto—noticed that Guy had his face down and elbowed him right in the face. What a shot; Guy was flattened while blood poured from his head. The thing that hurt him the most was the dumb helmet everybody has to wear over there. It came down and cut him on the nose.

Our players had to help him off the ice and I was beside myself. If I could have gotten hold of that player I would have killed him; Guy said, "I can't win. I fall asleep driving my car and I fall asleep on the ice."

My frustration was showing and I continued to betray a certain impatience as the series progressed. Who wouldn't? When we went up against the Russians the first time around we decided to play a cautious, close-checking game and we got our butts whipped. So, we altered our tactics against the Czechs and decided to play offensive hockey and we got our butts whipped, again, because our goaltending fell apart in the first period.

Next came the Swedes and naturally, a reporter asked: "How do you plan to cope with them?" I told him he should have asked me three weeks ago when we were still in Canada. At that time they were billing me as a hockey expert. Now, three weeks later in beautiful downtown Gothenburg, I was just another dumb hockey coach whose team was playing .500 hockey. Although we were playing only .500 hockey, I noticed a strange thing. The games were fast and furious and we were playing to the largest and most boisterous crowds. I would watch the Russians play the same team the following day to small crowds and it was about as exciting as watching paint dry. Please don't tell me they play exciting hockey; I know they are great and technically super, but I sure wouldn't want to watch them for 80 games. The people flocked to see *us*, and their booing of the opposition was great.

In terms of the play itself, our worst fears were realized. Lack of practice time for our club to jell hurt us right from the start. By contrast, the team play of the Russians and Czechs was giving us a good lesson. The Czechs and Russians had six-man units. The goalie, two defensemen and three forwards knew instinctively where every man was going to be, every split second. These six-men units had been practising and playing together for 800 hours getting ready for the tournament. Our guys had been working together for only two weeks. We were breaking down occasionally because our defense pairings hadn't had time to get accustomed to the forward lines they were playing with.

Despite the adversity, I was proud of our guys, especially Lafleur. He was giving it his best shot and so was Larry Robinson, except that Larry fell victim to one of his own little pranks and we all were the worse for it. In a giddy moment after a practice he decided to play Martian. He gathered a bunch of extra-long Q-Tips and inserted them in his ears and ran around shouting, "Look, I'm a Martian!" It got a few laughs until he tried to remove the Q-Tips from his ears. Apparently, Robinson forgot that they were extra-long and when he reached for one of them, instead of grabbing it, he accidentally drove the thing *into* his ear, right into the ear drum. Blood spurted out of his ear and the doctor had to be called.

Robinson was given pain-killers and sent back to his hotel room to recuperate. Unfortunately, he couldn't recuperate fast enough for us. He missed three games but, worse than that, the poor guy was suffering excruciating pain. (He told me that during that first night he had never been in such agony in his life. "If I had had a gun," he told me, "I would have shot myself.")

Eventually, Larry recuperated and played superbly. Hockey players being what they are, provided him with a warm welcome on his return to the dressing room. Everyone stood at attention—with Q-Tips in his ears. It produced the required laugh but, I must admit, my sense of humour took a few dips around this time. One of the problems concerned Morris Lukowich and Dave Babych, a forward and defenseman, respectively, from the Winnipeg Jets, employees of John Ferguson.

Babych had just completed his rookie year with Winnipeg while Lukowich had been around a few years. Each was a good player in his own way but they had been playing badly in this tournament. (For some reason—probably the coaching.) The way I run a team, if a guy is screwing up and there's someone around who could do a better job, the one who could help the team most gets the nod. To be true to myself and the team I had to bench Lukowich and Babych. But the minute I made that decision I began to hear my brother's voice—"Don't get Fergie mad at you."

I have to admit I had second thoughts. I began talking to myself. ("Don, when are you going to learn to be a politician? Play the 'game.' Save yourself some grief. Do what'll make Fergie happy.") But deep down, I knew all along what I was going to do.

Needless to say, I paid the price for my decision. Fergie was never the same with me after that. Not that he fired me or second-guessed me in the media. (At least not *then*.) But there *was* a certain detectable coolness that didn't exactly make me the most comfortable coach in Scandinavia. I figured the only way things would straighten out would be if we could somehow come up with a win over the Russians. But how? One theory was: you can't out-Russian the Russians; play your own game, take the man, finish the check.

The plan worked—to a certain extent. We had a 3-1 lead and were outplaying them by a long shot, outshooting them two-to-one. But, the Soviets came from behind and tied us. In a sense, it was a moral victory so, that night, for the first time since I had arrived in Scandinavia I went out and had a good time. I found myself a cozy bar and just nursed a few drinks well into the night. Before I knew it the clock had struck two in the morning and I was the only one left in the joint. Time to return to the hotel.

I picked up a beer mug with a Swedish emblem on it—my souvenir—and began making my way back to the hotel. The streets were completely deserted; creepy is the word for it. No cars, no people, and not much light. I headed for the river, where the hotel was located. Suddenly I looked up and, a few yards ahead of me, saw a large figure leaning against a street light, smoking a cigarette. The hotel was eight blocks away and there was no way I could get to it without actually walking past this guy. Whatever street-wise toughness I might have developed in Kingston had vanished in this scary moment. I began imagining headlines: DRUNK CANADIAN HOCKEY COACH MUGGED IN STOCKHOLM.

Closing my right hand on the beer stein, I prepared for the worst. I took another few steps while the stranger took a long drag on his cigarette. I took another step and now we were eye-to-eye. The man took another puff on his cigarette and, in almost perfect English asked: "How's Blue?" That was almost as good as beating the Russians.

So we finished in fourth place, losing the final game 4-2 to the Czechs. I wasn't all that discouraged.

I was very proud of our effort although I realized that the people back home wanted at least a medal. Still, I had managed to get behind the bench again, and that felt good. Even John Ferguson was friendly toward me when we sat together on the flight home from Sweden. When we arrived in Toronto I shook hands with Fergie and figured that any differences we might have had over Lukowich and Babych had been resolved. Three days later a story broke out of Winnipeg. Some reporter had asked Ferguson about the job I had done. He told the fellow that as a coach I make a good television commentator. (Nice, here we go again!) I talked to Fergie about it. He assured me that he had never said what had been printed, that he was quoted out of context and he was sorry about what had made the papers.

"John," I said, "that reminds me of the guy who's accused of rape and gets front-page headlines because of it. Then, when he's found innocent the story is buried on page 60."

My gut feeling is that Fergie *was* misquoted. When we returned home somebody asked Guy Lafleur whether I'd be a good choice to coach the Montreal Canadiens. He said he thought I'd be ideal for the job. Which only proves that Lafleur is not only a gentleman, a scholar, and a fine athlete but also a great judge of coaching talent.

I have been asked why Canada sends a team over to the World Tournament without our best players, fully aware that they're going to get stiffed. (A good example was 1982. Canada could have won a silver medal if Russia had beaten the Czechs. Naturally the game ended in a 0-0 tie.) The real reason we send a team is that if we don't go over there, they will not come to Canada and participate in the Canada Cup. Somebody has to go and pay the price.

Before the last Canada Cup Eagle was in a dilemma. He felt

obligated to have me as one of the coaches since I had been one of the sacrificial lambs in the earlier World Tournament. But Eagle was having a tough time with some of the g.m.s.

"Quite simply," said Eagle, "it's this way. I want you, Scotty wants you, but some of the g.m.s. don't like your attitude, or you."

I let Eagle off the hook. I said, "That's okay, Eagle, but do me a favour. Tell them I don't like them or *their* attitudes."

Another little piece of gratitude I received a year later when they were considering the coach for the next World Tournament in 1982. It was said in the newspapers that "we want somebody employed by the NHL to coach, not like Cherry. He was too independent and couldn't be controlled." (I liked that.)

EPILOGUE

If I had a dollar for every guy who stopped me on the street and said, "Don, you should be coaching again," I'd be as rich as Gretzky. Sometimes, though, I can't tell whether they say that because they want me back in coaching, or whether they want me *out* of TV!

At one point in my life I wanted very much to coach in the NHL, but I have almost cured myself of that affliction; and I *do* mean it's a sickness. Think about it: if a coach is worth his salt, he has to devote 24 out of 24 hours to his job, whether his family likes it or not. There have been over sixty coaching changes in the last four years in the NHL.

I would not only take the game home with me—because I used to take every loss personally—but I'd drive my family nuts. No, I don't miss that hassle at all. What I do miss is the camaraderie—the morning skates at the practice rink, the fooling around after practice, having fun with the young players, and, of course, the friendships that developed over the years with both the players and the media alike.

Perhaps I wouldn't be so offhand about it, if I hadn't gotten very lucky during my last weeks with the Colorado Rockies. Even though it wasn't certain that I would be fired, the handwriting *was* on the wall. My radar told me that I would be out of a job, so the time had come to find another means of earning a living. It was just about then that I got a call from the people at *Hockey Night in Canada* asking if I'd be interested in doing some television work. The idea was for me to host a feature called "Coach's Corner," in which I'd discuss various aspects, of hockey technique.

216

I was pretty tired at the time, and as I was about to say no, they said, "Come on down to Toronto, do a few tapes and see your mother in Kingston." Well, when they put it that way, I thought, why not? I did four tapes of "Coach's Corner" and flew back to Denver. I had barely gotten back when they called to say that the show had gone over well and they wanted me to do eight more.

The next thing I knew I was a TV personality! In no time at all I realized I was enjoying a lot of the benefits of coaching without any of the headaches. I was still around hockey people, I still had a certain amount of preparation to do, but best of all I was *involved* with the game. The producers not only allowed me, they encouraged me to express my opinions.

A lot of thanks has to go to Ralph Mellanby, executive producer of *Hockey Night in Canada*, for his encouragement. After my first Stanley Cup finals as a commentator, Ralph said that he didn't want me to change, the only promise he wanted from me was that I would never "turn professional." If any of you readers have seen me, you know I've kept that promise! So thanks to Ralph and my friend and advisor, Gerry Patterson, my TV career suddenly took off. I wonder where I'd be today without them?

The TV experience proved very enlightening and quite a balm for the ego of a twice-fired NHL coach. Look at it this way: I played sixteen years of professional hockey and won four championships in five years. Then I'd go home and my mother would say,"Where did you play *this* year, Don?" When I coached the Bruins, a few people knew me. Since I've become a television personality, everybody on the street seems to know me. I've been invited to do commercials, I've been invited to more banquets than there are rubber chickens and my ego became so inflated at one point that it required a quick puncture which, fortunately, happened before I became totally unbearable. It happened at Toronto's International Airport, where I was waiting in line for a ticket. An old gentleman and his wife were standing in front of me. They turned around and looked me over, whereupon the old gentleman said to his wife, "Do you know who this is?"

"I sure do," replied his wife, "I see him all the time on TV." (By now I'm feeling pretty good, as usual.)

"Well," asked the old gent, "who is he?"

"Why," his wife replied, "he's the Friendly Giant!" (For the uninitiated, The Friendly Giant is host of a Canadian children's TV show, and has been for 25 years. I'm surprised they recognized me without my giraffe!)

Another deflation occured at the Nassau Coliseum during the Islanders-Nordiques semi-final series in April, 1982. I was in the broadcast booth, when a voice blared out of the crowd: "Hey, Cherry, when are you gonna' get yourself an honest job?" I looked up and who should my heckler be, but Mrs. Mike McEwen.

I shot back, "How come Mike's got you up here in the cheap seats? Did he scalp his good ones?"

Whether Mrs. McEwen cares to believe it or not, I think I have a better feel for hockey now than I did at any time in my career. I talk to the referees, to the managers, the owners, the press and most important, I talk to the players. When I coached, I didn't have this opportunity or scope, because I mostly devoted my time to my own team. My contact with the players has really touched me.

For example, after one of the Islanders-Nordiques games, I was talking to some fans at the Nassau Coliseum parking lot, when, at a distance, I noticed Islander left wing Bob Nystrom (whom I've never met and always admired) getting into his car. Our eyes met. He waved to me and then gave me the thumbs-up sign.

You may wonder why I've made such a big deal over such a trivial gesture, but it meant a lot to me. Nystrom epitomizes the good, honest grinder. I like to feel that I'm a good, honest grinder. Being acknowledged that way by Nystrom was better than winning any lottery. It told me that he liked me just the way I am.

That incident, in turn, reminds me of an evening I once spent alone at our home on Wolfe Island, just across the St. Lawrence River from Kingston. The house is located on an isolated part of the island. Rose and Tim had gone back to Denver; it was September, late in the tourist season and that part of the island was deserted. It was just me and Blue and a few pints, watching a storm rage over the river, late at night.

I was feeling low. The Soviets had beaten Team Canada and I was suffering doubts about my future. I thought about brother Richard's lectures on conformity and others who had suggested I change my ways "for the better," whatever that meant. Suddenly, I flashed back to a talk I had had with an old gentleman who thought it would be wise for me to take the straight-and-narrow path and not antagonize so many people. As I mulled over the old man's message, I peered over toward the lighthouse beacon that pierced the black night. Then I recalled the old fellow's very words: "Keep fighting the world, Mr. Cherry, and you'll wind up being a lighthouse keeper on that island of yours."

So I sat there in the silence with Blue sitting beside me, sipping my brew, watching the waves crash over the docks. I began to think that, maybe, the old guy had been right. Maybe I wouldn't have blown hundreds of thousands of dollars by being stubborn, if, in fact, I had bent with the wind. But, as I cracked another pint, I said to Blue: "Ah, to hell with it, Blue. It's too late for me to change now.

"And I'll tell you another thing, Blue: if I do end up a lighthouse keeper on this island, I'll run it my way and it'll be the best damn lighthouse this island ever had."

Blue looked up at me and clearly said: "Damn right, Grapes, Damn right!"